Towards Gender Equality in the Music Industry

Towards Gender Equality in the Music Industry

Education, Practice and Strategies for Change

Edited by

Sarah Raine
and
Catherine Strong

BLOOMSBURY ACADEMIC
NEW YORK • LONDON • OXFORD • NEW DELHI • SYDNEY

BLOOMSBURY ACADEMIC
Bloomsbury Publishing Inc
1385 Broadway, New York, NY 10018, USA
50 Bedford Square, London, WC1B 3DP, UK
29 Earlsfort Terrace, Dublin 2, Ireland

BLOOMSBURY, BLOOMSBURY ACADEMIC and the Diana logo
are trademarks of Bloomsbury Publishing Plc

First published in the United States of America 2019
Paperback edition first published 2021

Volume Editors' Part of the Work © Sarah Raine and Catherine Strong, 2019
Each chapter © of Contributor

For legal purposes the Acknowledgments on p. xii constitute
an extension of this copyright page.

Cover design: Louise Dugdale
Art direction and photography by iandaviesphoto.com
Original cover design by Adam Kelly-Williams

All rights reserved. No part of this publication may be reproduced or transmitted in any form or by any means, electronic or mechanical, including photocopying, recording, or any information storage or retrieval system, without prior permission in writing from the publishers.

Bloomsbury Publishing Inc does not have any control over, or responsibility for, any third-party websites referred to or in this book. All internet addresses given in this book were correct at the time of going to press. The author and publisher regret any inconvenience caused if addresses have changed or sites have ceased to exist, but can accept no responsibility for any such changes.

Whilst every effort has been made to locate copyright holders the publishers would be grateful to hear from any person(s) not here acknowledged.

Library of Congress Cataloging-in-Publication Data
Names: Raine, Sarah, 1985- editor. | Strong, Catherine, editor.
Title: Towards gender equality in the music industry: education, practice and strategies for change / edited by Sarah Raine and Catherine Strong.
Description: New York : Bloomsbury Academic, 2019. | Includes bibliographical references (pages 212-213) and index. | Summary: "Presents a global overview of current research examining the ways in which gender equality is still an issue in the music industry."–Provided by publisher.
Identifiers: LCCN 2019026068 (print) | LCCN 2019026069 (ebook) | ISBN 9781501345500 hardback | ISBN 9781501345517 electronic book | ISBN 9781501345524 electronic book
Subjects: LCSH: Women in the music trade. | Music trade–Social aspects. | Music–Instruction and study–Social aspects. | Popular music–Social aspects. | Feminism and music. | Women musicians–Social conditions.
Classification: LCC ML82.T69 2019 (print) | LCC ML82 (ebook) | DDC 338.4/778–dc23
LC record available at https://lccn.loc.gov/2019026068
LC ebook record available at https://lccn.loc.gov/2019026069

ISBN: HB: 978-1-5013-4550-0
PB: 978-1-5013-8322-9
ePDF: 978-1-5013-4552-4
eBook: 978-1-5013-4551-7

Typeset by Integra Software Services Pvt. Ltd.

To find out more about our authors and books visit
www.bloomsbury.com and sign up for our newsletters.

Contents

List of Illustrations		vii
Notes on Contributors		viii
Acknowledgements		xii

1 Towards Gender Equality in the Music Industry: An Introduction
   Catherine Strong and Sarah Raine   1

Part One Education

2 Gender and Popular Music Education in North America: We Need to Talk *Kelly Bylica and Ruth Wright*   15

3 Preparing for the 'Real World'? Exploring Gender Issues in the Music Industry and the Role of Vocational Popular Music Higher Education *Helen Elizabeth Davies*   29

4 Engineering a Place for Women: Gendered Experiences of the Music Technology Classroom *Emma Hopkins and Pauwke Berkers*   45

5 Qualified Careers: Gendered Attitudes towards Screen Composition Education in Australia *Catherine Strong and Fabian Cannizzo*   59

Part Two Current Practice

6 Gender, Policy and Popular Music in Australia: 'I Think the Main Obstacles Are Men and Older Men' *Maura Edmond*   73

7 Setting the Stage for Sexual Assault: The Dynamics of Gender, Culture, Space and Sexual Violence at Live Music Events *Bianca Fileborn, Phillip Wadds and Ash Barnes*   89

8 South-West England Open Mics: Gender Politics and Pints? *Sharon Martin*   103

9 Gender Mainstreaming in the Music Industries: Perspectives from Sweden and the UK *Sam de Boise*   117

10 The Gatekeeper Gap: Searching for Solutions to the UK's Ongoing Gender Imbalance in Music Creation *Emma Hooper*   131

Part Three *Strategies for Change*

11 Queer Noise: Sounding the Body of Historical Trauma *Samuel Galloway and Joseph Sannicandro* — 147

12 'There's No Money in Record Deals and I'm Not Looking to Be Taken Advantage Of': Princess Nokia and Urban Feminism in a New Era of Hip-Hop *Hodan Omar Elmi* — 163

13 'Kill It in a Man's World': Gender at the Intersection of the British Asian and Bollywood Music Industries *Julia Szivak* — 175

14 Keychanges at Cheltenham Jazz Festival: Issues of Gender in the UK Jazz Scene *Sarah Raine* — 187

15 Queer(ing) Music Production: Queer Women's Experiences of Australian Punk Scenes *Megan Sharp* — 201

Index — 214

Illustrations

Figures

5.1	Educational Attainment of Screen Music Composers	61
10.1	PRS Membership Numbers by Gender, 1994–2015	134
10.2	PRS Average Earnings by Year and Gender, 1994–2015	134

Tables

8.1	Performance Settings and Gender Percentages	108
8.2	Gender and Preferred Instrument of Interviewees	109

Contributors

Ash Barnes is a PhD candidate of Criminology at the University of Tasmania. Research interest include transgression, deviancy and music cultures and how these areas of interests can explain how and why physical violence and sexual assault occur and become normalized. Ash is also an activist with a passion for justice for all non-human animals and queer and indigenous rights.

Pauwke Berkers is Associate Professor of Sociology of Arts and Culture at the Erasmus School of History, Culture and Communication, Erasmus University Rotterdam. He is author of *Gender Inequality in Metal Music Production* (2018, with Julian Schaap) and published widely on gender in popular music in *Gender & Society, Journal of Gender Studies* and *IASPM@Journal*. He is PI of the HERA project FestiVersities: European music festivals, public spaces and cultural diversity and NWO project POPLIVE – Staging popular music.

Sam de Boise is Senior Lecturer in Musicology at the School of Music, Theatre and Art, Örebro University, Sweden, His research focuses on music participation and engagement from critical, feminist perspectives and particularly the role of cultural policy in this process. He has also written on music, affect and emotions in relation to critical studies on men and masculinities. He is the author of *Men, Masculinity, Music and Emotions* (Palgrave Macmillan 2015).

Kelly Bylica is currently a PhD candidate in music education at Western University in London, Ontario, Canada, and former vocal and general music teacher in the Midwestern United States. Her research interests include critical and creative learning projects, composition in the classroom, experiential learning, and issues relating to diversity and inclusion in the music classroom. Kelly holds Music Education degrees from Valparaiso University and Northwestern University.

Fabian Cannizzo is an independent social researcher at RMIT University in Melbourne, Australia. His latest publications include *The Social Structures of Global Academia* (Routledge, edited with Nick Osbaldiston) and 'Tactical Evaluations: Everyday Neoliberalism in Academia' (*Journal of Sociology*). His research focuses on the career development and inequalities experienced in the creative and cultural industries, including in the music industry and academia. He is currently the co-convenor of The Australian Sociological Association's Work, Labour & Economy thematic group.

Helen Elizabeth Davies is Lecturer in Music at the Liverpool Institute for Performing Arts. Having undertaken doctoral research into music in the everyday lives of young teenage girls, she is currently researching gendered experiences and practices of young popular musicians in the contexts of popular music higher education and the music industry. Her key research interests are gender and sexuality, music performance, music education, music in everyday life and ethnographic research.

Maura Edmond is Lecturer in the School of Media, Film and Journalism at Monash University where she is a founding member of the Gender and Media Lab. Her research explores the sociology of creative scenes and subcultures, and has examined visual art, music, podcasting, radio, fashion, film and fandom from this perspective. Her writing on media, art and culture has been published in outlets such as *New Media and Society, Television and New Media, Art and Australia, Senses of Cinema, Overland* and *The Routledge Handbook of Global Cultural Policy* (2018).

Hodan Omar Elmi is a feminist researcher based in London. Her research focus is migration, diasporas, gendering, critical race theory, performance studies and music. Further to her academic pursuits Hodan is a radio producer and presenter and DJ under the alias '1poundfashionista'.

Bianca Fileborn is Lecturer in the School of Social & Political Sciences, University of Melbourne. In 2019, Bianca was appointed as an ARC Discovery Early Career Research Award Fellow. Her research is concerned with examining the relationships between space/place, identity, culture and sexual violence, and justice responses to sexual violence. Bianca is the author of *Reclaiming the Night-Time Economy: Unwanted Sexual Attention in Pubs and Clubs* (2016), and co-editor of *#MeToo and the Politics of Social Change* (2019), both published through Palgrave Macmillan.

Samuel R. Galloway researches political and queer theory at the University of Chicago, where he is a doctoral candidate in Political Science (2019). His dissertation, *Cruising Politics*, reconstructs a conceptual pre-history of post-Fordist contentious political activism. His current project, tentatively titled *Betraying Sovereignty*, explores the elaboration of a non-sovereign political practice in the works of Melville, Arendt and Genet.

Emma Hooper is Reader in Music and Creative Writing at Bath Spa University, with research areas including gender, pop music and robots. As a violist she has performed with Peter Gabriel, the Heavy and numerous other artists, as well as released two albums (about dinosaurs and insects, respectively) as solo artist Waitress for the Bees. She has authored two internationally best-selling novels: *Etta and Otto and Russell and James* (2015) and *Our Homesick Songs* (2018). She lives in England but goes home to cross-country ski in Canada whenever she can. (emmahooper.ca)

Emma Hopkins has graduated the master program Arts, Culture & Society at the Erasmus School of History, Culture and Communication, Erasmus University Rotterdam. She presented her research Engineering a place for women at the IASPM

Benelux/KVNM Student Music Conference in Amsterdam. She is a singer, songwriter and producer, having studied Electronic Music Production at Manchester's Spirit Studios.

Sharon Martin is a songwriter, singer, musician and teacher. She has taught sociology in Further and Higher Education for many years, and worked as a subject leader, tutor, course manager and advanced practitioner. She has carried out action research for the Institute for Learning and been published in *Association of Teachers of Social Science* journal. In addition to her undergraduate studies in History and Sociology at Goldsmiths University, and her PGCE at Cardiff University, Sharon completed an MMus at Bath Spa University (2017) and an MA in Women's Studies at Exeter University (2000). She was a Global Association of Liberal Arts scholar at Bath Spa University. Her main research interest is the relationship between gender and places of performance. As a musician, Sharon performs under Sharon Lazibyrd and released her debut solo album *Half Shame and Half Glory* in 2018. She has been played on BBC 6 Music and was *BBC Music Introducing* artist of the week in January 2018.

Sarah Raine is a Postdoctoral Research Fellow at the Birmingham Centre for Media and Cultural Research (BCMCR) at Birmingham City University. Sarah is currently a Creative Economy and Enterprise Fellow (AHRC), working in partnership with Cheltenham Jazz Festival on their *Keychange* (PRS Foundation) pledge to achieve a gender balanced program by 2022. She researches and has been published on a range of subject to include northern soul, women in jazz, jazz and the everyday, popular music heritage and curation, and gender politics within music industry and scene. Sarah is the Co-Managing Editor for *Riffs: Experimental Writing on Popular Music*, the Review Editor for *Popular Music History* and a Series Editor for Equinox Publishing.

Joseph Sannicandro is a doctoral candidate in the Department of Cultural Studies and Comparative Literature at the University of Minnesota, where he is completing a dissertation on the history of (un)popular culture in Italy during the social movements of the 1960s and 1970s. He regularly publishes art and music criticism, including in-depth conversations with musicians discussing their creative practices via his series Sound Propositions. He also records under the moniker *the new objective* and under his own name, and in a duo with Stefan Christoff.

Megan Sharp is a queer researcher currently working with the Faculty of Medicine, Dentistry and Health Sciences at the University of Melbourne. As the faculty research assistant for diversity and inclusion, Megan's research explores institutional practices of exclusion based on gender and sexuality as well as the affective and dynamic practices of resilience and solidarity found in minoritised groups. Megan earned her PhD in sociology at the University of Newcastle, Australia, in 2018. Her work has been published in *Queer Studies in Media and Popular Culture*, *The Journal of Youth Studies*, and *Emotion, Space and Society* as well as publicly via the Australian Sociological Association's Youth and Gender blog platforms.

Catherine Strong is Senior Lecturer in the Music Industry program at RMIT in Melbourne, Australia. Among her publications are *Grunge: Popular Music and Memory* (2011), *Death and the Rock Star* (2015, edited with Barbara Lebrun) and *The Routledge Companion to Popular Music History and Heritage* (edited with Sarah Baker, Lauren Istvandity and Zelmarie Cantillon). Her research deals with various aspects of memory, nostalgia and gender in rock music, popular culture and the media. She is currently Chair of IASPM-ANZ and co-editor of *Popular Music History* journal.

Julia Szivak is a PhD candidate in Media and Cultural Studies at Birmingham City University, where she researches the transnational networks of British Asian music production. She completed her MA in Hindi Literature from the ELTE University, Budapest, and in Comparative History from the Central European University, Budapest. Her research interests include South Asian popular culture, with a special focus on Bollywood music.

Phillip Wadds is Lecturer in Criminology at the University of New South Wales in Sydney, Australia. His research interests include policing, the night-time economy and related leisure, alcohol and other drugs, gender and violence, urban governance and the crime/media nexus.

Ruth Wright is Professor of Music Education in the Don Wright Faculty of Music at Western University in Canada. She has served as Chair of Music Education and Assistant Dean of Research at this university. Her 2010 book *Sociology and Music Education* (Ashgate Press) is a frequently used textbook in courses exploring this field. With colleagues at Western University, she founded Musical Futures Canada, a popular music education program in Canada.

Acknowledgements

This edited collection is a testament to the hard and innovative work of the contributors. It exists due to their enthusiastic response to a call made by the editors in 2017 in our attempt to in some way address a gap in the work on gender politics in the music industry. Thank you for sharing your work with us, for listening to our suggestions and contributing in a very significant way to a complex and intersectional issue. It has been a pleasure working with you all.

The editors would also like to thank Bloomsbury Academic for seeing the potential in this work and for their support throughout the publication process, especially when we experimented a little with the normal form. And on that note, we also wish to thank Ian Davies and Adam Kelly-Williams for their evocative front cover.

The editors wish to thank their respective institutions – RMIT (Melbourne, Australia) and Birmingham City University (UK) – for their support during this project. We hope that our efforts continue to place our research centres at the forefront of inquiry and critical thinking, and that this book inspires a new generation of scholars to ask new questions and to address the gaps that remain.

Lastly, we would like to thank all the people who contributed to this book in the sharing of data and stories, policy and experiences. Without your contributions and your trust, all this research would be hollow and empty. We hope that each chapter represents the beginning of a purposeful and collaborative relationship between academia and industry, and that by working together we can move towards gender equality in the music industry.

1

Towards Gender Equality in the Music Industry: An Introduction

Catherine Strong and Sarah Raine

During the 2010s, an unprecedented amount of attention has been brought to bear on the subject of gender in the music industry, with an upsurge in reports and studies focusing on this issue. What has emerged is a picture of overwhelming and entrenched inequality. This is not new information: for decades, scholars have examined the ways people who identify as women are marginalized, including through: lack of access to spaces associated with music (Björck 2013); sexist attitudes, including assumptions that they cannot use instruments or technology (Clawson 1999); the existence of a 'boys' club' that makes it hard for women to access information and networks (Leonard 2016); and through mechanisms of taste-making and archiving that create canons and histories that focus on men (Reddington 2007; Schmutz and Faulpel 2010; Strong 2011). Ethnographic, audience and scene- and location-based research has documented exclusionary practices, and interrogated the way women are particularly under-represented as performers in genres such as electronic music (Farrugia 2012; Gadir 2017) and heavy metal (Hill 2016; Berkers and Schaap 2018).

Recently, however, data has begun to emerge that approaches this issue of inequality through a more industry-based perspective. This data – often coming from industry reports or media articles as well as academic works – shows that people identifying as women are earning less in royalties (Strong and Cannizzo 2017), played less on radio (McCormack 2017), under-represented in the charts (Lafrance et al. 2011), de-emphasized in Spotify playlists (Pelly 2018), more likely to have shorter careers (Lieb 2013) and few in number in key decision-making positions in the industry (McCormack 2017). Research looking at the relationship between education and gendered outcomes in industry has contributed an extra dimension to this work, particularly by showing how structural issues in education and education policies have an impact on who ends up with the skills to succeed in these industries (Born and Devine 2015; de Boise 2017). Importantly, industry bodies have begun to participate in data collection on a much wider scale than before. Studies such as those by the

PRS Foundation (2017a) in the UK, Buma/Stemra in the Netherlands (Smeulders and Berkers 2017) and the Media, Entertainment and Arts Alliance (Cooper, Coles and Hanna-Osborne 2017) in Australia have finally provided larger-scale and whole-industry numbers that bear out what smaller and qualitative studies have been trying to convey for decades: that women face an uphill battle in almost every area of the industry and in some specific areas are almost completely locked out. As just one example, in February 2019, Smith, Choueiti and Pieper released a report analysing 600 songs in the Billboard end-of-year charts from 2012 to 2017. They looked at who was involved in the creation of these songs, from studio personnel to performers to songwriters. The findings were stark: women made up only 22 per cent of artists, 12 per cent of songwriters and 2 per cent of producers. The data did not even hint at any improvement in these figures, with 2017 actually being the lowest point for women performers in the sample. The chapters in this volume provide further detail on many other studies recently released, so a recitation of all the emerging data will not be provided here, suffice to say that a similar picture to that painted by Smith, Choueiti and Pieper is apparent across the board.

This volume presents research that uses an industry-based approach to examine why this gender imbalance has proven so hard to shift, and explores strategies that are being adopted to try and bring about meaningful change in terms of women and gender-diverse people establishing ongoing careers in music. In particular, it aims to bring together some of the empirical research that is being done at this point in time, to further flesh out our understanding of what is actually happening in the industry. This is done by focusing on three key areas. First, music education has often been identified as a place where people who identify as women and girls encounter early barriers to their full participation in music making. Contributors to this book look at the links between education and music industry careers, and extend this observation to gender-diverse students. Next, the book presents a series of case studies that consider practices in the music industry, examining what happens in day-to-day interactions between musicians and industry workers that reinforce or challenge gender biases. Finally, the book explores activist spaces, looking at both insider and outsider approaches to understanding structural issues in the industry and organized attempts to enable change. This is done bearing in mind Leonard's (2016: 37) assertion that while there has been a strong focus on performers in popular music studies, 'relatively little attention has been given to how gender structures the experiences of those within other areas of employment in the music industries'. This book does also examine performers; however Chapters 4 and 15 include the perspectives of those training for or working in support roles such as sound engineers, while other chapters look at the roles of policy makers (Chapter 6) and gatekeepers of various types (Chapters 8, 10 and 14) in maintaining or challenging gender inequality, and Chapter 7 includes audience experiences. It should be noted also that the book grew out of a call for papers for a special edition of *IASPM@Journal* (volume 8, issue 1) on gender politics in the music industry. In response to this call, we received many more excellent abstracts than could be accommodated in that issue, so made a decision to publish this book as well. Reading that issue alongside this volume is recommended, as this would add further insights, including on industry insiders such as producers (Reddington 2018), record company employees (Bennett 2018) and venue owners (Attrep 2018).

In terms of the inclusion of different perspectives, it should also be noted that although gender is the key focus of this volume, most chapters also incorporate an intersectional (Crenshaw 1991) consideration of how other elements of identity, particularly sexuality, impact on people's experiences in the music industry. While some chapters present gender in binary terms, this is generally because the data authors are working with is presented in this way. This includes in Chapter 10, where an industry body has given access to data that could not be meaningfully analysed in a non-binary way, in Chapter 5 where respondents to a survey only identified as male or female despite being given alternative options, and in Chapter 6 where the historical data being examined is all framed in binary terms. These examples give us insight into both the dominance of certain narratives about gender within the music industry, and the exclusion of people who do not fit within this way of seeing the world. In terms of other aspects of identity, Chapters 12 and 13 explicitly explore race and ethnicity as factors in how women engage with the industry, and Chapters 11, 12 and 15 foreground queer actors and perspectives. However, despite an emerging body of work (see, for example, Hawkins 2017; Maus and Whiteley 2018) there is clearly more to be done to bring us to a point where our understanding of how inequality works in music is truly intersectional, particularly in terms of fully incorporating the experiences of gender non-conforming and trans*[1] persons into this story, and ensuring that the ways in which the experiences of women of colour differ from white women is understood.

In order to understand how gender inequality persists in the music industry, it also needs to be placed in the context of changing work conditions and the rise of the 'creative industries' as a framework through which artistic work is often viewed. The label 'creative industries' has become a catch-all term for fields such as music, film, television, visual art, creative writing and, in some cases, IT and advertising (as in the UK's Cultural and Creative Industries framework). While the reframing of creative activities as central to economic prosperity in many countries has increased the perception of their worth in various ways, this also reflects a neoliberal approach that uses economic value as the main way to judge the worth of an activity, and which puts the individual at the centre of discussion (Gill et al. 2017). This focus on the individual has consequences for how creative workers can confront inequality. Cultural workers often strongly buy in to the notion of the existence of a 'meritocracy' which supposedly ensures the success of the most talented and hardworking people regardless of their identity (Strong and Cannizzo 2017). This works in combination with a 'postfeminist sensibility' (Gill et al. 2017) that positions feminist goals as obsolete to de-emphasize structural approaches to gender inequality (see also McRobbie 2008). So while the creative industries as a whole have a reputation for being liberal and tolerant, this has not translated into greater actual inclusivity, and a strong belief in the 'fairness' of these industries may prevent closer interrogations of whether this is actually the case, especially by those holding privileged positions in the system (Taylor and O'Brien 2017).

The precarious nature of work and the 'gig economy' that is typical in creative industries (and becoming more common in all areas of work) also leads to disadvantageous gendered outcomes, as risk is transferred to workers and any characteristics or circumstances that prevent a worker from being endlessly flexible and responsive to the requirements of the market can easily derail a career (Gill 2002; Hesmondhalgh and Baker 2015; Gill et al. 2017). Greater caring responsibilities and a lack of access to the 'masculine subjectivities' (Miller 2016) necessary to succeed in such an environment make women more vulnerable than their male counterparts. These then are some of the defining characteristics of the environment that the chapters in this book attempt to engage with and provide greater understanding of.

At the same time, the experiences of those working in music cannot be entirely understood using a broader 'creative industries' lens. There are aspects of music making that differ greatly from what happens in film, or television, or advertising, and that require investigation in their own right. Maura Edmonds, in Chapter 6, shows how, for example, music has been treated quite differently on a policy front than other areas of the arts in Australia, and the four chapters on education show that the collaborative processes in music making impact on gendered outcomes as they are reproduced in the classroom. Subsuming music under the 'creative industries' label risks missing these nuances. Furthermore, while we have used the term 'music industry' for the title of this book and in this introduction, we understand – and the chapters in the book demonstrate – that what is under consideration is not a monolithic entity, but a range of different practices, scenes, genres and stakeholders that are held together loosely by the artform they have in common (see Williamson and Cloonan 2007). The recording industry associated with Bollywood that Hard Kaur works within (Chapter 13) is in many ways very different to the punk scene in Australia (Chapter 15), or the jazz festival circuit of the UK (Chapter 14). Equally, the three parts of this book include different theoretical and methodological approaches, engage with genre-specific notions of gender or authenticity, and, contain threads that overlap with the themes of the other sections. They all, however, offer pertinent examples, provocations and models for examining issues relating to gender in the music industry.

Part I: Education

The first section of this book focuses on issues relating to music education. Success in the music industry – particularly in popular music – has not always been clearly linked to education. In fact, one of the great tropes in popular music is that it is an art form that enables anyone with talent, regardless of their background, to succeed. Stories of under-educated or working class musicians becoming household names against the odds abound in pop music histories, from blues to rock to hip-hop and beyond. Myths like these can, however, be used to shore up inequality, by focusing on notions of individual talent and avoiding discussion of structural issues. Music education in the classroom, for instance, has been shown to be highly gendered, with boys and girls encouraged to go down different musical paths and develop relationships with music that are seen to be 'appropriate' for their gender (Green 1997). This has ongoing effects for the musical expression of women throughout their lives. In addition to this, education for the music industry is increasingly becoming formalized, with courses in this area growing exponentially in the last ten to fifteen years (Born and Devine 2015). This growth has not been gender-neutral; many of these new courses have a technology focus that is associated with lower enrolments of women. We therefore felt that a volume on gender in music needed to include material on education as one way to consider how entry to the industry is facilitated.

The section starts with an overview of gender in the music classroom in North American compulsory education. Kelly Bylica and Ruth Wright outline the belated inclusion of popular music in the classroom in this region, before moving on to an exploration of how this education can often centre the male, cisgendered subject. They suggest that this is connected to three key issues: difference in communication styles between boys and girls, and the way that this impacts on group dynamics; the replication of the masculine culture of popular music in the classroom; and differences in boys' and girls' socialization in regards to technology. The chapter concludes with an exploration of how these problems could be addressed, including practical actions such as creating separate spaces for girls to learn in, but ultimately coming back to the need for educators to revisit some of the fundamental assumptions in music pedagogy about who and what music is for. The following chapter, by Helen Davies, moves on to an examination of vocational popular education in music in the UK, and highlights a number of similar issues. She draws on the results of a study commissioned by UK Music looking at how gender and sexuality shape experiences in music education institutions, with data gathered from educators and students. Students – men, women and gender non-conforming – all reported that they felt constrained by gender stereotypes in the classroom, and that it is difficult to step outside these. They found that social networks created during their time in education were already becoming dominated by men, particularly because there were simply fewer women in the classroom.

The following two chapters provide case studies of issues relating to specific areas in post-compulsory education. In their chapter, Emma Hooper and Pauwke Berkers look at an area that remains one of the most resistant to change in terms of gender representation: music technology. The chapter begins with a recap of how producers and engineers are still overwhelmingly men, and enrolments in music technology courses do not suggest that this will change any time soon. Their study on women's experiences in music technology education spaces found that they were highly aware of their 'token' status in the classroom, and had to adapt to the masculine nature of the culture there. While they found their teachers to generally be supportive, the fact that they were being taught almost exclusively by men again reinforced their marginal status. Ultimately, finding additional ways to get more women into these classrooms may be required to effectively challenge the status quo in this area. In their closely related chapter, Strong and Cannizzo draw on data from a study of screen composition careers in Australia to explore the role that education plays in finding success in that part of the industry. Their study showed that women screen composers tended to be more highly qualified than the men in the field, and this chapter tries to unpack some of the reasons for this. Interviews with composers showed that most respondents came to screen composition after careers elsewhere in the music industry, and in making this change men were less likely to see education as being necessary, taking instead a 'try it and see' approach. Women, on the other hand, used further education as a way to bolster their confidence, and to create connections and networks that they then drew upon after leaving education. In studying the educational institutions offering screen composition-specific courses, the authors report that while music courses are split close to 50/50 in terms of gender, in composition and music technology courses the proportion of women students drops off dramatically. When they do take these courses, women have to contend with a 'hidden curriculum' that mirrors and helps reproduce the masculine environment of the screen industries. However, there is growing awareness of this issue in education institutions, where many – but not all – are actively trying to increase the numbers of women in their courses.

Part II: Current Practice

The second section of the book, 'Current Practice', provides a range of case studies from across the music industry that give us an insight into what is currently happening 'on the ground' in mainstream music industry spaces. More than merely interesting case studies, these offer a range of models for engaging with policy, industry data, audience research and participant narratives to explore the ways in which gender politics and inequalities play out in a range of contexts, and indeed the ways in which individuals, communities and legislative bodies are attempting to address these. Many, also, take as their focus under-theorized topics, purposefully establishing new discussions or continuing emerging conversations.

Maura Edmond starts the section with her historical overview of policy in the Australian arts sector, and notes the tendency for issues of gender to be ignored for long periods of time, and for the same problems to be identified time and time again when attention is paid to this area. These problems include the tendency for caring responsibilities to derail women's careers, women's relative lack of confidence in comparison to men making it harder for them to access career opportunities, and women being locked out of networks that are seen as 'boys' clubs'. In addition to this, women experience sexual harassment and lack role models, particularly in leadership positions within the industry, both of which create barriers to women feeling as though they belong to it. Edmonds also notes that alongside the repeated identification of these same problems comes the reiteration of the same ideas to change the situation, usually in the form of short-lived programs that are not properly evaluated or supported beyond one or two iterations. She argues that a new approach is needed that more carefully tracks change over time and the effectiveness of programs that try to help women, and points to a more successful track record in the film industry in Australia, and ideas emerging from grassroots activism, as possible ways forward.

In Chapter 7, Bianca Fileborn, Phillip Wadds and Ash Barnes consider sexual assault at live music venues in Australia through an ethnographic and audience-focused study. Having usefully framed sexual violence and harassment in relation to issues of gender and music – an area which has so far attracted little academic attention within popular music studies – the authors consider the dominant gender inequality in the Australian live music scene, and the subcultural norms, liminality, anonymity and sexualization of music spaces as the 'cultural scaffolding' (citing Gavey 2005) for sexual violence. This combination of elements also means that live music venues are difficult to police as these potentially harmful behaviours are deeply ingrained within the culture of festivals and live venues. The authors conclude by noting that such elements provide an opportunity for perpetrators, and victims are later called upon to downplay the severity of sexual violence and harassment.

Continuing a discussion of the cultural construction of gendered space, Sharon Martin examines how the space and place of open mic events can form a barrier to women's participation at these events. This is important, as open mics are a place where musicians often get their first opportunity to play in front of others, and exclusion from these may amount to exclusion from public music making altogether for some people. Martin's field work focuses on the difference between open mics held in pubs, which are run by men and almost exclusively have men as participants, and community music nights, which are held in halls and are more likely to be run by women. She notes that while the pub is already marked as a masculine space, halls can be configured to create a more inclusive atmosphere. In particular, halls can allow for the presence of children, which means women with caring responsibilities are more likely to be able to attend these events.

From local open-mic venues to national music industries, Sam de Boise compares how 'gender mainstreaming practices' have been implemented in the UK and Sweden, two countries with different legislation and cultural policy structures. By focusing on the similarities of the approaches, their successes and limitations, and by applying a frame of musical labour, de Boise considers gender mainstreaming strategies and the limitations of national and industry-driven data in understanding the extent of the gender imbalance within the music industry. Drawing on empirical research with nine representatives of the industry within the UK and Sweden, de Boise illustrates how concerted industry-responses, against a background of state-supported initiatives, may improve gendered representation. The chapter concludes with a call for intersectional and non-essentialist feminist approaches in addition to 'gender mainstreaming' strategies in order to address limitations and, for example, to engage beyond the binary.

Emma Hooper follows this up with an examination of the role of gatekeepers in the UK music industry. Her chapter draws on data produced through a partnership between a group of researchers (including herself) and the Performing Rights Society (PRS) in the UK, including quantitative data that shows the gender divide in the PRS membership and in members' earnings. Interviews with musicians and other industry participants examined in her chapter have highlighted how the people who stand between musicians and audiences, or gatekeepers, play a significant role in preventing women from gaining access to the networks and opportunities that are vital to building a career. Understanding how these gatekeepers make choices about what music to include and what to exclude is therefore vital, and Hooper concludes by suggesting that the introduction of quotas might be the only way to counteract the unconscious bias and ingrained habits of this group.

Part III: Strategies for Change

The final section of this edited collection contains a very different selection of case studies. This section concentrates more on resistance to the norms of the industry and how people have tried to affect meaningful change, or work outside the structures that marginalize women. These case studies present different ways of thinking about the music industry, or attempts to create new practices that fundamentally challenge the status quo. The examples in this section are more focused, looking at single acts, scenes or genres, in an effort to draw out the specifics of what has enabled different approaches to emerge and what effect this has had.

To begin the section, Sannicandro and Galloway uncover a fascinating aspect of the history of industrial and noise music in their case study of the band Fistfuck, composed of Diana Rogerson and Jill Westwood. Contemporaries of Coil and Nurse with Wound, Fistfuck have not been accorded the same respect in histories of these genres despite also doing groundbreaking work. Sannicandro and Galloway argue that there are a number of reasons for this; the very confronting nature of the use of BDSM imagery and practices on stage by the band; the diminution of their contribution because one of the band members, Diane Rogerson, was in a relationship with one of the members of Nurse with Wound; and the lack of recorded material by the band. The authors argue, however, that it is this very lack of material that opens up space for more interesting readings of the band and the potentials of the music industry itself. They consider how both noise and BDSM practices implicate the body in ways that mean capturing a performance for posterity in a meaningful form may not even be possible, and the potentialities hinted at in the tiny fragments of their work available to us may do more to open up queer spaces for thinking about bodies, trauma and gender. This raises questions about how the history of the music industry is written around records that best suit its capitalist form.

Following this with a further critique of the limits of the music industry, Hodan Elmi's chapter considers the career of Destiny Frasqueri, who performs under the name Princess Nokia. After her initial experiences in the industry were unsatisfactory, Nokia has sought to carve out a place for her music making that allows her to incorporate all aspects of her identity and values, including her queerness, her heritage and her spirituality. This involves also finding ways to empower others, particularly through what she calls 'Urban Feminism', a form of feminism that seeks to include all women, especially poor, inner-city women of colour who may be alienated by feminism's middle-class ways of speaking. Nokia therefore strives to bring her activism and her music-making together in a way that benefits others. This detailed consideration of a single musician is continued in the following chapter with Julia Szivak's study of the British Asian rapper, Hard Kaur. Placed within the gendered context of the Bollywood and the British Asian music industries, Szivak uses Hard Kaur as a case study through which to examine the construction and perception of femininity in both contexts, exploring the ways that this has been subverted by rapper during her career. Although this subversion of gendered expectations has at times proven problematic for Hard Kaur, Szivak argues that this liminal position at the intersections of diaspora and the nation has ultimately led to the rapper's successful negotiation of the strictly gendered roles in Bollywood and British Asian music.

Placing musician experiences within a specific music industry context, Sarah Raine presents the initial findings of a partnership research project with Cheltenham Jazz Festival in the UK, a project which aims to support the festival with their *Keychange* pledge (PRS Foundation) to a gender balanced program by 2022. Having set the scene for the gender politics of the UK jazz scene and the genre more widely, Raine considers the everyday music making activities of four women musicians in the UK as they detail the barriers to their access and progression in jazz in relation to formal education, DIY strategies and engagement with jazz festival gatekeepers. Again, the partial nature of UK data on the gender imbalance with the music industry is highlighted and the interpretative nature of the *Keychange* 50/50 gender balance target is problematized through an analysis of the festival's current and historic demographic data on musicians. With recommendations relating to Cheltenham's future strategy in mind, Raine ends by highlighting issues of visibility and access for women jazz musicians and considers the role of the academic in relation to these initiatives and gender politics.

Finally, Megan Sharp's chapter on the punk scene in Australia examines the contributions of queer women in support roles in the scene – such as sound engineers and stage technicians – and how they use a Do It Together ethos to create space for other non-cis male persons. By working 'within the margins' rather than trying to inhabit the centre of these scenes, these women can draw other like-minded people to them, and construct a supportive community that has the potential to ultimately reconfigure normative ideas of who can be part of punk. Sharp demonstrates how music itself is an important part of this process.

Sitting at the intersection between musical production, the creative industries and gender politics, this volume brings together research that considers the gender politics of the music industry itself. It takes a global approach to these issues, and incorporates a range of genres and theoretical approaches. At a time when more attention than ever is being paid to gender and music, this volume presents contemporary research that contributes to current debates and offers insights into possible solutions for the future. Moving forward, it is important that this attention is maintained, and that work is done to not just document the strategies being implemented, but to rigorously assess these to find out what is effective in the long term for increasing women's participation in all aspects of music making. At the moment this is the vital missing piece in the work being done, and tackling this challenge will ensure that we truly move forward towards gender equality in the music industry.

Note

This chapter contains material previously published as part of Strong, C. and S. Raine (2018) 'Gender politics in the music industry', IASPM@Journal, 8 (1): 2–8.

1 The asterisk is used here and throughout the book as a Boolean operator to indicate that there are a number of people who identify as transgender beyond binary gender (m/f) identities.

References

Attrep, K. (2018), 'From Juke Joints to Jazz Jams: The Political Economy of Female Club Owners', *IASPM@Journal*, 8 (1): 9–23.

Bennett, T. (2018), '"The Whole Feminist Taking-Your-Clothes-Off Thing": Negotiating the Critique of Gender Inequality in UK Music Industries', *IASPM@Journal*, 8 (1): 24–41.

Berkers, P. and J. Schaap (2018), *Gender Inequality in Metal Music Production*, New York: Emerald.

Björck, C. (2013), 'A Music Room of One's Own: Discursive Constructions of Girls-Only Spaces for Learning Popular Music', *Girlhood Studies*, 6 (2): 11–29.

Born, G. and K. Devine (2015), 'Music Technology, Gender, and Class: Digitization, Educational and Social Change in Britain', *Twentieth-Century Music*, 12 (2): 135–172.

Clawson, M.A. (1999), 'When Women Play the Bass: Instrument Specialization and Gender Interpretation in Alternative Rock Music', *Gender & Society*, 13 (2): 193–210.

Cooper, R., A. Coles and S. Hanna-Osborne (2017), *Skipping a Beat: Assessing the State of Gender Equality in the Australian Music Industry*, Sydney: University of Sydney.

Crenshaw, K. (1991), 'Mapping the Margins: Intersectionality, Identity Politics, and Violence against Women of Color', *Stanford Law Review*, 43 (6): 1241–1299.

De Boise, S. (2017), 'Gender Inequalities and Higher Music Education: Comparing the UK and Sweden', *British Journal of Music Education*, 35 (1): 23–41.

Farrugia, R. (2012), *Beyond the Dance Floor: Female DJs, Technology and Electronic Dance Music*, Bristol: Intellect.

Gavey, N. (2005), *Just Sex? The Cultural Scaffolding of Rape*, London & New York: Routledge.

Gadir, T. (2017), 'Forty-Seven DJs, Four Women: Meritocracy, Talent and Postfeminist Politics', *Dancecult*, 9 (1): 50–72.

Gill, R. (2002), 'Cool, Creative and Egalitarian? Exploring Gender in Project-Based New Media Work in Europe', *Information, Communication and Society*, 5 (1): 70–89.

Gill, R., E.K. Kelan and C.M. Scharff (2017), 'A Postfeminist Sensibility at Work', *Gender, Work & Organization*, 24 (3): 226–244.

Green, L. (1997), *Music, Gender and Education*, Cambridge: University of Cambridge Press.

Hawkins, S. (ed.) (2017), *The Routledge Research Companion to Popular Music and Gender*, Oxford: Oxford.

Hesmondhalgh, D. and S. Baker (2015), 'Sex, Gender and Work Segregation in the Cultural Industries', *The Sociological Review*, 63 (S1): 23–36.

Hill, R. (2016), *Gender, Metal and the Media: Women Fans and the Gendered Experience of Music*, London: Palgrave.

Lafrance, M., L. Worcester and L. Burns (2011), 'Gender and the Billboard Top 40 Charts between 1997 and 2007', *Popular Music and Society*, 34 (5): 557–570.

Leonard, M. (2016), 'Girls at Work: Gendered Identities, Sex Segregation, and Employment Experiences in the Music Industries', in J. Warwick and A. Adrian (eds.), *Voicing Girlhood in Popular Music: Performance, Authority, Authenticity*, 37–55, New York: Routledge.

Lieb, K. (2013), *Gender, Branding, and the Modern Music Industry*, New York: Routledge.

Maus, F.E. and S. Whiteley (2018), *The Oxford Handbook of Music and Queerness*, Oxford: Oxford.

McCormack, A. (2017), 'By the Numbers: The Gender Gap in the Australian Music Industry'. *triple j Hack*. Available online: http://www.abc.net.au/triplej/programs/hack/by-the-numbers-the-gender-gap-in-the-australian-music-industry/8328952 (accessed 14 June 2018).

McRobbie, A. (2008), *The Aftermath of Feminism: Gender, Culture and Social Change*, London: Sage.

Miller, D.K. (2016), 'Gender and the Artist Archetype: Understanding Gender Inequality in Artistic Careers', *Sociology Compass* 10 (2): 119–131.

Pelly, L. (2018), 'Discover Weakly: Sexism on Spotify', *The Baffler*. Available online: https://thebaffler.com/latest/discover-weakly-pelly (accessed 5 April 2019).

PRS Foundation (2017(a)), *Women Make Music Evaluation 2011–2016*. Available online: http://www.prsformusicfoundation.com/wp-content/uploads/2017/03/PRS-Foundation-Women-Make-Music-evaluation-report-2017-FINAL.pdf (accessed 27 August 2017).

Reddington, H. (2007), *The Lost Women of Rock Music*, Sheffield: Equinox.

Reddington, H. (2018), 'Gender Ventriloquism in Music Production', *IASPM@Journal*, 8 (1): 59–73.

Schmutz, V. and A. Faulpel (2010), 'Gender and Cultural Consecration in Popular Music', *Social Forces*, 89 (2): 685–707.

Smeulders, E. and P. Berkers (2017), *Women Music Creators in the Netherlands*, Rotterdam: Buma/Stemra.

Strong, C. (2011), 'Grunge, Riot Grrrl and the Forgetting of Women in Rock'. *Popular Communication*, 44 (2): 398–416.

Strong, C. and F. Cannizzo (2017), *Australian Women Screen Composers: Career Barriers and Pathways: Research Report*, Melbourne, Australia: RMIT University. Available online: http://apraamcos.com.au/about-us/industry-research/australian-women-screen-composers/ (accessed 17 November 2018).

Taylor, M. and D. O'Brien (2017), '"Culture Is a Meritocracy": Why Creative Workers' Attitudes May Reinforce Social Inequality', *Sociological Research Online*, 22 (4): 27–47.

Williamson, J. and M. Cloonan (2007), 'Rethinking the Music Industry', *Popular Music*, 26 (2): 306–322.

Part One

Education

2

Gender and Popular Music Education in North America: We Need to Talk

Kelly Bylica and Ruth Wright

Introduction

It is important not to overlook the seminal role that experiences in compulsory music education can play for students in preparation for entry to the popular music industry. To define our perspective, this chapter will, therefore, concentrate on matters of gender and popular music education within compulsory schooling in the North American context. The chapter will begin with an overview of the comparatively recent entrance of popular music into music education as a field and its even later appearance in North American music education. We will then consider issues affecting gender equality in popular music education at the compulsory schooling level in North America and possibilities for change to engage, enable and equip more students regardless of gender and sexual identity to enter the music industry.

History of popular music in North American education

In comparison to music education systems in the UK, Europe and the Nordic countries, popular music as a genre, and its associated pedagogies as curricular approaches, has received comparatively little attention until recently in North America. North American scholarship on popular music and education is therefore still in its infancy.

The Scandinavian countries led the way in the introduction of popular musics to music education, with established traditions in these genres dating from as early as the 1930s in Denmark (Wright 2017). The current status in these countries places popular musics and musicking practices in a central place in school music curricula, a situation also reflected in Scandinavian music education practices and curricula in post-compulsory education (Wright 2017). In Europe, Germany has included popular music in education from the 1950s onwards (Rolle 2010) and since the 1980s, popular music has become a frequent if not preferred genre in the classroom. In Britain, the place of popular music in the curriculum has been proposed and debated since the late 1960s (Swanwick 1968; Vulliamy and Lee 1982; Vulliamy and Shepherd 1984) and gradually assumed a peripheral place in the classroom. It was not until Green's (2001) *How Popular Musicians Learn* highlighted the essential role that authentic pedagogy must play when engaging in popular music learning in schools that a pedagogic breakthrough occurred. Subsequent to this, and the work of the Musical Futures project in the UK of which Green's research comprised a significant part, popular music became a central part of the UK music curriculum in many schools.

Despite expressions of support for popular music at the important Tanglewood Symposium on music education (Choate 1968), popular music has been much slower to gain entry to the school curriculum in the United States and Canada (Mantie 2013). Reasons for this appear to be numerous, but Mantie (2013) attributes the situation to a fundamental pedagogical if not epistemological dichotomy between the two national approaches to music education in the United Kingdom and the United States. Music educators in the UK and Europe may be seen to adopt a process-driven approach to music education, with a focus on student experience, partly due to the history of student musical composition in the classroom (Mantie 2013). Mantie views the North American approach, however, as more product-oriented with a concentration on high quality, large ensemble performance, the study of challenging repertoire and the conservation of a long-held tradition. In this context, the US discourse is centred around quality of repertoire, learning and teaching. As Mantie (2013: 343) observes:

> The conflation of quality with taste ... has factored significantly in the history of music education in the United States, evident in such things as the music appreciation movement and ongoing lists of 'best' music for school ensembles. It is not surprising, then, to find concerns about quality echoed in the American PMP [popular music pedagogy] discourses, where the potential use of popular music is accompanied by attendant fears over the erosion of quality teaching of quality music.

At the root of such differing transatlantic outcomes in music education in terms of the role of popular music may be matters of voice according to Mantie (2013). He suggests that, in the case of North America, the voices of those advocating for the introduction of popular music into the curriculum may simply not have been heard in the same way as those of their colleagues across the Atlantic. He attributes this to a number of contributory factors linked to Foucauldian theory of power and discourse and the sociolinguistic theory of Jan Bloomaert. Here, the failure to recognize both the culturally grounded context of certain discourses of popular music education and their linkage (or indexing) to certain specified social locations and powerful gatekeeping institutions in the originating context can neutralize their power to effect change in other global contexts.

Pedagogical views in England and across Europe often focus on the process of interweaving popular music pedagogy with the greater tapestry of music education (Wright 2017). Much of the focus in North American education, however, seems to separate popular music from the larger context of music education. Popular music is often offered either as a specialized, elective course that privileges specific ways of knowing and understanding (i.e. mixing, producing, songwriting, etc.), or through the inclusion of popular music repertoire in large ensemble programs, often still taught with traditional pedagogical techniques (Abramo 2011a, 2011b; Mantie 2013; Tobias 2013, 2014, 2015, 2016). In this context, progress has however been made in North America in the inclusion and introduction of music technology, recording, and producing programs as well as rock, pop, and jazz music in the curriculum (Wright 2016).

Gender and popular music education in North America: Current issues and possibilities for change

Music education is entrenched in a long tradition of patriarchy. Attention to feminist issues in this area therefore only began in the 1970s (Lamb, Dolloff and Howe 2002). Studies have explored missing female role models and gendered approaches to compositional and performance activities, among other issues (Koza 1993; O'Toole 1994; Gould 1996), but only in the last decade have scholars in the United States and Canada begun to explore gender in relation to popular music education and to widen their conceptions beyond the gender binary including considerations of sexual identity.

The majority of research in North American popular music education has focused on popular music elective courses offered to high school students (i.e. Abramo 2011a, 2011b; Tobias 2013, 2014, 2015). Research has suggested that while such course offerings are an important first step in introducing popular music to North American curricula, they raise questions concerning replication of issues of gender disparity (as noted by Abramo 2011a, 2011b; Tobias 2013, 2015; Cobb 2016). While Campbell, Connell and Beegle (2007: 222) suggest 'that the informal processes of making popular music, such as improvisation and group composition, could make the educational experience more stimulating and more enjoyable for adolescents', Abramo (2011b) posits that in our efforts to integrate a new pedagogical approach, we may have used hetero-normative, masculine popular music practices as the foundation of this new pedagogy. He suggests that our 'very definition of the popular music process [modelled on guitar-based, rock music] might render the girls' practice invisible and push them away' (37). This raises even wider issues when we consider popular music education from a non-binary gender/sexual identity perspective. What of students from the LGBTQ+ community? How might the replication of hetero-normative masculine popular music practices affect these students? What popular music learning spaces and pedagogical approaches might be needed to include and enable future students from across the gender/sexual identity spectrum?

Elementary general music has been even slower to embrace change (Regelski 2002; Benedict 2016). This phase of North American music education is still predominantly centred around the implementation of a number of long-standing pedagogical methods such as Orff, Kodaly, Dalcroze and Gordon. These methods are approaches that can be used to teach musical concepts; each has its own underlying philosophy, objectives, systems and goals. Critiques of an uninterrogated, singular implementation of these methods have been offered (Benedict 2009, 2016), and several studies have considered the inclusion of popular musics and popular music pedagogy within the primary school classroom (Jaffurs 2004; Lewis 2016; Linton 2016). Programs such as Little Kids Rock and Musical Futures have attempted to challenge traditional ways of thinking about general music learning (O'Neill and Bepsflug 2011; Wright 2011, 2016; Weiss, Abeles and Powell 2017 among others). Few studies, however, have considered the privileging of popular music gender narratives in the North American elementary music education context.

Existing studies can be analysed as demonstrating the perpetuation and replication of issues of gender inequality in popular music education related to three central issues: communication, replication of culture and technology. Each of these three central issues related to replication of gender inequality, as evidenced through empirical studies, will now be explored.

We would be remiss, however, in writing a chapter about gender and popular music education if we did not also include possibilities for change. According to sociologists such as Bourdieu (Bourdieu and Passeron 1990) and Bernstein (2000), beliefs and dispositions cultivated in compulsory education both reflect and reproduce those of dominant forces in society. Within such a conceptualization of education, however, there lies inherent the possibility that change at the level of the school might effect change at the level of society. Active reflection on how to reorient gendered practices in popular music in North American schooling and subsequent pedagogical innovation and implementation may therefore begin to impact the way we understand gender and sexual identity in relation to popular music more broadly.

Communication and group dynamics

Abramo's (2011a, 2011b) research on group compositional processes within a secondary school songwriting course noted gendered differences in the communicative styles of males and females. He found males were more likely to communicate in short bursts of conversation, more frequently opting for nonlinguistic communication or communication through musical gesture as opposed to female preference for verbal communication. These differences in communication also spilled over into songwriting styles. In his examination of two single-gendered secondary school rock bands and one of their original compositions (Abramo 2011a: 7), he noted that the girls' group composition with its 'integrated form, lyrics about personal relationships, standard tuning, clean timbres, and consistent tempo ... affirmed a certain type of femininity and also embodied the girls' "feminine" collaborative process'. The boys' group composition, on the other hand, with its 'rigid hierarchical form, unfettered sense of self and rebellion in the lyrics, drop D tuning, distortion, and manipulation of tempo ... projected a form of masculinity'. Each of these groups affirmed their gender through their use of characteristics associated with gendered norms.

Popular music pedagogy often involves groupwork, with students performing, composing, and improvising in friendship groups (Green 2001). Friendship groups strive to create spaces where students feel comfortable working together, emulating real-life practices of popular musicians. Tobias (2014), however, found that girls faced difficulty accessing male-dominated friendship groups. Girls felt as though they were held to higher expectations than boys or exhibited an inability to trust that male-dominated groups would offer opportunities for collaboration and compromise, often electing to find a female group to join or opting to work alone. In an ongoing project with Grade 7 and 8 students (ages 12–14) in a Musical Futures popular music class, we found similar themes, with girls in mixed groups dismayed that their female friends were not in their class, or all-girl groups who deliberately elected to remain all-female in an effort to make sure there was greater communicative harmony.

Replication of culture

A second issue to be considered is the replication of culture. Many of the gender norms that can be observed in the popular music classroom are replications of larger cultural and social structures. Abramo (2011b) notes that students and schools are not in a social vacuum, a conviction in evidence since the writings of John Dewey (1899). Every action and choice students make is either borrowed from or in reaction to the rules that shape their social world. Their compositions and creations, therefore, are 'not only products of musical knowledge, but also products of cultural knowledge expressed musically' (Abramo 2011b: 9). Because music is a social construction, consideration must be given to the delineated (extra-sonic) meanings created by the context and individuals who are experiencing the music (Green 2010). This means that engaging in popular music requires an awareness of the gendered relationships we have with music, and the awareness that popular music pedagogy cannot ever be a neutral endeavour, requiring awareness and vigilance on the part of the educator as to the reproduction of gender norms.

Within popular music education, and popular music as a whole, there is a history of gendered spaces as well as the perpetuation of a heteronormative discourse (Tobias 2014; Smith 2015). Popular music can be misogynistic, exclusionary and sexualized. Lyrical insinuations, objectification and sexualisation of women, and the relegation of women to restrictive gendered musical roles – as singer or bass player – can contribute to these practices. Dialogues and conversations that challenge these discourses and others as they relate to non-binary conceptualisations of gender and sexual identity are important to future change and do exist in some popular music classrooms.

In Cobb's (2016) study, students challenged the exclusive use of heterosexual gender pairings in their music video production. Through the process of producing a music video, they explored romantic narratives of love and loss from a variety of viewpoints, using their experiences in this class to interrogate both their own – and society's – views. The space created in this popular music class enabled students to have difficult conversations that challenged heteronormative narratives, creating opportunities for students to explore their own identities, and welcoming a diversity of perspectives and opportunities.

Abramo (2015) explored ways of challenging the sexism, heteronormativity and racism that can be present in popular music through different readings of a popular work. He advocates for a listening and discussion model that welcomes, but also critically examines popular music that is brought into the classroom. Not every popular music classroom operates in this way, however.

The LGBTQ+ community is often excluded from or silenced within the music classroom and within popular music, particularly if we are unwilling to see a spectrum of possibilities in how we encourage popular musicking in classes. The girls in Tobias's (2014: 5) study ask us to challenge 'gendered societal norms ... and the exclusionary nature of the music industry', but we must also be willing to look past gender as a duality. There is a significant gap in popular music education literature concerning those students who do not identify within the traditional gender binary. This suggests that conversations that address existing gender inequalities within the popular music industry and the ways in which these might intersect with a multiplicity of student identities are needed in our classrooms. This is especially important if our conception of education is that it can, and should, be a response to marginalization and heteronormativity, not a perpetuation of current narratives.

Technology

Technology, particularly at the intermediate and secondary levels, has often been cited as a source of alienation for females (Comber, Hargreaves, and Colley 1993; Armstrong 2001; Pegley 2006). Armstrong (2001) linked this to *technophobia* (fear of technology). Technophobia is part of a larger debate in popular music studies, as Bayton (1998) and Hollows (2000) note that women are often excluded from decision-making positions in the production side of the music industry due, in part, to perceived or realized technophobia. Technophobia is historically associated with women, and Armstrong suggests that girls may avoid technology as it is socially constructed as a male domain. In Pegley's (2006) case study of two technology-driven Ontario intermediate schools in the mid 1990s, ensemble-based choral and band programs were abolished in favour of sound editing and production courses. Girls had more adverse attitudes towards the technological classes than boys and expressed concern that too much technology was replacing meaningful live interaction within the school environment.

More recently, Tobias's (2013, 2014, 2015) study of a secondary songwriting and technology course noted that of the few girls in the class, all were engaged in the technological processes. While girls in this study occasionally found themselves frustrated with technology, they remained engaged in the process. One girl in his study purposefully chose to work alone in order to gain technological production skills. Alice, another student in Tobias's (2013) study, worked almost exclusively with technology for her projects and found that she was able to record/create her entire track based on her ability to manipulate MIDI. Editing and mixing were central to the work of several of the girls in this study. These differences suggest that this issue may be changing over time, or may manifest differently in distinct contexts.

Simoni and Younker (2008) found that girls in a single-gendered, after-school composition and technology program appreciated the freedom to play with technology in a safe environment, suggesting the benefits of all-girl spaces. Comber, Hargreaves, and Colley (1993) echo this, suggesting that girls may take a bit longer to feel comfortable with technology, but quickly catch up to boys, indicating that confidence, rather than skill, is the issue here. Technology and technophobia should not prevent girls from engaging at the same level as boys in technological endeavours. These studies demonstrate that young women are both interested in technology and willing and able to challenge male domination in the field. What is perhaps necessary is a safe space for girls, girl-identified and other non-hetero or cis-gendered students, away from the hetero-male gaze, in which they might be able to develop confidence, explore and learn among like role models and away from stereotypes. However, it is equally important to note that 'female-only activities can be seen as prohibiting' and that flexibility must be maintained in order to help students of different genders and sexual identities to learn to work together with technology (Baker and Cohen 2008: 330). These are complex issues and will require considerable research and inquiry to unravel.

Tobias (2013) noted that, despite their commitment to engaging with technology, one of the female participants in his study felt that the technological course name, as well as the focus on technology, kept other female songwriters from electing to take the course. This suggests that the labelling and pigeonholing of popular music courses as inextricably connected to technology may keep girls from participating in them. As students continue to enter compulsory schooling as digital natives, this technological imbalance may even out. This may be especially so if, as Tobias (2014) suggests, educators consider varied pathways to engaging with technology, rather than forcing a singular approach to technological musicking. One way to combat concerns of technology is to rethink the naming, labelling and focus of popular music education courses.

It is apparent from the discussion above that the relationship between gender and music technology is not the simple binary previously supposed. If, however, one of the goals of popular music pedagogy is to affirm the skills and interests of all students through popular music offerings, it may be beneficial to consider how we label and choose these offerings. Perhaps it is particularly necessary to consider whether our course offerings and designations are affirming the interests and skills of all students, or merely the interests and skills of some (McPhail 2013).

Tobias (2014) asserts that recording, production and mix engineering are often inherently male-dominated fields and links this perception to the reluctance of some girls to partake in these courses. This connects back to previous discussions of technophobia (Bayton 1998). Tobias suggests that, had the curricular priorities in the course he researched been broader, considering the creative songwriting process in addition to the emphasis on the technological aspects of recording and producing, more girls might have expressed interest in the course. Discussions surrounding the interaction of expression and meaning-making through songwriting with the technological skills necessary for recording and producing may have opened space for 'dialogue addressing gendered meanings and identities' (Tobias 2014: 20).

This brings us to consideration of issues of power and the problems inherent in uninterrogated replication of gendered stereotypes (Hollows, 2000). It also raises questions as to whether the role of pedagogy in relation to gender equality in the classroom is to work within the confines of dominant gendering to 'balance' curriculum, or to address the wider gendered assumptions at the root of these stereotypes.

Possibilities for change

The issues presented above: communication and group dynamics, replication of culture, and technology are intertwined. Considering possibilities for change within one invariably impacts the others. Therefore, each of these suggestions, though certainly not an exhaustive list, responds to multiple issues.

Female-only spaces have been explored as a response to counter some of the male-domination that can occur in popular music classrooms. Girls have been noted as more willing to speak out in all-girl spaces, and all-girl spaces offer the opportunity to try out roles and modes of communication usually claimed by boys (Björck 2013; Warwick and Adrian 2016). Our current ongoing research, however, suggests that girls may still reproduce dominant roles within an all-girl group, leaving the opinions of some group members muted, thereby eliminating the communicative 'leg up' that all-girl musicking might offer female students. Additionally, Tobias (2014) noted that in the elective class offering in his study, few girls were present in the class, leaving few options for girls to find all-girl spaces in which to work within the classroom structure. Therefore, while all-girl musicking may offer possibilities in elementary or compulsory music education courses, elective classes pose a different challenge.

This then begs the question: why were so few girls in Tobias's study participating in non-compulsory popular music offerings? Perhaps a critical look at how we are conceptualizing these classes – and what we are asking students to do in them – is necessary. As educators, we may be privileging one way of knowing or doing in popular music, all while failing to ask ourselves why that particular form of knowledge is important (Abramo 2011b). We may be complicit in perpetuating gendered stereotypes of popular musicking rather than addressing the underlying assumptions.

Rather than insisting that students operate within larger, often gendered, structural understandings of popular music participation, educators might create spaces for exploration within popular music. These explorations may or may not include technology, and they may or may not be guided by a particular genre within the popular paradigm. Allowing students to 'choose their own processes regardless of the labels' (Abramo 2011b: 37) requires active reflection in our assumptions and epistemologies that may be blinding us as educators to the ways in which we are reproducing gendered inequality. By changing the expectations we communicate to students and aiming to treat classrooms as places for students to gain awareness and connection with others, we avoid the reproduction of any singular way of *doing* popular music, instead creating spaces for exploration and curiosity. Students are agents of change. They are not in music classes only to learn established traditions privileged and taught by the educator; they are in music classes to '*shape* musical traditions and social traditions that live and breathe and transform the world in which we live' (Allsup and Sheih 2012: 50). It is our responsibility to listen to what they are saying.

Tobias (2016: 113) suggests considering a hybrid approach when conceptualizing popular music classes. A hybrid approach 'reflects a comprehensive curricular model that allows for students to emphasize particular foci or specializations while developing multifaceted or hyphenated musicianship in varied contexts.' In this way, 'students might emphasize different roles or ways of knowing and doing music to varied degrees in the same class as opposed to focusing solely on musicianship specific to a particular way of being musical'. Instead of excluding or focusing on one way of doing popular music, students investigate and explore, engaging in a multifaceted, individualized approach to creating popular music that allows them space to create and learn meaningfully.

The deliberate inclusion of different ways of experiencing and doing popular music also comes with questions about difficult topics surrounding aspects of human experience. How do we have conversations that challenge music that reifies gendered norms, objectifies young women and men, and expresses topics of sexuality, desire and sexual orientation? How do we address issues of inequality, gendered norms and objectification within the popular music industry writ large? These are questions that are often messy, scary and difficult for educators to introduce into the classroom, but we know that ethically, we cannot ignore them. While conversations may look different in elementary and secondary contexts, we must break down the narratives that may be preventing some from participating if we want to make the popular music classroom a space for all to explore. Noticing inequities, identifying them, and naming them requires conversations that require courage, both on the part of the educator and also on the part of students. How can we hope to create spaces for change and transformation if we do not acknowledge current inequities? Changing how we conceptualize popular music education requires ethically aware, critically self-reflective practitioners willing to take the time and emotional investment to recognize and respond to current inequity and to cultivate the same qualities in their students.

Abramo (2011b) warns of reducing gender in popular music education to an *a priori* dichotomy that does not include space for a continuum of experiences. What may be true for some girls, will not be true for all, and the same for boys. Furthermore, an exploration that insists on male and female dichotomous categories excludes issues facing the LGBTQ+ community. Rie's story (as documented by Nichols 2013) shares the journey of a transgendered student who uses popular music composition as an avenue to explore identity and self-becoming. When Rie is denied access to her school music programs, she finds ways to express herself musically through composition, alone, in a space devoid of music educators and expectations. She subsequently finds a musical community through the sharing of her works both live and online. We must ask ourselves whether our popular music programs and classes are truly welcoming to students like Rie. If not, why? And more importantly, how can we consider pedagogical mindshifts that create spaces in popular music education that welcome all students, regardless of gender or sexual identity?

Concluding thoughts

Addressing the complexities of the replication of gender inequalities within popular music education is not as simple as encouraging girl and girl-identified students to join and contribute to popular music classes. While addressing gender imbalances in student participation and acknowledging misogynistic, heteronormative, exclusionary and sexualized popular music tropes is a step forward, it is inadequate without 'critical analyses of the systems that perpetuate ... exclusion and gendered norms' on the part of both educators and students collaboratively (Tobias 2014: 16). This can lead to spaces that welcome and support students of any gender or sexual identity. This much needed pedagogical mindshift will require active reflection that examines 'how and why these processes come to be, and why students, as active musicians in the popular music process, make the decisions they do' (Abramo 2011a: 9). As popular music education matures in North America, we, as educators will need to reach beyond traditional boundaries and narratives, challenging our own and our students' conceptions of ways of knowing and doing popular music if we are to contend with gender inequality in popular music classrooms and ultimately in the popular music industry.

References

Abramo, J.M. (2011a), 'Gender Differences in the Popular Music Compositions of High School Students', *Music Education Research International*, 5: 1–11.

Abramo, J.M. (2011b), 'Gender Differences of Popular Music Production in Secondary Schools', *Journal of Research in Music Education*, 59 (1): 21–43.

Abramo, J.M. (2015), 'Negotiating Gender, Popular Culture, and Social Justice in Music Education', in C. Benedict, P. Schmidt, G. Spruce and P. Woodford (eds.), *The Oxford Handbook of Social Justice in Music Education*, 582–597, New York: Oxford.

Allsup, R.E. and E. Sheih (2012), 'Social Justice and Music Education: The Call for a Public Pedagogy', *Music Educators Journal*, 98 (4): 47–51.

Armstrong, V. (2001), 'Theorizing Gender and Musical Composition in the Computerized Classroom', *Women: A Cultural Review*, 12: 35–43.

Baker, S. and B.M.Z. Cohen (2008), 'From Snuggling and Snogging to Sampling and Scratching: Girls' Nonparticipation in Community-Based Music Activities', *Youth and Society*, 39 (3): 316–339.

Bayton, M. (1998), *Frock Rock: Women Performing Popular Music*, Oxford: Oxford University Press.

Benedict, C. (2009), 'Processes of Alienation: Marx, Orff and Kodaly', *British Journal of Music Education*, 26 (2): 213–224.

Benedict, C. (2016), '"Reading" Methods', in C. Abril and B. Gault (eds.), *Teaching General Music*, 368–374, New York: Oxford University Press.

Bernstein, B. (2000), *Pedagogy, Symbolic Control and Identity*, Lanham: Rowman and Littlefield.
Björck, C. (2013), 'A Music Room of One's Own: Discursive Constructions of Girls-Only Spaces for Learning Popular Music', *Girlhood Studies*, 6 (2): 11–29.
Bourdieu, P. and J-C. Passeron (1990), *Reproduction in Education Society and Culture*, London: Sage.
Campbell, P.S., C. Connell and A. Beegle (2007), 'Adolescents' Expressed Meanings of Music in and out of School' *Journal of Research in Music Education*, 55 (3): 220–236.
Choate, R.A. (ed.) (1968), *Music in American Society: Documentary Report of the Tanglewood Symposium*, Music Educators National Conference.
Cobb, G. (2016), 'Music Video Production (MVP), Education and New Musical Literacies for 21st Century Music Learners', in R. Wright, B.A. Younker and C. Beynon (eds.), *21st Century Music Education: Informal Learning and Non-Formal Teaching Approaches in School and Community Contexts*, Waterloo, ON: CMEA/ACME.
Comber, C., D.J. Hargreaves and A. Colley (1993), 'Girls, Boys and Technology in Music Education', *British Journal of Music Education*, 10: 123–134.
Dewey, J. (1899), *The School and Society: Being Three Lectures*, Chicago: University of Chicago Press.
Gould, E.S. (1996), 'Initial Involvements and Continuity of Women Band Directors: The Presence of Gender-Specific Occupational Models' (Doctoral dissertation). Retrieved from ProQuest Dissertation and Theses Global (UMI No. 9626111).
Green, L. (2001), *How Popular Musicians Learn: A Way Ahead for Music Education*, Cambridge, England: Cambridge University Press.
Green, L. (2010), 'Gender Identity, Musical Experience, and Schooling', in R. Wright (ed.), *Sociology and Music Education*, 53–66, New York: Routledge.
Hollows, J. (2000), *Feminism, Femininity, and Popular Culture*, Manchester, U.K.: Manchester University Press.
Jaffurs, S.E. (2004), 'The Impact of Informal Music Learning Practices in the Classroom, or How I Learned How to Teach from a Garage Band', *International Journal of Music Education*, 22 (3): 189–200.
Koza, J.E. (1993), 'The 'Missing Males' and Other Gender Issues in Music Education: Evidence from the *Music Supervisors' Journal*, 1914–1924', *Journal of Research in Music Education*, 41 (3): 212–232.
Lamb, R., L. Dolloff and S.W. Howe (2002), 'Feminism, Feminist Research, and Gender Research in Music Education: A Selected Review', in R. Colwell and C. Richardson (eds.), *The New Handbook of Research on Music Teaching and Learning*, 648–674, New York: Oxford University Press.
Lewis, J. (2016), 'Musical Voices from the Margins: Popular Music as a Site of Critical Negotiation in an Urban Elementary Classroom' (Unpublished doctoral dissertation). Teachers College: New York.
Linton, L. (2016), '"When Are You Going to Start Teaching Us?" Primary Music Education and Informal Learning: Expectations and Outcomes', in R. Wright, B.A. Younker and C. Beynon (eds.), *21st Century Music Education: Informal Learning and Non-Formal Teaching Approaches in School and Community Contexts*, Waterloo, ON: CMEA/ACME.
Mantie, R. (2013), 'A Comparison of "Popular Music Pedagogy" Discourses', *Journal of Research in Music Education*, 61 (3): 334–352.

McPhail, G. (2013), 'The Canon or the Kids: Teachers and the Reconceptualization of Classical and Popular Music in the Secondary School Curriculum', *Research Studies in Music Education*, 35 (10): 7–20.

Nichols, J. (2013), 'Rie's story, Ryan's Journey: Music in the Life of a Transgender Student', *Journal of Research in Music Education*, 61 (3): 262–279.

O'Neill, S. and K. Bespflug (2011), 'Musical Futures Comes to Canada: Engaging Students in Real-World Music Learning', *The Canadian Music Educator*, 53 (2): 25–27.

O'Toole, P. (1994), 'I Sing in a Choir But I Have "No Voice!"', *Quarterly Journal of Music Teaching and Learning*, 4, 5 (4, 1): 65–77.

Pegley, K. (2006), 'Like Horses to Water: Reconsidering Gender and Technology within Music Education Discourses', *Women and Music: A Journal of Gender and Culture*, 10: 60–70.

Regelski, T. (2002), 'On "Methodolatry" and Music Teaching as Critical and Reflexive Praxis', *Philosophy of Music Education Review*, 10 (2): 102–123.

Rolle, C. (2010), 'Über Didaktik Populärer Musik. Gedanken zur Un-Unterrichtbarkeit aus der Perspektive ästhetischer Bildung', in J. Terhag and J. Terhag (eds.), *Musikunterricht heute Bd.8. Zwischen Rock-Klassikern und Eintagsfliegen. 50 Jahre Populäre Musik in der Schule* [About teaching popular music. Thoughts on un-teachability from the perspective of aesthetic building. Music lessons today, Vol. 8. Between rock classics and ephemera. 50 years of popular music at school], 206–220, Oldershausen: Lugert Verlag.

Simoni, M. and B.A. Younker (2008), 'Project Lovelace: Teenage Girls and Technology Based Composition'. International Computer Music Conference, Belfast, N. Ireland, International Computer Music Association.

Smith, G.D. (2015), 'Masculine Domination in Private-Sector Popular Music Performance Education in England', in P. Burnard, Y. Hofvander Trulsson and J. Söderman (eds.), *Bourdieu and the Sociology of Music Education*, 61–78, Surrey: Ashgate.

Swanwick, K. (1968), *Popular Music and the Teacher*, Oxford: Pergamon.

Tobias, E.S. (2013), 'Composing, Songwriting, and Producing: Informing Popular Music Pedagogy', *Research Studies in Music Education*, 35 (2): 213–237.

Tobias, E.S. (2014), 'Solo, Multitrack, Mute? Producing and Performing (Gender) in a Popular Music Classroom', *Visions of Research in Music Education*, 25: 1–28.

Tobias, E.S. (2015), 'Crossfading Music Education: Connections between Secondary Students' in-and out-of-School Music Experience', *International Journal of Music Education*, 33 (1): 18–35.

Tobias, E.S. (2016), 'Learning with Digital Media and Technology in Hybrid Music Classrooms', in C. Abril and B. Gault (eds.), *Teaching General Music*, 112–140, New York: Oxford University Press.

Vulliamy, G. and E. Lee (eds.) (1982), *Pop, Rock and Ethnic Music in School*, Cambridge: Cambridge University Press.

Vulliamy, G. and J. Shepherd (1984), 'Sociology and Music Education: A Response to Swanwick', *British Journal of Sociology of Education*, 5 (1): 57–76.

Warwick, J. and A. Adrian (eds.) (2016), *Voicing Girlhood in Popular Music. Performance, Authority, Authenticity*, New York: Routledge.

Weiss, L., H.F. Abeles and B. Powell (2017), 'Integrating Popular Music into Urban Schools: Examining Students' Outcomes of Participation in the Amp Up New York City Initiative', *Journal of Popular Music Education*, 1 (3): 331–356.

Wright, R. (2011), 'Musical Futures: A New Approach to Music Education', *The Canadian Music Educator*, 53 (2): 19–21.

Wright, R. (2016), 'Informal Learning in General Music Education', in C. Abril and B. Gault (eds.), *Teaching General Music*, 209–240, New York: Oxford University Press.

Wright, R. (2017), 'The Longer Revolution: The Rise of Vernacular Musics as "New Channels of General Learning"', *Journal of Popular Music Education*, 1 (1): 9–24.

3

Preparing for the 'Real World'? Exploring Gender Issues in the Music Industry and the Role of Vocational Popular Music Higher Education

Helen Elizabeth Davies

Introduction

At *Billboard*'s 2015 'Women in Music' event, after receiving the 'Woman of the Year' award, Lady Gaga described the music industry as 'a f***ing boys' club' (Shepherd 2015). In 2016, having been repeatedly under-credited for her work, Björk criticized the music press for being a 'boys' club' (Earls 2016). For Carla Marie Williams, songwriter and founder of support network Girls I Rate, equality in the music industry 'definitely doesn't exist' as it is still a 'boys' club' (Khomami 2018). These views reflect increasing discussions relating to gender issues in the music industry,[1] where there have been calls for and action to bring about change. This is occurring at a time when the links between the music industry and the growing number of vocational popular music degree courses are being strengthened. For example, UK Music's[2] Music Academic Partnership is a collaboration between music educational institutions and UK Music members focused on 'preparing individuals who want to build careers out of their passion for music' (UK Music n.d.). Given the continuing development of connections between the music industry and popular music higher education, and the gender issues identified in the industry, taking account of gender in the popular music higher education context is crucial.

This chapter discusses a UK Music-supported research project that aims to explore experiences and issues relating to gender and sexuality[3] for young musicians. Using data generated primarily from qualitative research with UK-based musicians who are in vocational popular music higher education or graduates in their early careers, the chapter focuses on the intersections between education and industry to argue that, when preparing students for a career in the music industry, popular music higher education currently contributes more to the maintenance than to the disruption of the music industry 'boys' club', due to gender inequalities earlier in the musical pipeline. The chapter begins with a consideration of gender in popular music higher education, then an outline of the research project aims, participants and methods. The final sections analyse the research data in relation first to gender norms and stereotypes, then to networking and opportunities, focusing on education contexts and strategies.

Gender in music higher education

The study of gender has particular importance for courses offering a popular music education that is practical, vocational and music industry facing (Whiteley 2015: 369), of which there is an ever-increasing number. In 1996, there were 'over 80 courses of various levels available in the UK for students of the music business, instrumental skills and music technology' (Laing 1999); twenty years later, around 1500 similar courses were listed (Ariadne Publications/UK Music 2016). For students taking many of these courses, work in the music industry is not only future activity for which they are being prepared, but ongoing activity that is integral or additional to the curriculum. There are, as Hebert, Abramo and Smith (2017: 458) recognize, 'ethical challenges' for educators and institutions who are 'working towards equitable ends in and through music education' at the same time as seeking to 'prepare students for an industry that endorses and perpetuates sexism and even misogyny'. For Woodward (2017: 401), 'masculine domination of popular music performance and music production makes the demand for gender equity in the popular music classroom all the more challenging'.

The importance of addressing gender issues in music at school level cannot be overstated. Green's (1997) research in schools shows how musical meanings, discourses and practices are produced and reproduced as gendered. Singing, for example, is affirmed as a feminine practice while technologies and composition are constructed as masculine. Following Green, Dibben (2002) highlights the gendering of instruments among older children, with boys preferring to play 'masculine' instruments such as drums, guitar and trumpet and girls tending to choose the more 'feminine' flute, piano and violin (O'Neill and Boulton cited in Dibben 2002: 122). Research published in 2015 by the National Association for Music in Higher Education shows the extent to which the gendered tendencies and assumptions prevalent at school level filter through to music higher education, reporting 'the gendering of roles, disciplines, practices and behaviours plays a big part in Music, resulting in the underrepresentation of women in many areas and particularly at management and policy making levels' (Bogdanovic 2015: 19). Although this research did not involve student participants, staff offered observations about students' gendered practices, such as: 'You generally see females singing or playing the keyboard and even if that's not the thing that they're good at. Similarly, you will see the boys doing all quote-unquote masculine parts' (Bogdanovic 2015: 12). The gendering of instruments affects the gendering of academic roles resulting in unevenness of role models, which in turn has an impact on student choices, thereby contributing to the 'perpetuation of the established gendered musical pathways' (Bogdanovic 2015: 10).

The comments made by Bogdanovic's research participants align with Green's school level research, suggesting that by the time musicians reach higher education, their gendered roles and practices are well established. Research carried out by de Boise (2017) comparing gender inequalities in music higher education in the UK and Sweden, confirms that 'gender divisions in instrument selection, and activity in secondary education' are amplified in music higher education (de Boise 2017: 32).

Due to the vocational nature of many music higher education courses, it is clear that 'inequalities in formal music education relate to and further impact inequalities in wider music practice' (de Boise 2017: 23). As Born and Devine (2015: 149) assert, musical instruments can 'serve as key avenues through which larger musical formations such as genres are constructed as gendered communities of practice'. Direct and in-depth research into the gendered experiences of musicians in higher education, therefore, can contribute valuable perspectives on the role of vocational popular music higher education in the maintenance or disruption of the music industry 'boys' club'.

Young musicians research project

In 2016, UK Music commissioned a scoping study for research into experiences and issues relating to gender and sexuality for performers of popular music aged eighteen to twenty-five, in higher education, training or early career, investigating:

1. the ways in which they identify with, experience and perform gender and sexuality in their musical practices;
2. their key issues and challenges relating to gender and sexuality;
3. how popular music higher education and community-based music organizations currently respond to these issues and challenges, and what needs to change.

In the first instance, seven professionals working in the music industry or music support roles were asked to share their insights into the key challenges relating to gender and sexuality for young musicians.[4] They identified a range of issues including: low levels of female membership of music industry bodies; the masculinization and male domination of music facilities and scenes; lack of female participation in music scenes, projects and programs; few female leaders, tutors, staff and role models; low visibility and recognition of female participation; gender stereotyping of musical roles; sexualization of female musicians; and barriers to non-hetero sexualities in some communities.

Following this, as part of a pilot study, I conducted semi-structured, one-to-one interviews based on the research questions outlined above, with seven young musicians at the Liverpool Institute for Performing Arts (LIPA), a higher education institution in the UK. Lise, Lucy, Georgia, Kristian and Ian were final year LIPA music undergraduates, and Kamilla and Simon are LIPA music graduates in their early careers. In addition, Ash, a music undergraduate from another institution, shared his experiences with me via email. Georgia, Kamilla, Lise and Lucy are female; Ian, Kristian and Simon are male; Ash is transgender.[5] All are white and either British, North American, North European or Scandinavian, and were in their early to mid-twenties at the time of the interviews.[6] Although gender inequality most obviously disadvantages females, it is central to this research project to involve participants of all gender identities. Gender is relational and requires a holistic analytical approach, as 'one of the primary means through which young men and women define themselves is through and against one another' (Nayak and Kehily 2008: 4). However, it is also important to transcend binary gender models and engage 'pluralistic understandings of gendered expression and identity' (de Boise 2017: 34). On a practical level, involving everyone in the movement for gender equality is essential 'if we want to change things from within, with input from those who currently hold the most power' (Reed 2016).

The benefits and drawbacks of the research methodology cannot be fully explored here, but it is recognized that, from a constructivist viewpoint, interviews offer only 'indirect "representations"' of experience (Silverman 2006: 117), as the interviewer and interviewee actively co-create a version of the world deemed to be mutually appropriate (Silverman 2006: 118). Analysis of interview data, therefore, needs to take account of not only the 'official topic' of the interview (Silverman 2006: 137), but also the 'identity work' undertaken by the interviewee to present themselves in a way they consider to be appropriate to the interview, as well as the wider discourses that might be drawn upon to explain beliefs and experiences (Rapley 2004: 16 cited in Silverman 2006: 137). As all but one of the interviewees were students to whom I had taught popular music studies for three years, each interview took place in the context of a student-lecturer relationship, giving rise to particular identity work on the part of each student and myself. Furthermore, the interview discussions were informed by cultural discourses relating to popular music, gender and sexuality, interviewees' understanding of which was, to some extent, informed by a curriculum that I designed. Bearing this in mind, the next two sections analyse some of the themes generated by the interview data, focusing primarily on the perspectives offered by the interviewees, within the context of an awareness of the research 'social encounter' (Rapley 2004: 16). The analysis is organized around two themes: gender norms and stereotypes; and networking and opportunities.

Gender norms and stereotypes

Gender norms, i.e. 'what is considered proper behaviour', have a 'profound effect on both the personal and social, the micro and macro levels of our lives' (Järviluoma, Moisala and Vilkko 2003: 1). The concept of stereotyping enables the consideration of 'the way in which prevailing and repeated categorizations might influence the treatment of individuals and groups' (Hesmondhalgh and Baker 2015: 30). As outlined above, existing research (e.g. Green 1997; Bogdanovic 2015; de Boise 2017) highlights the gendering of musical practices and roles in education at school and higher education levels, focusing on musical instrument choice as the core of gender stereotyping of musical practice. At LIPA, music students gain their places by applying and auditioning on an instrument (e.g. drums, guitar, bass, keys) or as a vocalist. On the music degree courses since LIPA's first year of operation (1996) to the present, male students have been in the majority overall, most vocal students have been female, and most instrumentalists have been male. In 2017–18 for example, there were 458 applications in total: 44 per cent were from females and 56 per cent from males. Of the 245 applications from instrumentalists, 16 per cent were from females and 84 per cent from males. Of the 213 vocalists who applied, 76 per cent were female and 24 per cent were male. Places were awarded to eighty-two applicants of which 38 per cent were female. There were thirty-seven students studying vocals, of which 65 per cent were female. Of the forty-five students studying an instrument, 16 per cent were female. Efforts to increase the proportion of female students result in a higher number of female vocalists because the majority of female applicants are singers. Consequently, although a gender diverse musical culture is sought actively at LIPA, due to imbalance at the application stage, teaching and learning currently take place in gender-imbalanced environments within which musical roles are predominantly gendered in stereotypical ways.

The effects of gender stereotyping in relation to musical instrument choice and musical roles were experienced in various ways by the musicians in my research. Two of the female interviewees are instrumentalists, and both had negative experiences of male-dominated learning environments. Drummer Georgia found the confidence she gained during her early single-sex education challenged by moving into mixed education aged sixteen: 'Even though I'd been drumming for at least eight or nine years at this point, I was more self-conscious than I ever had been.' For Lise, a strings player, learning to play her instrument in male-dominated groups had a detrimental effect on her confidence and, at LIPA, the fact that she was often 'the only girl' in music improvisation classes consolidated her insecurities: 'If you're put on the spot in front of eight or seven boys it's gonna be a lot more intimidating than if it's with a roomful of girls.' Some male interviewees also commented on low confidence they perceived in their female peers. Ian, for example, noticed that, for some female musicians in improvisation classes 'there's a sort of timidness sometimes, even if they're fantastic'. Arguably many of these tendencies might not be solely attributable to gender, as it is difficult to fully distinguish the effects of gender from other traits. As Beard argues, however, 'our mental, cultural template for a powerful person remains resolutely male' (Beard 2017: 53), and so it is unsurprising that male-dominated learning environments present a challenge for some female music students. As Lise put it, 'a lot of women feel less than a man, if you're put next to each other'.

For vocalist Lucy, in contrast, gender stereotyping created a concentration of female students in her classes that she found problematic: 'One of the things that's really bothered me is the fact that most of the vocalists are female and you spend a lot time together as vocalists.' This issue was exacerbated by timetable constraints, as she explained: 'Last year with production, everyone else was put in groups based on ability apart from the vocalists because our timetable clashed.' In addition to the tendency for most female students to study singing, there is a relative lack of experience and/or confidence of females in relation to music production, arguably due to 'long standing symbolic links between technology and masculinity' (de Boise 2017: 33). Because Lucy was grouped according to instrument (i.e. voice) and consequently gender, she found the level of her music production group too low: 'I didn't really feel like I was at their standard.'

Musicians of all gender identities can be challenged by musical instrument gender stereotyping in education environments. Transgender male drummer Ash, despite support from staff, found getting involved in musical projects at college difficult due to the social and emotional challenges of being 'misgendered constantly': 'I still get called she most of the time/by most people, staff included.' An additional cause of frustration for Ash was the fact that there were 'proportionally very few instrumentalists that aren't men, including in the staff', leading to a lack of relevant role models, and giving rise to feelings of 'being excluded as a "girl"/non-binary/not-a-cis-man drummer'.

As well as musical instruments and roles, several students spoke about the gender norms and stereotypes associated with songwriting and performance. Lise attributed to gender norms her reluctance to fully express herself in her songwriting: 'I feel like it's less likely that you'll be taken seriously if you're a girl and you're singing about important subjects. I'm really scared of discussing anything important.' Kristian was also aware of the relationship between gender norms and his musical practice: 'what I'm aiming to do musically is a lot about emphasizing vulnerability, which is often considered a little bit away from the traditional masculine persona'. Ian too explained how his musical role involved qualities stereotyped as feminine: 'I feel like almost in a way to be a singer-songwriter you have to have a little femininity to be able to express and be in touch with your emotions.' As Biddle and Jarman-Ivens (2007: 9) note, 'musical genres are gendered spaces and operate according to highly codified conventions'. Arguably, both male musicians were conscious of the constraints of gender norms but felt able to challenge them in their songwriting in accordance with the expectations of genre, in a way that Lise found more difficult. Her perception that 'important' subjects are stereotypically masculine confirms the prevalence of hegemonic masculinity in popular music culture and arguably suggests a tendency towards 'emphasized femininity' among some women in the cohort (Connell cited in Kearney 2017: 34).

Although both Ian and Kristian recognized the advantages of being, in Ian's words, 'a straight white guy', the constraints of gender norms were experienced in other ways by the male interviewees. In relation to performance, Ian sometimes felt the pressure of normative masculinity: 'sometimes when I'm on stage there's this need to be masculine.' He explained masculinity in this context as 'grown-up', 'commanding' and 'guarded and cautious', as opposed to femininity, which he characterized as more childlike and playful. Popular music 'has always offered privileged space for gender ... play' (Middleton 2007: 103), and 'the appeal of pop lies in playfulness and diversity' (Hawkins 2016: 14). In relation to masculinity specifically, Biddle and Jarman-Ivens (2007: 15) argue that the relationship between masculinity and popular music 'operates as one of the dominant sites for the working through of masculine identities'. The feelings expressed by these young musicians, however, suggest that, while 'gender play' is prevalent in popular music performance, creative possibilities are also shaped and sometimes limited by an internalized pressure to conform to gender norms and stereotypes. For some male musicians, the discourse of 'toxic masculinity' with its associated characteristic of male fragility, can lead to more rigid masculine norms and stereotypes, with femininity considered more 'negotiable and mutable' (Lang 2016). As Dyer (1993: 16) argues, the more enforced the stereotype, the greater its degree of 'rigidity and shrillness'.

These examples suggest that the challenges created by gender norms and stereotypes in music higher education are complex and require more than one approach. Two representatives of community-based music organizations interviewed as part of my scoping study mentioned similar issues and their strategies for addressing them. Stewart Baxter spoke about the challenge of encouraging young women to use the music facilities at The Warren Youth Project, a support service for marginalized young people in Hull. Similar to the local music scene that is dominated by 'white male guitar bands', the music rehearsal spaces at The Warren are used mostly by males, with female participation typified by 'getting on the mic and singing a Rihanna song'. The organization runs specific projects to try to engage more young women and counter their feelings of exclusion from 'masculine spaces' such as studios. Similarly, Kate Lowes reported low levels of female participation in the projects and programs run by Brighter Sound, a creative music charity for young people in Manchester. She explained the organization's aim to enable female musicians to 'break out of one-dimensional singer-songwriter stereotypical female musician roles' by encouraging greater participation and creative freedom through female-only projects such as the *Both Sides Now* program (Brighter Sound 2018).

The impact of female-only music projects on gender stereotyping and inequality is discussed by Baker and Cohen (2008) and Marsh (2018). Girls Rock Camp, a worldwide alliance of community-based all-female music project, empowers young females to participate in music making by 'creating productive spaces that encourage accessibility, promotion of female and female-identified artists, and connection amongst girls and female professionals' (Marsh 2018: 89). Female-only projects in which young female musicians can feel empowered to take creative risks and develop skills in a non-threatening environment can often involve a 'female takeover' of male-dominated spaces such as recording studios, as mentioned above by Stewart Baxter. In addition, The Warren provides a 'women's room', a female-only 'safe space', to which young females can withdraw from the male-dominated main facility. Baker and Cohen (2008: 326) similarly point out the value of community-based music organizations providing a separate 'protective' space for women, although they conclude that facilitating young women's participation in music 'does not always necessarily mean female-only groups' (Baker and Cohen 2008: 334). In my research, as mentioned earlier, Lucy found the experience of learning in all-female groups challenging for several reasons and, despite her difficulties in male-dominated groups, Lise did not advocate female-only music education because 'you don't learn how it works and how to deal with it'. Similarly, while Georgia found her formative single-sex education valuable, she recognized the need to be able to work with men: 'I think for me it was positive but obviously in the real world you can't work with women all the time.' According to Baker and Cohen (2008: 334): 'Young women require single-sex groups at the initial stages of "getting started" with an activity yet want the option of mixed groups when they have built up enough experience and confidence'. It seems female-only groups can be beneficial for some female musicians, but do not offer a sustainable solution to preparing them for the 'real world'.

While the efficacy of female-only projects and spaces as a strategy for addressing gender issues in music higher education is debatable, access to relevant role models is arguably as crucial to music students as it is to female participants in community-based music programs. Marsh (2018: 89) notes the importance of the involvement in Girls Rock Camp of 'women and female-identified persona as performers, instrumentalists, technicians, engineers, organizers, managers, et cetera'. Baker and Cohen (2008: 335) highlight the value of female facilitators, as these are 'important role models for encouraging young women to get involved in more music-based activities'. This was the case for Georgia who, for several years before joining the degree course, participated in music summer schools at LIPA, rebuilding her confidence by working with a female mentor and role model:

> That was when I became more confident working with men. In the first year I just didn't speak but then as time went on I got more confident and became quite assertive. I think I was quite lucky because I had a mentor who was a bass player and she was like 'you're the one who holds all this together, you've got to be the assertive one.' When you see someone like her doing well for herself and a woman as well. She doesn't take any crap from anyone and she plays with men all the time.

Baker and Cohen (2008: 333) note the difficulties experienced by some community-based organizations in providing female facilitators/mentors, due both to funding issues and to the lack of 'suitably qualified women'. This latter problem is identified in relation to music higher education in Bogdanovic's (2015) research mentioned earlier, due to the gender stereotyping of musical instruments and roles.

As well as describing their various challenges arising from gender norms and stereotypes in relation to their musical practice, several of the interviewees in my research emphasized the importance of raising gender awareness among the cohort. Alongside considerations of intersections between gender and other identity characteristics such as ethnicity and class, it is clear that gender should 'not be thought of as simply concerned with dichotomies of men/women or masculinity/femininity' (de Boise 2017: 34). For example, Simon pointed out the importance of avoiding 'talking about gender in such a binary way, [as] it's such a spectrum for many people', and Ian advocated including in the curriculum more examples of musicians who do not conform to gender norms to inspire students to 'be themselves and experiment more'. For Georgia, discussion of gender should be 'part of every module'. She suggested that a male tutor discussing gender inequality in a music production lecture could effectively demonstrate that gender issues are not solely the concern of female students and tutors. Baker and Cohen (2008: 336) argue that addressing issues of gender inequality in music making and music learning contexts through 'interventions ... with or for young women' frames the problem as female. Therefore, it is important to undertake work with young men in order to challenge 'their attitudes to girls' music making and inclusivity' (Baker and Cohen 2008: 336). Raising awareness of the effects of gender across the curriculum for the whole cohort is clearly an important factor in challenging gender norms and stereotypes in music higher education.

Networking and opportunities

In their analysis of the cultural and creative industries, Conor, Gill and Taylor (2015: 6) note that gender inequality persists, with women 'consistently faring less well than men'. Within the sector, 'networking and maintaining contacts' is a key activity for nurturing reputation, and informal 'word-of-mouth' recruitment is typical. This 'contacts culture' disadvantages women, who benefit from more formal and transparent recruitment settings (Conor, Gill and Taylor 2015: 10–11). Focusing more specifically on the music industry, Leonard's (2016) research with women in non-musician roles found similar issues arising from the existence of 'a "boys' club" or fraternity':

> male colleagues repeatedly cemented their social bonds with one another through leisure activities that are closely associated with particular forms of masculinity … the sharing of such practices allowed for the blending of work and leisure that further excluded women colleagues who missed out on networking opportunities. (Leonard 2016: 42)

The proliferation of female musicians' networks such as Girls I Rate and Women in Music attests to the need for dedicated networks for women due to these issues in the music industry. In the context of vocational popular music higher education, developing students' skills in relation to working practices such as collaboration and networking is central to preparing them for their future careers. At LIPA, for example, music students are encouraged and expected to collaborate in relation to all aspects of the curriculum, including performance, songwriting and music production. Their professional practice involves seeking and creating work opportunities, such as forming bands and performing in a professional capacity in a range of 'real world' contexts.

Clearly, the impetus exists at LIPA for networking and collaboration to take place, as it is part of the curriculum. However, some of the female interviewees in my research gave accounts of musical networking as exclusionary of women. In Kamilla's experience, males tend to 'band together' and help each other, even if they don't know each other well. Similarly, Georgia felt the strong presence of a 'lads' club' among musicians at LIPA: 'They always go to each other before me for work – they always forget I'm a drummer', although she did not believe this practice to be deliberate: 'none of them have directly ever gone out of their way'. Lucy observed: 'Boys naturally without them realising are a little bit more involved in their own sex group than they think', suggesting a perception that homosocial networking is a 'natural' tendency, at least among males. For Georgia, the social bonds between males are mirrored in her own networking and musical relationships with other women: 'I'd probably more so go to a woman than a man, so I think it works the other way as well'; however, inequality in numbers is problematic: 'There are less women than men.' As discussed in the previous section, females constitute around 30–40 per cent of the music cohort at LIPA which, combined with the low proportion of female instrumentalists, can disadvantage them in relation to homosocial networking. If the imbalance created by male dominance in terms of numbers is detrimental to female networking, female-only projects, such as those discussed in the previous section, can provide a solution, as Marsh (2018: 97) found in relation to Girls Rock projects: 'an unexpected and important outcome has been the evolution of a network of supportive collaborators'.

While some interviewees gravitated towards working with other women, however, others discussed an apparent lack of support and cooperation between female musicians. In contrast to Georgia's preference for networking and working with other females, some women reported perceptions of female competitiveness. Despite a strong friendship and working relationship with another female musician, Kamilla observed, in herself and other women, problems with forging relationships with other female musicians. Her explanation for this, given with a measure of dry humour, is the fear that they will 'steal each other's boyfriends'. Lucy also reported stronger negative feelings in her working relationships with females than with males: 'I get more conscious of girls judging me than men judging me. Men make me feel more comfortable than women do.' It is possible that, in order to flourish in an environment where there are relatively few women, some female musicians, deliberately or not, become 'one of the lads'. As Leonard (2016: 44) points out, it is common practice for women to 'adopt the trappings of masculinity in order to adapt to and be accepted' within male-dominated cultures. On the other hand, in such an environment, it could also be beneficial to use difference as an advantage, capitalizing on the unique position of being 'the only girl'. In order to avoid simplistic and negative misconceptions about female networking and working relationships, however, this issue needs further analysis, taking account of wider social contexts and structural constraints.

Effective networking can be crucial to finding work, and several points arose from my research in relation to work opportunities and gender issues for young musicians. Students studying on vocational popular music courses need to engage with 'real world' work opportunities, and the fact that opportunities for performing musicians depend on strong networks can be disadvantageous to women. However, as Simon reported, the importance of image in performance, combined with gender stereotyping of particular instruments, can also have a negative impact on work opportunities for females: 'Brass is often perceived as quite masculine and I know that I've been picked over female candidates before for image reasons'. While this bias can be detrimental to female musicians, some can benefit from the situation, as mentioned above. Georgia explained: 'I've been hired for gigs because I'm a woman before. There was a function band that wanted all women because it looks a bit more different.' Ian also pointed out the benefit of having a female band member: 'It's almost like a selling point to have a girl in the band. I think we got way more gigs because we had a female lead singer.' Overall, though, the live music industry does not favour female musicians, as recent research highlights (Larsson 2017). The Liverpool live music scene, in which most LIPA music students participate, has been depicted as particularly male-dominated (Cohen 1991, 1997). For Georgia this continued to be the case, as in her experience of playing a Liverpool venue: 'we were the only two women in the gig, of five bands'. Similarly, Simon perceived the Liverpool music scene as: 'very masculine. It doesn't feel like you can go there and be gay or feminine or whatever.' In his experience, many venues do not even cater for the possibility of female musical participation in the scene: 'Every venue I've been to, there's never a female dressing room or a separate area for them. There's no expectation that women will be there on stage I think.'

It can be argued that, despite the advantage that can sometimes be gained from difference, the fact that female musicians are in the minority and their relative lack of power in male-dominated music environments can create weaker networks and perpetuate inequality in relation to work opportunities. In vocational popular music higher education, the curriculum aims, at least implicitly, to facilitate networking and work opportunities without gender bias. However, factors such as gender imbalanced student cohorts and gender stereotyping in relation to musical instrument choice, combined with masculinized 'real world' music scenes, can present female musicians with stronger challenges in relation to networking and finding work opportunities. Along with seeking to create greater gender diversity and challenge gender stereotyping within the cohort and curriculum, therefore, it could be worthwhile to encourage female students to join existing women's music networks, and/or establish female musician networks within vocational popular music higher education such as those that exist in the 'real world'.

Conclusion

Existing research and recent statistics show that gender issues exist in the music industry, and work towards greater equality and diversity in the industry is ongoing. In relation to vocational popular music higher education, my research so far shows that, for some young musicians, issues such as those associated with gender stereotyping and networking can have a detrimental effect on their learning experiences and musical practices. In relation to LIPA, one example of a vocational popular music higher education institution in the UK, gender issues are, alongside and within a context of broader socio-cultural inequalities, created by instrument choice and stereotyping earlier in the pipeline. However, as Green (2001: 213) argues, musicians and their teachers are 'in a strong position to resist the music industry's power to dictate commercially driven notions of musical success and failure'. Continuing efforts to address gender issues in the music industry, and broader gender equality movements such as The Everyday Sexism Project and #MeToo, point to the need for vocational popular music higher education to contribute to change. Hawkins (2002: 12) observes, 'pop culture forms a site where identity roles are constantly evolving to fit social needs', and so vocational popular music higher education, although by definition music industry facing, should take account of this shift rather than replicating and reinforcing inequalities in the industry.

The data discussed in this chapter were generated from a small sample and, as Conor, Gill and Taylor (2015: 12) suggest, 'we have to be aware of both the "realities" of gendered lives, and, simultaneously, of how our own stories may cement or challenge these'. From the research so far, though, potential strategies could include: creating more equal and diverse gender representation in student cohorts and teaching teams through positive action; raising awareness across the curriculum of a wider diversity of gender identities, as well as issues and inequalities in the music industry; encouraging and empowering students who want to push boundaries and challenge gender norms; and facilitating and strengthening networks for female musicians. It would also be beneficial to forge strong relationships with music industry bodies, such as UK Music's Music Academic Partnership, and community-based music organizations, such as Brighter Sound, to collaborate on furthering the equality/diversity agenda.

These potential solutions arguably raise more questions than they answer. Further research that expands and diversifies the participant group will help to illuminate the effects of the interview context and enrich the data by taking account of a wider range of identities, experiences and perspectives, to find ways in which vocational popular music higher education could more effectively prepare all young musicians for the 'real world' and contribute to the disruption of the 'boys' club'.

Notes

1. Although Williamson and Cloonan (2007) point out that there are several interconnected but distinct music industries, for simplicity I am using the all-encompassing singular term 'music industry'.
2. UK Music is a campaigning and lobbying group which represents the recorded and live music industry (UK Music n.d.).
3. While the research project aims to explore both gender and sexuality, this chapter focuses on experiences and issues relating to gender.
4. Telephone interviews were carried out with: Vick Bain, CEO of BASCA (4 July 2016), Stewart Baxter, Arts Development Worker, The Warren Youth Project, Hull (31 August 2016), Dai Davies, Strategic Development Manager, Ebbw Vale Institute (30 August 2016), James Hannam, Senior Grants Manager, PRS for Music Foundation (2 December 2016), Andy Inglis, artist and tour manager and music industry mentor (1 July 2016), Kate Lowes, Head of Programmes, Brighter Sound, Manchester (4 July 2016), Carrie Mansfield, Creative Director, The Garage, Norwich (7 September 2016).
5. At the time of the research, Ash was in the process of transitioning physically from female to male.
6. Most of the interviewees are anonymized at their own request.

References

Ariadne Publications/UK Music (2016), *Music Education Directory 2016/2017*. Available online: https://www.ukmusic.org/assets/general/Music_Education_Directory.pdf (accessed 30 November 2018).

Baker, S. and B.M.Z. Cohen (2008), 'From Snuggling and Snogging to Sampling and Scratching: Girls' Nonparticipation in Community-Based Music Activities', *Youth and Society*, 39 (3): 316–339.

Beard, M. (2017), *Women and Power: A Manifesto*, London: Profile Books/London Review of Books.

Biddle, I. and F. Jarman-Ivens (2007), 'Introduction. Oh Boy! Making Masculinity in Popular Music', in F. Jarman-Ivens (ed.), *Oh Boy! Masculinities and Popular Music*, 3–17, London: Routledge.

Bogdanovic, D. (2015), *Gender and Equality in Music Higher Education. A Report Commissioned and Funded by the National Association for Music in Higher Education*. Available online: http://www.namhe.ac.uk/publications/reports/gender_and_equality_2015.pdf (accessed 30 November 2018).

Born, G. and K. Devine (2015), 'Music Technology, Gender, and Class: Digitization, Educational and Social Change in Britain', *Twentieth-Century Music*, 12 (2): 135–172.

Brighter Sound (2018), *Both Sides Now*. Available online: https://www.brightersound.com/bothsidesnow/ (accessed 30 November 2018).

Cohen, S. (1991), *Rock Culture in Liverpool: Popular Music in the Making*, Oxford: Clarendon Press.

Cohen, S. (1997), 'Men Making a Scene. Rock Music and the Production of Gender', in S. Whiteley (ed.), *Sexing the Groove. Popular Music and Gender*, 17–36, London: Routledge.

Conor, B., R. Gill and S. Taylor (2015), 'Introduction: Gender and Creative Labour', in B. Conor, R. Gill and S. Taylor (eds.), *Gender and Creative Labour*, 1–22, Chichester: John Wiley and Sons Ltd.

de Boise, S. (2017), 'Gender Inequalities and Higher Music Education: Comparing the UK and Sweden', *British Journal of Music Education*, 35 (1): 23–41.

Dibben, N. (2002), 'Gender Identity and Music', in R. MacDonald, D. Hargreaves and D. Miel (eds.), *Musical Identities*, 117–133, Oxford: Oxford University Press.

Dyer, R. (1993), *The Matter of Images: Essays on Representations*, London: Routledge.

Earls, J. (2016), 'Björk Speaks Out against Sexism in Music and Film Industries', *NME*, 1 June. Available online: http://www.nme.com/news/music/bjork-6-1191804 (accessed 30 November 2018).

Green, L. (1997), *Music, Gender, Education*, Cambridge: Cambridge University Press.

Green, L. (2001), *How Popular Musicians Learn: A Way Ahead for Music Education*, Aldershot: Ashgate.

Hawkins, S. (2002), *Settling the Pop Score: Pop Texts and Identity Politics*, Aldershot: Ashgate.

Hawkins, S. (2016), *Queerness in Pop Music: Aesthetics, Gender Norms, and Temporality*, New York: Routledge.

Hebert, D.G., J. Abramo and G.D. Smith (2017), 'Epistemological and Sociological Issues in Popular Music Education', in G.D. Smith, Z. Moir, M. Brennan, S. Rambarran and

P. Kirkman (eds.), *The Routledge Research Companion to Popular Music Education*, 451–477, London: Routledge.

Hesmondhalgh, D. and S. Baker (2015), 'Sex, Gender and Work Segregation in the Cultural Industries', in B. Conor, R. Gill and S. Taylor (eds.), *Gender and Creative Labour*, 23–36, Chichester: John Wiley and Sons Ltd.

Järviluoma, H., P. Moisala and A. Vilkko (2003), *Gender and Qualitative Methods*, London: Sage.

Kearney, M.C. (2017), *Gender and Rock*, New York: Oxford University Press.

Khomami, N. (2018), 'Music Industry Is Still a Boys' Club, Says Beyoncé Songwriter', *The Guardian*, 8 March. Available online: https://www.theguardian.com/music/2018/mar/08/music-industry-still-boys-club-beyonce-songwriter-carla-marie-williams (accessed 30 November 2018).

Laing, D. (1999), 'The Economic Importance of Music in the European Union: 6. Music in Education', *Journal on Media Culture*, 2 July. Available online: http://www.icce.rug.nl/~soundscapes/DATABASES/MIE/Part1_chapter06.shtml (accessed 30 November 2018).

Lang, N. (2016), 'Gender Fluidity Has a Toxic Masculinity Problem', *Daily Beast*, 3 February. Available online: https://www.thedailybeast.com/gender-fluidity-has-a-toxic-masculinity-problem (accessed 30 November 2018).

Larsson, N. (2017), 'Live Music Acts Are Mostly Male-Only. What's Holding Women Back?' *The Guardian*, 12 October. Available online: https://www.theguardian.com/inequality/2017/oct/12/tonights-live-music-acts-will-mostly-be-male-only-whats-holding-women-back (accessed 30 November 2018).

Leonard, M. (2016), 'Girls at Work: Gendered Identities, Segregation, and Employment Experiences in the Music Industries', in J. Warwick and A. Adrian (eds.), *Voicing Girlhood in Popular Music: Performance, Authority, Authenticity*, 37–55, London: Routledge.

Marsh, C. (2018), '"When She Plays We Hear the Revolution": Girls Rock Regina – A Feminist Intervention', *Journal of the International Association for the Study of Popular Music*, 8 (1): 88–102. Available online: http://iaspmjournal.net/index.php/IASPM_Journal/article/view/890 (accessed 30 November 2018).

Middleton, R. (2007), 'Mum's the Word: Men's Singing and Maternal Law', in F. Jarman-Ivens (ed.), *Oh Boy! Masculinities and Popular Music*, 103–124, London: Routledge.

Nayak, A. and M.J. Kehily (2008), *Gender, Youth and Culture: Young Masculinities and Femininities*, Basingstoke: Palgrave Macmillan.

Rapley, T. (2004), 'Interviews', in C. Seale, G. Gobo, J. Gubrium and D. Silverman (eds.), *Qualitative Research Practice*, 15–33, London: Sage.

Reed V. (2016), 'Gender Equality in Music: The Beginnings of a New Movement Involving Men and Women', *Huffington Post UK*, 15 June. Available online: http://www.huffingtonpost.co.uk/vanessa-reed/gender-equality-music_b_10475886.html (accessed 30 November 2018).

Shepherd, J. (2015), 'Lady Gaga Calls Out Music Industry for Being a 'Boys Club' in Emotional Speech at Billboard's Women in Music Event', *The Independent*, 13 December. Available online: https://www.independent.co.uk/arts-entertainment/music/news/lady-gaga-calls-out-music-industry-for-being-a-boys-club-in-emotional-speech-at-billboards-women-in-a6771371.html (accessed 30 November 2018).

Silverman D. (2006), *Interpreting Qualitative Data: Methods for Analysing Talk, Text and Interaction*, 3rd edn, London: Sage.

UK Music (n.d.), *Music Academic Partnership*. Available online: https://www.ukmusic.org/assets/general/UK_MUSIC_ACADEMIC_BROCHURE_FINAL_WEB_spreads.pdf (accessed 30 November 2018).

Whiteley, S. (2015), 'Blurred Lines, Gender and Popular Music', in A. Bennett and S. Waksman (eds.), *The Sage Handbook of Popular Music*, 365–380, London: Sage.

Williamson J. and M. Cloonan (2007), 'Rethinking the Music Industry', *Popular Music*, 26 (2): 305–322.

Woodward S.C. (2017), 'Social Justice and Popular Music Education. Building a Generation of Artists Impacting Social Change', in G.D. Smith, Z. Moir, M. Brennan, S. Rambarran and P. Kirkman (eds.), *The Routledge Research Companion to Popular Music Education*, 395–411, London: Routledge.

4

Engineering a Place for Women: Gendered Experiences of the Music Technology Classroom

Emma Hopkins and Pauwke Berkers

Introduction

In an interview with *Rolling Stone*, singer-songwriter-producer Grimes (Claire Boucher) stated: 'I don't think there are few female producers because women aren't interested. It's difficult for women to get in. It's a pretty hostile environment' (Hiatt 2016). Data confirms that music producers are almost always male (Doubleday 2008). For example, the Music Producers' Guild in the UK reports that only 4 per cent of its members are women (Savage 2012). Moreover, the work of female producers largely goes unrecognized: only four women have received Brit nominations for best producer, none of whom won (Savage 2012). Previous research has explained this alignment between masculinity and technology as being the result of, amongst others: music socialization – gender stereotyping of instruments (Clawson 1999a) and instrument preferences of children (Wych 2012); gendering of genres (Bayton 1998; Baker, 2013; Gavanas and Reitsamer 2013) in that both rock and electronic music are associated with masculinity and technology (electric guitar, DJ equipment), whereas pop, which requires little to no technological skill (singing, acoustic music), is associated with femininity; gendered music talk among participants (Werner and Johansson 2016) and in the media (Davies 2001); and the absence of female role models (Berkers and Schaap 2018) and experts (Straw 1997).

Another possible – yet understudied – explanation for the lack of female producers might be the near absence of women in specialized educational programs. UK data show that students in music technology degrees are 90 per cent male to 10 per cent female. Figures also demonstrate a decline in the numbers of women studying music technology from one educational level to the next (Born and Devine 2015: 146-147). Consequently, music technology education has the characteristics of a 'leaky pipeline', an analogy often used to describe similar drop-off rates observed in science, technology, engineering and mathematics subjects (Blickenstaff 2005). While STEM disciplines have witnessed a discernible improvement in gender representation, the 'leaky pipeline' analogy remains a rather fitting description for the relationship between gender and music technology education (Born and Devine 2015: 148).

Music technology is a vital cornerstone of the music industry, both practically and artistically. It is essential to the practical reproducibility of music and, consequently, its evolution. In addition, music producers and sound engineers possess a significant amount of creative control over the artists whom they work with and affect the sound of these artists. However, as in society at large, gender prejudice, discrimination and harassment remain prevalent in music industries and communities (Gadir 2016: 115). With this in mind, the marginalization of women in popular music has largely been attributed to their lack of control over male-dominated, essential parts of the music industry including the domains of production, management and journalism (Farrugia 2009: 337).

This research aims to shine a light on women's experiences within music education as future producers and engineers. It focuses on women as students pursuing a masculinized topic (music technology), in male-dominated spaces (music technology classrooms), that often feed into careers in a male-dominated field (music industry). Drawing on nine in-depth interviews, we ask the question: how have these women experienced music technology education in relation to gender? To answer this question, we have examined (1) classroom experiences, (2) interactions with (male) classmates and (3) experiences with (male) teachers.

By addressing this understudied topic, this chapter makes several contributions. First, few studies have explored the educational experiences of women within the technical areas of the music industry, particularly music production and sound engineering. Existing studies on music technology and gender have mainly focused on women as DJs or DJ/producers, particularly within the field of electronic music (see, for example, Rodgers 2010; Farrugia 2012; Gavanas and Reitsamer 2013). Second, previous research on music technology, gender and education has been largely centred on music technology as a sub-topic within the broader taught subject of Music, with school-aged students (Comber, Hargreaves and Colley 1993; Armstrong 2008; Armstrong 2011). Instead, this research concentrates on the post-compulsory tiers of education, more closely preceding music technology careers. Additionally, higher education classes place greater responsibility on individual student performance and are therefore subject to less supervision from teachers; this makes it possible to explore gender in the social context of the classroom, since behaviour and choices of language are subject to fewer constraints. This has gone unexplored by prior research, since, generally, teachers heavily moderate class discussions and work in compulsory, school-level education. Examining varying levels of music technology education contributes further to understanding the apparent 'leaky pipeline' theory. Third, this chapter uses the personal and lived experiences of women studying music technology to explore the effects of structural issues in education.

Data and methods

The focus of our study is on the experiences of women studying music technology. We therefore opted for semi-structured interviews, as this type of interviewing allows respondents to elaborate where they please, make connections to the topics they feel are most relevant and to develop their own narrative (Gubrium and Holstein 2002). Our interviewees were selected on the basis of the following criteria: (1) people identifying as women, who (2) were in the process of completing, or who had completed, post-compulsory education courses (diploma and bachelor degree) related to music technology, sound engineering and/or music production in the last ten years, (3) in Manchester (United Kingdom) or Berlin (Germany). Both cities have been centres of cultural and creative production as a result of deindustrialization, with Berlin now having arguably superseded the reputation of Manchester, despite the latter's enduring night-time and electronic music scene (Bader and Scharenberg 2010). Snowball-sampling techniques were used: contact was made with informants via Facebook based on referrals from individuals inside and outside our social networks. Relevant informants were then able to suggest respondents who had been studying at the below named institutions in Manchester and Berlin.

In total, nine interviews were conducted between April and June 2017. Respondents were between twenty-one and thirty-seven years old. The majority (seven) had studied, or were studying, in Manchester at the School of Electronic Music, School of Sound Recording, Futureworks, or University of Salford; two respondents were in the process of completing studies at dBs, Berlin. Three interviews were held face-to-face in casual café/bar settings in Manchester, while the remaining six were conducted via Skype. Interviews were recorded and transcribed verbatim using transcription software ExpressScribe. Interviews lasted between fifty and ninety minutes. All names mentioned in this chapter are aliases to warrant anonymity.

Interviews were structured in three main parts using an interview guide (available on request). First, we discussed their classroom experiences, encouraging respondents to talk about their feelings about being one of few women in the class. Second, we addressed their interactions with (male) classmates in terms of types of experiences and the effects such a male-dominated environment had on women, and vice versa. Third, we addressed questions relating to teachers, i.e. how respondents felt about having few female teachers, gendered experiences with teachers and whether and how teachers addressed gender imbalances. The data were analysed in Atlas.ti using thematic analysis as it has proved to be an effective method for reporting on the 'experiences, meanings and the reality of participants' (Braun and Clarke 2006: 80–81).

Classroom experiences

Being token in class: Empirics and reasons

All respondents reported being either the only woman, or one of few women in class. As such, they are tokens i.e. members of the numerical minority (less than 15 per cent) in skewed groups (Kanter 1977; Berkers and Schaap 2018). The observations of our interviewees are consistent with estimates that music technology degrees are comprised of a majority of men (Born and Devine 2016). Moreover, while three respondents mentioned that a number of their female peers dropped out, the majority of applicants were male to begin with, similar to previous studies (Born and Devine 2015: 146). Respondents highlighted two main reasons for this gender imbalance.

First, construction of music technology as a masculine profession discouraged women from enrolling in such programs. Our interviewees held media socialization, advertising and the schools themselves (including masculinized logos and online content as well as course materials lacking in visible women) responsible for this. They co-construct men as technologically able and on the flipside of this, women as technologically incompetent (Cockburn 1983; Wajcman 1991). Second, some interviewees expressed a belief that women lack awareness of (and interest in) the subject area, or that women are, generally speaking, innately more interested in the on-stage solicitation of attention, as opposed to the off-stage aspects of music-making. This latter notion – that 'men and women are innately and fundamentally different in interests and skills' – has been referred to as gender essentialism (England 2010: 150).

Feelings about being a token in the class

Feelings about being one of the few women in their classes tended to fall into predominantly two categories: (1) adaptation disguised as neutrality and (2) negativity. First, three respondents reported feelings of what initially sounded like neutrality, saying 'I don't mind it' (Anna) or 'I'm just not that fussed' (Alex). However, when interviewees expanded on these initial answers, they were less straightforward. For example, Sara said she became accustomed to being the only woman in the class, 'To be honest, after my college course, I was quite used to it because it was the same thing back in college.' Another respondent, Victoria, reported that she 'tried not to feel the difference' whereas Georgia stopped voicing aloud her worries about her capabilities within the course in order to 'behave like them'. Perhaps this does not convey neutrality but rather an effort to accept the maleness of music technology. Other respondents who expressed 'neutral' feelings also highlighted their comfort and familiarity with men, as well as not identifying themselves as particularly feminine, perhaps as justifications for their alleged neutrality on the gender imbalance: 'I don't really care, doesn't bother me I'm the only girl. I don't like sitting here talking about makeup, straightening my hair for my Saturday night and the stilettos I haven't ever bought in my life' (Alex). Familiarity with men and presenting stereotypically masculine traits may enable for better adaptation to a male environment i.e. becoming an 'honorary male' (Dryburgh 1999; O'Shea 2008). Previous studies have, however, shown that 'women can become caught in a gender-oriented "twilight zone" in which they do not truly belong to the female gender in the mainstream world as a result of a constant effort to tone down their femininity' in male-dominated spaces (Nordström and Herz 2013: 465).

Second, four respondents drew attention to negative feelings surrounding being one of few women in their class: they included feeling intimidated, self-conscious ('I was definitely very, very quiet, very self-conscious'), isolated, concerned about gender ('Do those guys think the question I asked is stupid?'), lonely and misunderstood. Respondents related these feelings to the behaviour of male classmates. For example,

Olivia described the frustration felt when her male classmates seemed unwilling to empathize with her perspectives on gender in electronic music: 'I felt like I just got shot down by like everyone and I was just kind of like, "Damn." I do think that if there was another female, you know, maybe ... they kind of would have been like, "Yeah, no actually I can see where you're coming from," but all these guys could not understand where I was coming from'. Similarly, Davina recognized the relationship between feeling uncomfortable and the behaviour of male classmates: 'I didn't feel too comfortable and especially when sexist, misogynistic jokes were coming out'. We will address these feelings in more detail below.

Interactions with (male) classmates

Experiences with male classmates

First and foremost, almost all respondents had an overall good or satisfactory relationship with their predominantly male classmates, 'The atmosphere was great with the boys, relationship was brilliant. The class was tight knit' (Jessica). Further to this, two respondents went on to emphasize the collaborative nature of their courses, 'It was very collaborative, very supportive, very friendly' (Georgia). However, relationships were also gendered.

One of the most common observations made was that male classmates tended to display stereotypically masculine or boyish behaviours (West and Zimmerman 1987): 'It is very obvious when you are in the school like this that they are not used to, still not very used to women's presence ... in the corridors they would still, for example, provoke each other by shouting things and sometimes even like playing, like wrestling ... but it's usually in a funny, friendly way' (Georgia). This included reverting to 'guy talk', i.e. openly and frequently broaching topics that are stereotypically of male interest, including heterosexual male perspectives on women and sex. For example, Sara said: 'They're just very laddish with each other ... just chatting about all the girls like, "She's hot" and talking about football, you know, things that I cannot join in. Just how they behave with each other ... it's a different dynamic'. At times, guy talk descended into toxic masculinity (see Haider 2016): 'They were all quite misogynist, a lot of rape jokes and I had to go to the college at one point 'cause they were really intimidating. I'd be in the studio with thirteen boys all joking about raping a girl' (Jessica). Such behaviours are perhaps reflective of the homosocial, collective nature of musical activity (Clawson 1999b). As a result, five respondents described feelings of social disconnection: 'Sometimes we [respondent and another female classmate] felt a bit detached from the group because the guys were on their guy talk and it was very difficult to actually have a conversation about something' (Victoria).

In addition, the gendered interactions between the female respondents and their male classmates are affected by perceived competitive hyper-intellectual 'nerd' attitudes. While working with computers seems at odds with quality characteristics (physical strength, aggression or authority) of traditional hegemonic masculinity, in some societal domains rhetoric has shifted from 'only the strong will survive' to 'the geeks will inherit the earth' (Royal 2014: 177). Suzanna described her male classmates as, 'If you imagine Big Bang Theory, that kind of guys?' who would 'alienate other people with terminology'. This eventually led her to the conclusion that 'they weren't interested in getting to know me even though I put quite a lot of effort in'. It has been theorized that this kind of technical one-upmanship and gratuitous use of technical language by male musicians and technicians is used as a power move to exclude women from technical spaces (Bayton 1997). Olivia expressed a similar sentiment when discussing her feeling that male classmates positioned themselves as experts:

> I remember I didn't know what one thing was on the [mixing] desk ... I asked him [a male classmate] and he goes, 'How do you not know that?' ... There was a part of me that felt like, 'Aw okay, you just think I'm just some stupid girl,' or also cause they were older as well like, *[sarcastic tone]* 'Oh, I'm so much more experienced than you.' (Olivia)

These findings resonate with previous research that has established a strong association between masculinity, technological skill and control (Cockburn and Ormrod 1993; Wajcman 2004). Consequently, the recording studio as a technological environment has been coded as a masculine space due to the prevailing connotation between masculinity and the mastery of 'complex' technologies (Leonard 2007).

Male spaces and women's behaviour

Being a woman in a mostly male class (a token) had an impact on the behaviour of our respondents. First, they participated less in class discussions, became quieter, or meticulously planned what they would say before speaking aloud. This results in girls having to conform to 'malestream' processes and ways of thinking, or be silenced (Caputo 1994). Respondents were mostly worried that contributing to class discussion and being wrong would lead male classmates to criticize them harshly, or apply this judgement to their gender, i.e. being a 'stupid girl':

> Guys saying dumb things are just funny guys or are just jokey guys, oh how hilarious. But when girls say that kind of thing then it immediately becomes a fact that she's dumb, that she doesn't know what she's talking about, that she can't ... being a woman in my class for instance, I know I have to be more careful with what I say and I have to be more sure that what I'm saying is right, because if I say something stupid or something that doesn't make sense, I know that I'm going to be judged heavily on that, opposed to how a guy would be judged for saying something equally stupid. (Victoria)

Moreover, those in a token position are more often judged according to their group category (women) as opposed to on individual competencies (Roth 2004; Schaap and Berkers 2014). Three respondents reported being subject to such gendered evaluations:

> It definitely felt like there was a lot of comments that flew round, not from the lecturers, but from other students on the course about my skill levels, maybe? They've never seen any of my work, they've never heard any of my work, but just sort of assuming and making little remarks about it, [that it] might not be as good as the guys or that I might need extra help. (Suzanna)

Secondly, as a result of being highly visible as tokens, women are often evaluated as an object of erotic or romantic interest: the fulfilment of the 'male gaze' (Mulvey 1975). Surprisingly, only two respondents had experienced this. In one of these cases, male classmates suggested that the respondent was of romantic interest to the technical support staff and that she should use this to her advantage and theirs:

> They [male classmates] asked me to be the one to go and ask the studio staff for the things because they said I was a girl and the studio staff, like, fancy me, so we're more likely to get good equipment ... I went to go get the microphone out but they didn't have it in stock and so one of the studio staff gave me a microphone that only third year students should have access to, so he wasn't allowed to give me it, but he did ... the guys were like, 'What? Like, he would never do that for us and he only did that because he fancies you.' (Anna)

Not only does this example reflect the consequences of tokenism, it arguably feeds into discourses surrounding the role of women in music scenes as peripheral or the appendages of men (Cohen 1991: 206).

Female presence in male spaces

Interviews also addressed any perceived effect that female presence in a male space had on the behaviour of male classmates. For the most part, respondents did not report noticing their male classmates make any attempt to modify their behaviour in light of there being women in the class. Contrarily, three respondents suggested that their male classmates did alter their choices of words, language and conversation topics. Georgia further detailed this: 'Normally they would have manly banter about things ... I guess they were a bit more considerate in terms of the language that they would use and even though I'm not worried about cussing and swearing ... it's like, "Start behaving yourself, Georgia is standing there," but it was just usually as a joke'. Alex reported that her classmates initially adopted what she described as stereotypically feminine, caretaking (or arguably, paternalistic) behaviours towards her:

> Some of them are dead femme so it's actually just like being with a bunch of girls ... they're dead sensitive and dead nurturing. So like I would turn up on a Saturday and Ben would be like, 'Oh hiya babe, how's everything going? Y'alright? How was work? Oh I just brought you in a sandwich,' ... I think they realized maybe half way through the course that they didn't really need to be so sensitive around me. (Alex)

Thus, when male classmates were receptive to female presence, their actions – if any at all – were either not serious or essentialist.

Experiences with teachers

A predominantly male teaching staff

Respondents reported either being taught entirely, or predominantly, by men. In their initial interview answers, more than half of the respondents did not consider the lack of female teachers to be a problem per se. However, as they elaborated on their responses, positions differed. Three respondents (Alex, Anna and Victoria) echoed gender-blind ideas that the individual knowledge, experience and overall merit of the teacher are more important. Anna explained that 'It doesn't matter if they're a man or a woman, it just matters how good they are at the job'. Victoria expanded on this, acknowledging that while being taught by mostly male teachers is not problematic in itself, it is a reflection of the scarcity of women within the wider field of music technology. Yet, she alleges that women have to work harder to become successful (Kanter 1977): 'The teacher that I had here in Berlin, she's like a PhD, but that's the level of how good she had to be – and I had [male] teachers that don't even have a Master's degree, that don't even have a degree for that matter'. Second, Suzanna, Jessica and Anna highlighted the lack of role models for women in music technology, while a further four (Georgia, Suzanna, Davina and Jessica) expressed the belief that a greater number of female teachers would play a role in attracting more female students, or help to deconstruct the masculine image of the profession.

Teachers and gendered experiences

Gendered experiences involving teachers could be placed into three categories. First, most interviewees report indirect gender discrimination among teachers, i.e. teachers' own gendered preconceptions seep their way into interactions with and in assessments of students (Green 1997; Born and Devine 2015). Anna, Davina and Sara argued that teachers, on occasion, made statements suggesting that women were in fact better than male students in certain aspects of the course. On the surface, this may sound encouraging; however, explanations of the reasons why relied on stereotypical and essentialist notions of (emphasized) femininity or female physicality. For example, in an audio engineering class: 'The tutor said that women tend to make better foley artists, like making the sounds and like recreating the scenes than men do … he was like, well women just tend to like be lighter on their feet and have a closer eye for like, detail and attention' (Anna). While female bodies are thought to be advantageous in this area, Anna speculated that she was left out of a boom pole demonstration, due to her assumed lack of physical strength to hold the equipment. Similarly, a teacher praised an interviewee's efforts by making a connection between her femininity and emotional engagement with music. While working on a jazz track, her teacher said:

'You really thought about the emotion of the track ... because you as a female, you focus on details a lot more than the guys' (Sara). Another way that teachers revealed such implicit gender biases was in providing extra support for – and being extra attentive to – female students. Davina considered the possible gendered dimension to this: 'I'd say they're extra supportive 'cause they're aware that that you're in the minority ... If you're keen as well and you're dedicated, I'd say they're extra supportive most of the time, but even then that's a sort of special treatment assuming that you need it, isn't it?' These examples can be considered micro-aggressions: more subtle or covert forms of discrimination towards oppressed groups, particularly occurring where more obvious forms of discrimination are unacceptable (Nadal 2013). The above example raised by Sara demonstrates assumptions of traditional gender roles, while the example raised by Davina is a micro-aggression in its implicit and covert assumption regarding the inferiority of female students and their abilities (Nadal 2013: 39, 43).

Second, more explicit cases include the school's dismissal of complaints made about classmates or teachers, for what they felt were misogynistic remarks. An interviewee described reporting her male classmates to a class lecturer for repeatedly making rape jokes, to which she was told, 'It's just boys, you've got to get over it' (Jessica). Davina described taking a complaint about a member of teaching staff to the head of the school only to be told, 'That's just the way the industry is.' Third, it is also important to note that five respondents suggested feeling that the teaching staff tried to relate to students in a gender-neutral manner, although three of those same five interviewees also provided examples of gendered experiences with teachers. Perhaps it is important to consider these gendered experiences within the wider context of respondent's overall experiences of their teachers, suggesting that gendered encounters and interactions were not necessarily everyday experiences.

Addressing the gender imbalance

Six respondents identified ways that teaching staff attempted to address the gender imbalance in class. First, the most common strategy was the inclusion of, or drawing of attention to, the contributions made by women to the field of music technology in classes and course content. Indeed, actively drawing attention to the work of women where it appeared in class was perhaps an attempt to make the contributions of women more visible: 'He'd [male teacher] look at female examples as well, so if he was talking about a band he'd get another female band or one with a female singer or guitarist' (Jessica). Second, according to three respondents (Olivia, Jessica, Alex), teachers also addressed the gender imbalance directly and verbally: making the class aware of the vast gender imbalance in the wider industry, incorporating some acknowledgement of female students, or acknowledging gender inequality into opening dialogues. Olivia detailed:

> I did feel like they [the teachers] were very aware of it [the gender imbalance] ...
> I remember at the start of my degree one of the teachers was doing this big kinda

speech to all the students ... he said something along the lines of, 'Big respect to all the girls who are here to study because obviously there's not that many of them.' (Olivia)

Additionally, two respondents also reported being selected for class demonstrations over their male classmates; if a volunteer was required, a female classmate tended to be called upon. It was speculated that this was to encourage participation and to heighten feelings of comfort: 'It [the gender imbalance] was always like the elephant in the room, however sometimes in practical lessons ... if we were being shown something new, teachers would pick on me to be the person that they demonstrated this thing with' (Suzanna).

Respondents interpreted efforts to address the gender imbalance as ways that teachers had tried to be more inclusive of women within the class. These attempts have to be seen in the light of the hidden curriculum, that is, schools transmit concealed lessons that are taught as a means of social control, involve teaching differently within the class, political socialization and covert training in compliance (Giroux and Purpel 1983). If the concealed lesson in music technology education is that it is a male discipline, perhaps teachers' efforts to address the gender imbalance were also attempts to disrupt the apparent hidden curriculum that excludes women from music technology class content (see Strong and Cannizzo in this volume for a further discussion of this).

Conclusion and discussion

This chapter investigated gendered experiences of music technology education, by addressing their (1) classroom experiences, (2) interactions with (male) classmates and (3) experiences with teachers. First, being a token in a mostly-male classroom informs experiences of music technology education. Respondents' feelings on being one of few women in their class were generally negative and/or they felt they needed to adapt their behaviour to fit within a male-dominated environment. This reaffirms the masculine image of music technology, since even with women present, masculinity remains the norm. As a result, the masculinization of music technology as a profession continues.

Second, respondents generally reported having good or satisfactory relationships with their classmates. While this may be reflective of respondents' day-to-day experiences, these outcomes might result from selection of interviewees. Those who finished music technology training were able to adapt to a male-dominated environment – including its boyish and tech nerd posturing, occasional gendered evaluation, objectification of women and lack of accommodation of women. Others possibly dropped out. Future research might examine women who left the leaky pipeline.

Third, respondents were for the most part taught entirely by men. Most respondents drew attention to gendered interactions with teachers, mostly in terms of microaggressions. Women's performance was linked to essentialist ideas of feminine quality characteristics, such as emotion and lack of physical strength. However, teachers appeared to make attempts to address the gender imbalance in class through a variety of strategies, such as the inclusion of female contributions and examples in class content, addressing gender inequality in the music industry and picking female volunteers for demonstrations. Future research might further investigate the hidden curriculum by examining the content analysis of music tech school course materials and online content, in addition to classroom observations.

Additionally, the contemporary phenomenon of 'bedroom production' should not be underestimated as an alternative form of music technology education. Internet expansion and the development of user-friendly recording software opened the gates in terms of accessibility, but these informal educational pathways into music technology fall outside of the remit of this study. A small body of research addressing this topic is emerging (Rodgers 2010; Barna 2017); however, further research in this area should explore the use of online materials/self-teaching as a strategy for circumventing male dominated environments such as music technology schools.

All of this can be related back to the wider issue of the marginalization of women within popular music. The way by which music technology classrooms are constructed male spaces is connected to women students either self-excluding, or adapting to the masculine norms that are upheld. Understanding the gendered experiences of women studying at the educational levels preceding careers in music technology can therefore help us to make sense of the drop-out rates observed in women in music technology education – and consequently in the field of music technology. In another sense, perhaps this can go some way towards our understanding of where exactly the leaks in the 'leaky pipeline' occur and resultantly, where they can be fixed.

References

Armstrong, V. (2008), 'Hard Bargaining on the Hard Drive: Gender Bias in the Music Technology Classroom', *Gender and Education*, 20 (4): 375–386.

Armstrong, V. (2011), *Technology and the Gendering of Music Education*, Farnham: Ashgate.

Bader, I. and A. Scharenberg (2010), 'The Sound of Berlin: Subculture and the Global Music Industry', *International Journal of Urban and Regional Research*, 34 (1): 76–91.

Baker, S. (2013), 'Teenybop and the Extraordinary Particularities of Mainstream Practice', in S. Baker, A. Bennett and J. Taylor (eds.), *Redefining Mainstream Popular Music*, 14–24, New York: Routledge.

Barna, E. (2017), 'A (Translocal) Music Room of One's Own. Female Musicians within the Budapest Lo-Fi Scene', in E. Barna and T. Tófalvy (eds.), *Made in Hungary: Studies in Popular Music*, 59–70, New York: Routledge.

Bayton, M. (1997), 'Women and the Electric Guitar', in S. Whiteley (ed.), *Sexing the Groove: Popular Music and Gender*, 37–49, New York: Routledge.

Bayton, M. (1998), *Frock Rock: Women Performing Popular Music*, Oxford: Oxford University Press.

Berkers, P. and J. Schaap (2018), *Gender Inequality in Metal Music Production*, Bingley, UK: Emerald.

Blickenstaff, J. C. (2005), 'Women and Science Careers: Leaky Pipeline or Gender Filter?', *Gender and Education*, 17 (4): 369–386.

Born, G. and K. Devine (2015), 'Music Technology, Gender, and Class: Digitization, Educational and Social Change in Britain', *Twentieth-Century Music*, 12 (2): 135–172.

Born, G. and K. Devine (2016), 'Gender, Creativity and Education in Digital Musics and Sound Art', *Contemporary Music Review*, 35 (1): 1–20.

Braun, V. and V. Clarke (2006), 'Using Thematic Analysis in Psychology', *Qualitative Research in Psychology*, 3: 77–101.

Caputo, V. (1994), 'Add Technology and Stir', *Quarterly Journal of Music Teaching and Learning*, 4 (4): 85–90.

Clawson, M.A. (1999a), 'When Women Play the Bass: Instrument Specialization and Gender Interpretation in Alternative Rock Music', *Gender & Society*, 13 (2): 193–210.

Clawson, M. (1999b), 'Masculinity and Skill Acquisition in the Adolescent Rock Band', *Popular Music*, 18 (1): 99–14.

Cockburn, C. (1983), *Brothers: Male Dominance and Technological Change*, London: Pluto Press.

Cockburn, C. and S. Ormrod (1993), *Gender and Technology in the Making*, London: Sage.

Cohen, S. (1991), *Rock Culture in Liverpool: Popular Music in the Making*, Oxford: Oxford University Press.

Comber, C., D.J. Hargreaves and A. Colley (1993), 'Girls, Boys and Technology in Music Education', *British Journal of Music Education*, 10 (2): 123–134.

Davies, H. (2001), 'All Rock and Roll Is Homosocial: The Representation of Women in the British Rock Music Press', *Popular Music*, 20 (3): 301–319.

Doubleday, V. (2008), 'Sounds of Power: An Overview of Musical Instruments and Gender', *Ethnomusicology Forum*, 17 (1): 3–39.

Dryburgh, H. (1999), 'Work Hard, Play Hard: Women and Professionalization in Engineering – Adapting to the Culture', *Gender & Society*, 13 (5): 664–682.

England, P. (2010), 'The Gender Revolution: Uneven and Stalled', *Gender & Society*, 24 (2): 149–166.

Farrugia, R. (2009), 'Building a Women-Centred DJ Collective', *Feminist Media Studies*, 9 (3): 335–351.

Farrugia, R. (2012), *Beyond the Dance Floor: Female DJs, Technology, and Electronic Dance Music Culture*, Chicago, IL: University of Chicago Press.

Gadir, T. (2016), 'Resistance or Reiteration? Rethinking Gender in DJ Cultures', *Contemporary Music Review*, 35 (1): 115–129.

Gavanas, A. and R. Reitsamer (2013), 'DJ Technologies, Social Networks and Gendered Trajectories in European DJ Cultures', in B.A. Attias, A. Gavanas and H.C. Rietveld (eds.), *DJ Culture in the Mix: Power, Technology and Social Change in Electronic Dance Music*, 51–78, New York: Bloomsbury.

Giroux, H. and D. Purpel (1983), *The Hidden Curriculum and Moral Education: Deception or Discovery?*, Berkeley, CA: McCutchan.

Green, L. (1997), *Music, Gender, Education*, Cambridge: Cambridge University Press.

Gubrium, J. and J. Holstein (2002), *Handbook of Interview Research: Context and Method*, Thousand Oaks, CA: Sage.

Haider, S. (2016), 'The Shooting in Orlando, Terrorism or Toxic Masculinity (or Both?)', *Men and Masculinities*, 19 (5): 555–565.
Hiatt, B. (2016), 'Grimes on 'Art Angels' Follow-Up, Why She Loves Tool', *Rolling Stone*, 12 April. Available online: https://www.rollingstone.com/music/features/grimes-on-art-angels-follow-up-why-she-loves-tool-20160412 (accessed 4 April 2018).
Kanter, R.M. (1977), *Men and Women of the Corporation*, New York: Basic Books.
Leonard, M. (2007), *Gender in the Music Industry: Rock, Discourse and Girl Power*, London: Routledge.
Mulvey, L. (1975), 'Visual Pleasure and Narrative Cinema', *Screen*, 16 (3): 6–18.
Nadal, K. (2013), *That's So Gay! Microaggressions and the Lesbian, Gay, Bisexual, and Transgender Community*, Washington, D.C.: American Psychological Association.
Nordström, S. and Herz, M. (2013), '"It's a Matter of Eating or Being Eaten": Gender Positioning and Difference Making in the Heavy Metal Subculture', *European Journal of Cultural Studies*, 16 (4): 453–467.
O'Shea, H. (2008), '"Good Man, Mary!" Women Musicians and the Fraternity of Irish Traditional Music', *Journal of Gender Studies*, 17 (1): 55–70.
Rodgers, T. (2010), *Pink Noises: Women on Electronic Music and Sound*, Durham, NC: Duke University Press.
Roth, L.M. (2004), 'The Social Psychology of Tokenism: Status and Homophily Processes on Wall Street', *Sociological Perspectives*, 47 (2): 189–214.
Royal, C. (2014), 'Gender and Technology', in A. Trier-Bieniek and P. Leavy (eds.), *Gender & Pop Culture: Teaching Gender*, 175–189, Rotterdam: Sense Publishers.
Savage, M. (2012), 'Why Are Female Record Producers So Rare?', *BBC News*, 29 August. Available online: http://www.bbc.com/news/entertainment-arts-19284058 (accessed 23 January 2017).
Schaap, J. and P. Berkers (2014), 'Grunting Alone? Online Gender Inequality in Extreme Metal Music', *Journal of the International Association for the Study of Popular Music*, 4 (1): 101–116.
Straw, W. (1997), 'Sizing Up Record Collections', in S. Whiteley (ed.), *Sexing the Groove: Popular Music and Gender*, 3–16, London: Routledge.
Wajcman, J. (1991), *Feminism Confronts Technology*, Cambridge, UK: Polity Press.
Wajcman, J. (2004), *TechnoFeminism*, Cambridge, UK: Polity Press.
Werner, A. and S. Johansson (2016), 'Experts, Dads and Technology: Gendered Talk about Online Music', *International Journal of Cultural Studies*, 19 (2): 177–192.
West, C. and D.H. Zimmerman (1987), 'Doing Gender', *Gender & Society*, 1 (2): 125–151.
Wych, G. M. (2012), 'Gender and Instrument Associations, Stereotypes, and Stratification: A Literature Review', *Update: Applications of Research in Music Education*, 30 (2): 22–31.

5

Qualified Careers: Gendered Attitudes towards Screen Composition Education in Australia

Catherine Strong and Fabian Cannizzo

Introduction

This chapter is based on a study of Australian screen composers and the challenges and opportunities that shape their careers. It brings to light a number of very specific factors that influence women's participation in this field, and the relationship between successful careers and higher education. On the one hand, our study found a number of factors in play that have been well documented in other areas of the music industry that serve to limit women's participation, such as the existence of homosocial networks through which information and work flow (the 'boys' club'), and difficulties in balancing caring responsibilities with demanding work schedules. However, there are areas that appear to diverge from accounts in other studies. In particular, screen composition requires a different skill set and ways of working than performing as a musician, or being a composer, and as such the pathways through education are specific to this field. We suggest in this chapter that although Australia suffers from the phenomenon of the 'leaky pipe' when it comes to women entering education for screen composition as school leavers (Born and Divine 2015), there is a 'reentering' of the pipe that occurs as women who have had careers elsewhere come to view screen composition as a possible career option. While this re-entry into education can be beneficial in a number of ways for women, it also means exposure to the 'hidden curriculum' that closely resembles and reproduces the masculine culture of the industry itself. For men, on the other hand, this same masculine culture means that successful screen composition careers are possible without any formal education in this area. These gendered perceptions and decisions around screen composition education are shaped by contemporary labour and career practices.

The Australian screen composers study

The data in this chapter came from a mixed-methods study conducted between December 2016 and February 2017 (see Strong and Cannizzo 2017). The authors were commissioned by APRA AMCOS (the Australian Performing Rights Association and Australian Mechanical Copyright Owners' Society) to undertake research on the pathways and barriers to establishing a career in screen composition, with a focus on how gender makes a difference in this area. APRA AMCOS membership data shows that only 21.7 per cent of their members identify as female, with royalties to female members fluctuating between 15 per cent and 21 per cent. The percentage of female screen composers is lower again, with only 13 per cent of registered screen composers identifying as female. With women categorically underrepresented in registered musicianship and composition work, our study in part sought to question what role educational institutions played in creating this situation.

In order to interrogate the gendered disparity in membership numbers, a survey was sent to all current APRA AMCOS members who claimed royalties as screen composers. The survey consisted of twenty-eight questions, both closed and open ended. Overall, 159 usable surveys were completed, representing 7 per cent of the population. Thirteen per cent of female composers and 6 per cent of male composers responded. At the end of the survey, respondents were asked to provide contact details if they wished to participate in an interview. Interviews of approximately an hour each were conducted with eleven female and seventeen male composers, which were analysed using the software package NVivo. In this way, a combination of descriptive quantitative data and detailed qualitative data was collected. The limitations of this data should be noted however: the response rates are relatively low, and almost 70 per cent of the respondents (73 per cent of male respondents and 53 per cent of female) classified themselves as 'established' composers, suggesting our results are skewed towards this group. It should also be noted that while there was an option for respondents to give an identity other than 'male' or 'female', no participants did so. As such, this chapter is framed in terms of only these two categories, but this should not be read as a commitment by the authors to a binary approach to gender.

In addition to the data collected from APRA AMCOS members, research was also conducted with education providers. Anonymous interviews were conducted with academics at eight Australian tertiary institutions who provide courses related to screen composition. These covered a range of institution types, including universities, vocational training, and for-profit institutions. These interviews were focused specifically on gender issues, particularly relating to student numbers and institutional approaches to the gender imbalances.

Educated women composers, self-taught men

We will begin unpacking the relationship between screen composition careers and education by examining what the composers we surveyed and interviewed told us about their education. The data collected on composers' career paths suggested that the vast majority did not follow a pathway that lead from school, to a higher degree focused on composition, then into the industry. Rather, screen composers often came from other parts of the music industry: 82 per cent of male and 76 per cent of female respondents to the survey reported that they worked professionally as a musician prior to being a screen composer.

As part of the online survey for this study, we collected data on the highest level of education of our respondents. A curious pattern emerged whereby women composers were more highly educated than the male composers in our sample (see Figure 5.1). Only 34 per cent of men in our study held a degree higher than a bachelor's, compared to 62 per cent of women. Sixty-six per cent of men as opposed to 79 per cent of women reported that they had formal music education of some sort; however, when this was broken into the type of education received it was revealed that the most common type of music education reported by men was 'Music Lessons', which encompasses anything formal but non-accredited, including music lessons taken by respondents as children. Almost 30 per cent of males but only 10 per cent of females have moved into careers as screen composers with only this level of music education. Women, on the other hand, were more likely to have higher education degree relating to music. This difference became more pronounced again when respondents were asked about training specific to screen composition; 42 per cent of women but only 15 per cent of men had screen composition training. Overall, then, the women who are finding work in this field are much more likely to have formal education in this area.

The interviews for this study gave further detail on the pathways taken by composers through their careers, which provide insights into when and why composers undertook formal education, and how composers who had no qualifications established successful careers regardless. This data demonstrated gendered differences in that men were

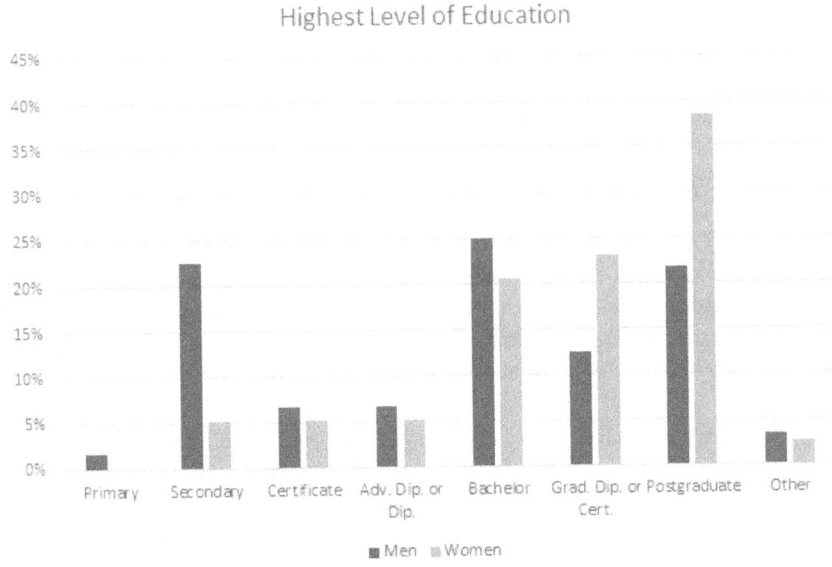

Figure 5.1 Educational Attainment of Screen Music Composers.

more likely to describe themselves as 'self-taught' and not consider formal education as necessary to supplement this. Men described the way that throughout their lives as musicians, they had adopted a 'try it and see' attitude:

> I saved up the cash that I had and what I could earn and I bought myself an Atari ST computer ... and then I guess tried out ideas I had, but without a band I could use a small little sound module to imitate drums and imitate bass guitar and keyboards and things like that. So I started doing that for myself and creating songs that way. (Steven)
>
> I basically had one lesson when I knew of a really good funk musician, and thought that I'd like to learn how to play funky guitar better than I was. Other than that, really, you may as well say no, I've had no lessons ... I'm self-taught. (Nathan)

This attitude continued over into their initial forays into screen composition:

> I got involved doing television music. [A colleague] was looking for a guitarist for something. So I started playing guitar for him. And then he asked me if I wanted to compose. So then I had this two-week crash course in how to use Logic, and was suddenly recording music ... I just basically got thrown in at the deep end ... I've always been the sort of person that's willing to learn in public, I guess. (Nathan)

No men interviewed returned to education after they had made the decision to move into screen composing. One male interviewee went as far as to explicitly reject the need for qualifications in order to succeed in the field:

> I guess I also knew that in terms of formal qualifications, they're not really needed in the industry, I mean, unless you want to be a teacher. Nobody ever asks you what level of qualification do you have, it's more about your work. So I guess the thing for me is that I haven't formally trained, but I've had a lot of mentors and I've had the kind of drive, I guess, to continue bettering myself. (Toby)

Women, by contrast, were more likely to take a default position that education was needed to advance their career. For example, the following woman already had a music degree, and had spent many years as part of a very successful band. For her, the idea of moving into screen composition was accompanied by an almost automatic assumption that returning to formal education would be required to do this:

> There I was with a music degree and absolutely no prospect of employment, and no idea what to do ... a friend of mine suggested [a screen composition course] to me. And it actually was the perfect thing for me, because I'd always had an interest in the visual arts ... And it was just like a perfect melding of art forms that seemed like – I was incredulous that it hadn't occurred to me before. (Caroline)

Women composers also used education as a way of trying to make further progress when they hit roadblocks in their careers. A composer who had been quite successful, but who felt that she could not get to the level she wanted to in the industry, discussed how she returned to education to try to get something extra to push her career further:

> I was working with international productions, and I just realized that I was kind of at the peak of where I could go. Not so much the level of the productions I was working on, but you know, I always wanted to be working on more features and more heavy hitting series, but I was working constantly. I was making a living, and I knew I needed to know more about my craft ... Surely, I can get to the level of writing those big feature films if I get my orchestral chops up, and that's really why I went back and got my Bachelor of Music degree – in order to have more certainly concert music, but also to break through the glass ceiling and get those big feature films. (Rachelle)

While this composer reported that this strategy was ultimately unsuccessful for a variety of reasons not related directly to education, the difference between this type of approach and the male composers' informal strategies for career progression is noteworthy.

There are a number of possible explanations for these differences, all of which are interrelated. The first is that women may be less likely to be hired as screen composers unless they have formal qualifications. This would be in keeping with the findings of other studies that have found women do not progress as far in their careers unless they are more qualified than the men they are competing with (OECD 2015; Carnevale et al. 2018). However, as this study did not investigate hiring practices by those using the services of screen composers, we can offer no firm finding on whether this is the case. The second possibility is that women use qualifications as a way of feeling confident that they do in fact have the skills to do the job. This relates to findings of other studies on gender in music and the creative industries more broadly (see, for example, Hesmondhalgh and Baker 2015; Leonard 2016; Gadir 2017; Gill et al. 2017), that suggest that women do not feel as confident in their abilities as men, and are also less likely than men to self-promote and take on challenges that they do not feel entirely secure in attempting. This was noted by some interviewees:

> Yeah, I feel like – it's so hard to tell what is a generalisation and what is what I experience as well but I feel like a lot of men just have the confidence to just accept it and just do it and I think a lot of women feel like they have to study for a million years and then they might be qualified to do a job beyond the score or whatever, you know. (Margaret)

This was also reflected in the way that men and women talked about themselves in interviews for this project; men were much more likely to express strong positive self-assessments (for example, male respondents described themselves as 'prodigies', 'geniuses', and one man simply declared that he was 'fucking brilliant'), whereas women offered much more restrained comments on their abilities. These differences can be seen in terms of men inhabiting an artistic masculine subjectivity that allows for expressions of confidence and for artistic experimentation that women are denied, or even punished for if they try to adopt it (Miller 2016). In lieu of the ability to self-promote or to confidently assert an ability to succeed at tasks never attempted before, women return to education.

A further factor at play here is the importance of informal networks. The so-called 'cool, creative and egalitarian' industries, have produced new forms of gendered inequality deriving from the informality, autonomy and flexibility associated with project-based work organized through networked gatekeepers (Gill 2002). As Gill (2002: 78) notes of her sample of European new media workers, freelancers in the industries found traditional means of finding work, such as advertised job postings, increasingly irrelevant in comparison to the importance of 'informal networks'. In industries where work is organized on an informal basis, networking has become a key tool for attaining job security (Ebbers and Wijnberg 2009; see also Castells 2010). The consequences of these changes for workers in creative and cultural industries is captured well by Wittel (2001), who describes contemporary work as being shaped by 'network sociality'. Whereas networking has always been an important business practice for upper management and the corporate world, it is now 'as much performed on the ground of the corporate world as at the top' (Wittel 2001: 56). Schmoozing, attending social events and taking charge of online 'data doubles' (Haggerty and Ericson 2000) have become commonplace among creative employees and contractors as much as CEOs, and this was reported as being very much the case by our respondents. In highly masculinized fields such as screen composition, men dominate these networks to such an extent that the women in our study referred to them as the 'boys' club'. Where such networks are nebulous and difficult to access, the path to and through education is clear, and offers alternative ways of creating networks. A number of women composers referred to the connections they made in education institutions as being of ongoing importance to their careers. However, as we will argue below, the male dominance of industry networks can be as difficult to challenge in educational settings as in the industry.

Education institutions and screen composition educators

Having demonstrated that women who have established a career in screen composition are more likely than men to have returned to higher education in order to do so, we move in this part of the chapter to a consideration of what they encounter in these institutions. As background, there is extensive research that explores the gendered dynamics of music education, and shows that from an early age boys and girls are socialized very differently in this area (see Abramo 2011; Tobias 2014). In terms of aspects of education directly related to this study, research has shown that music technology and composition are both gendered as masculine in classrooms, and women are less likely to pursue these elements of music making. Victoria Armstrong

(2008: 381) has pioneered research into gendered music education, finding that girls in her study were less confident with using music technologies than boys. The association of technology with masculinity may lead to perceptions in classrooms that 'women are less able and less interested in all things technological', which includes music technologies (Armstrong 2011: 3). Armstrong's claims support Lucy Green's now classic study of gender and music composition, in which Green (1997: 105) argues that 'the cerebral delineation of composition continues to carry overwhelmingly masculine connotations'. Gender-based assumption about learners are suggested to play a role in socializing boys and girls into differential attitudes towards music composition practice. Research in the higher education setting both in the UK (Bogdanovic 2015) and Australia (Zhukov 2006) suggests that masculine dominance of music education spaces, such as classrooms and conservatoria, may continue well beyond the secondary education setting (for a more extended discussion of gender differences in music education, see Hooper and Berkers, and Davies in this volume).

What emerged from our interviews with higher education providers is that despite enrolment in music courses being almost evenly split between men and women across all courses offered, courses relating to screen composition had much lower numbers of women than other music courses. Educators claimed that simply using the word 'composition' in a course title saw a drop in women students to between one-third to a quarter of all students, whereas in related courses that used terms such as song writing or performance numbers of men and women were usually even. Courses that had titles that suggested a greater use of technology (such as sound design) were likely to have even lower proportions of women, at around 10 per cent. This finding corresponds with the overseas research discussed in Born and Divine (2015), which suggests that the association between composition and technology is a barrier to female participation in education in this area. Another consideration in this area was the makeup of the teaching staff. For the most part, teaching staff for composition and music technology courses were reported to be all-male or mostly male. Between student and staff composition, learning was occurring in a male-dominated environment.

We wish to examine how this masculine environment constitutes part of the 'hidden curriculum' of music education, as a way of socializing students to work in a similar environment and thus helping to normalize it. A hidden curriculum is 'the unstated norms, values and beliefs that are transmitted to students through the underlying structure of meaning in both the formal content as well as the social relations of school and classroom life' (Giroux and Penna 1979: 22). This theory views education institutions as 'agent[s] of socialization' (Giroux and Penna 1979: 22), and in order for education to achieve ends that are about the pursuit of social justice, as opposed to social reproduction, the hidden curriculum needs to be made visible and disrupted. In music-related higher education, research has suggested that teaching students how to form social bonds is a central part of the hidden curriculum (Pitts 2003), and this emerged as a central aspect of gendered student experiences in this study, in ways that related to the centrality of networks to screen composition work in the industry.

When discussing their education experiences, the women screen composers in our study reported being quite aware of their minority status in their courses. They commented on feeling excluded from activities male students undertook together, whether these were formal classroom activities or informal socializing or projects outside the curriculum. This suggests the start of the creation of 'exclusionary networks' by men (Christopherson 2009). The discussion by Hopkins and Berkers in this volume of music technology students in the UK and Germany closely resembles our findings here, and is worth reading in conjunction with this chapter. Students also commented on interactions with teachers:

> From time to time I do feel like maybe one or two teachers, there is a bit of a masculine ego edge that comes through ... I think there's a certain amount of unwillingness to share what you've done, for fear of not really making the mark or not being on par. (Jennifer)

As a corollary, teachers also shared experiences of having female students in classes and sensing that they became isolated or discouraged:

> I remember going – just by virtue of the fact that she's the only woman in this class, and she was quiet, quite reserved person, I thought she's really at a disadvantage straight off the bat. Because there's three loud blokes in here and this quiet, reserved – because they're small classes – this quite reserved woman. (…) And I feel like at the end of my course, it might have actually been discouraging to her, rather than empowering. (Graham)

These experiences of women being outnumbered, excluded and feeling as though they do not 'fit' the culture they have found themselves in match what women composers told us about their experiences in the industry. As part of this hidden curriculum, however, some women talked about developing strategies during education to either resist this culture (for example, through cultivating women-centred networks) or to work with it, which have carried through into their professional lives.

There were other more subtle ways in which the gendered aspects of the industry were reproduced in classrooms. Interviews with educators suggested the lack of women teachers is related to the way information about jobs flows through the same types of informal networks as in the screen composition industry. In the case of jobs teaching music, these networks will overlap significantly, with educators hiring people from within their professional networks. Thus, the 'boys' club' can also impact on the gender make up of those teaching. One respondent from a for-profit institution described with frustration a scenario where he had been involved in a round of recruitment for new staff, and had put forward a short-list of candidates that was gender-balanced, only to see no women hired. He explained this outcome as follows:

> There was a lot of nepotism in there as well, and it's like, I know this person from back in the day, and I know this person from back in the day and they got the job. And there was actually one instance ... There's this one gentleman, he was not working. He was on the dole (…) and he ended up being offered a job because he

was someone's friend, and he was not the right person for the role – categorically not the right person for the role. (Finn)

This type of scenario leaves women students with few role models, which may increase feelings of isolation in courses where their fellow students are also mostly male (Armstrong 2008: 378). It also models to the students industry practices of 'jobs for the boys' and underqualified men being given opportunities because of their connections. This mirrors the situation for practitioners described in the first part of the paper.

The question then arises of whether – especially given the sheer difference in numbers between male and female students – formal education can be used to impact on outcomes for women in the industry, or whether the hidden curriculum simply prepares students for the inequality to come. The educators interviewed for this project showed awareness of the gender imbalances in their courses, and also of the broader imbalances in the industry, but responses to this varied greatly across (and possibly within) institutions. Almost every educator spoken to noted that the problems with getting women into composition and music technology courses were not at the level of tertiary education but came from primary and secondary school. There were simply not as many women as men applying to do these courses in the first place. In a minority of interviewees, this translated into a disinterest in pursuing any remedial strategies, as the educators saw the problem as beyond their control. In one case, the interviewee went further here in attributing this to a fundamental difference between men and women that could not be addressed. Other factors also impacted on educators' willingness to implement measures to shift gender levels among students; one respondent at a high-profile university reported that as the 30 per cent proportion of women in the composition course at his institution was higher than the proportion at another university seen as a close competitor, there was no need to do any work to improve this figure. So some institutions are happy to persist with the current situation.

On the other hand, staff at a number of institutions reported strategies that had been developed to try to either increase female representation, or improve the outcomes for their female students. In terms of seeing more women admitted, some institutions reported giving favourable treatment to women candidates; for example, one educator who taught a course with historically very low numbers of women applicants said he admitted almost every such applicant almost as a matter of course, whereas another institution gave women applicants extra 'points' on their admission score. In courses where there was an element of subjectivity in admission (for instance, where candidates had to do an audition, an entry task or an interview), some institutions reported changing and standardizing procedures in order to try to reduce gender-related bias. Interview data from current screen composers demonstrates how important changes such as these are, as they revealed that in the past a lack of stringency around entry processes had led to women being explicitly discriminated against. However, we would argue that a reliance on methods to increase the intake of women into courses is limited, because of the lack of control over numbers of applicants in the first place.

In terms of what happened once women were in the courses, interviewees tended to discuss ways they were attempting or succeeding at improving retention and graduate outcomes. In the institutions where there was a high level of commitment to trying to change the outcomes for women composers, strategies such as implementing mentorship programs or reserving key internships for women students were designed to improve early-career outcomes. Some went further than this in also considering what was happening in courses on a day-to-day level that could have a different impact on male and female students. One interviewee talked about engaging with the film-making students who worked with the screen composition students to challenge elements of their culture that could be considered unfriendly to women:

> A guy was getting a woman, a professional actor who retired, in for an exercise to do things that you just – that she was clearly uncomfortable with, and he just didn't see that that was wrong. We've had younger students make films involving violence on women, which I suppose, for me, is just kind of – just normal. Now people really will have that debate about is this – how much is this perpetuating a situation and how much – is it actually doing anything to question the norm of violence by men on women, or it is just exploiting that? Those are the questions which probably didn't occur 15 years ago, 10 years ago. Right there now, things get quite hammered now. How will this play? How is it really – what's the ideology going on here? What can we do about it? So there's been a shift, definitely. (Robert)

In addition to this, some institutions were changing processes around hiring to increase women teachers. Some institutions had implemented more formal hiring procedures that make it harder for people to just hire their friends. A female respondent discussed how the addition of new, female, staff members at the institution she was studying at, which had introduced such measures, made a difference to her experience, saying 'I really appreciated that. It made me feel a lot better actually being in the department and having more female teachers to look up to and to hear how they went through their journey.'

These types of strategies may have some effectiveness in changing the hidden curriculum in these courses. While there is no easy or quick fix to the imbalance in numbers, when educators act to send the message that women are valued in their courses (through targeted programs and mentorships), when they are aware of and challenge the culture of masculinity, and when students are shown that women can succeed in the industry through their inclusion in teaching staff, a different set of values may start to emerge. Of course this is never straightforward – a student may interpret a mentorship scheme, for example, as women needing more help rather than a statement on their value – but ultimately may be more effective than a focus on numbers.

Conclusion

While education is generally framed as an unqualified good, and something that will benefit individuals if they undertake it, for screen composers in Australia the relationship between 'being educated' and 'getting work' is not straightforward and is highly gendered. An ability to embody certain masculine characteristics such as self-confidence and self-promotion, and an ability to access networks that are already extremely male-dominated – the 'boys' club' – trump qualifications in terms of gaining work in the screen composition industry. Women return to higher education when trying to break into the industry as a way to counteract some of the disadvantages they face by not possessing these characteristics, whereas men do not need to do so. Higher education qualifications can indeed be beneficial to women; however, they can also subtly increase the disadvantages they face, through delaying their entry to the field, and by exposing them to a hidden curriculum in education institutions that can reinforce the expectation of a male-dominated industry. The use of industry networks to hire (sometimes unqualified) staff serves to reinforce the masculine nature of the field and can replicate the pattern where more qualified women are overlooked in favour of well-connected men. These findings lead to questions about who gains what benefits from higher education in screen music related subjects, and what type of changes can be implemented that will meaningfully challenge the status quo in this area.

The Australian Women Screen Composers project has revealed that screen composition education serves multiple functions in reproducing the screen and music industries, including both technical training and socialization. Screen composition education courses, as with education for the creative industries more broadly, need to ensure that they are fit for purpose to achieve not only skills-based outcomes, but also contribute to the equitable socialization of current and future professionals. As Giroux and Penna (1979: 27) have noted, 'any curriculum designed to introduce positive changes in classrooms will fail, unless such a proposal is rooted in an understanding of those socio-political forces that strongly influence the every texture of day-to-day classroom pedagogical practices'. Higher and vocational education organizations are authoritative institutions that can help to shape common discourses and expectations that marginalize women in music composition, such as the ongoing image of the artist as an 'implicitly masculine' archetype (see Miller 2016). Addressing gender inequalities and stereotypes in music education is as important to the career development of young adults, perhaps entering higher education from the high school setting, as it is for mature composition students, who have perhaps already worked for years in the creative industries and are seeking to refine or redefine their career trajectories.

References

Abramo, J.M. (2011), 'Gender Differences of Popular Music Production in Secondary Schools', *Journal of Research in Music Education*, 59 (1): 21–43.

Armstrong, V. (2008), 'Hard Bargaining on the Hard Drive: Gender Bias in the Music Technology Classroom', *Gender and Education*, 20 (4): 375–386.

Armstrong, V. (2011), *Technology and the Gendering of Music Education*, Farnham and Burlington, VT: Ashgate.

Bogdanivic, D. (2015), *Gender and Equality in Music Higher Education*. Available online: http://www.namhe.ac.uk/publications/reports/gender_and_equality_2015.pdf (accessed 3 March 2018).

Born, G. and K. Devine (2015), 'Music Technology, Gender, and Class: Digitization, Educational and Social Change in Britain', *Twentieth-Century Music*, 12 (2): 135–172.

Carnevale, A.P.N. Smith and A. Gulish (2018), *Women Can't Win*, Washington DC: Georgetown University Center on Education and the Workforce. Available online: https://cew-7632.kxcdn.com/wp-content/uploads/Women_FR_Web.pdf (accessed 10 February 2019).

Castels, E. (2010), *The Rise of the Network Society*, 2nd edn, Chichester: Wiley-Blackwell.

Christopherson, S. (2009), 'Working in the Creative Economy: Risk, Adaptation, and the Persistence of Exclusionary Networks', in A. McKinlay and C. Smith (eds.), *Creative Labour: Working in the Creative Industries*, 72–90, Houndmills, Basingstoke: Palgrave Macmillan.

Ebbers, J.J. and N.M. Wijnberg (2009), 'Latent Organizations in the Film Industry: Contracts, Rewards and Resources', *Human Relations*, 7 (62): 987–1009.

Gadir, T. (2017), 'Forty-Seven DJs, Four Women: Meritocracy, Talent and Postfeminist Politics', *Dancecult*, 9 (1): 50–72.

Gill, R. (2002), 'Cool, Creative and Egalitarian? Exploring Gender in Project-Based New Media Work in Europe', *Information, Communication and Society*, 5 (1): 70–89.

Gill, R., E.K. Kelan and C.M. Scharff (2017), 'A Postfeminist Sensibility at Eork', *Gender, Work & Organization*, 24 (3): 226–244.

Giroux, H. and A. Penna (1979), 'Social Education in the Classroom: The Dynamics of the Hidden Curriculum', *Theory and Research in Social Education*, 4 (1): 20–42.

Green, L. (1997), *Music, Gender, Education*, Cambridge: Cambridge University Press.

Haggerty, K.D. and R.V. Ericson (2000), 'The Surveillant Assemblage', *British Journal of Sociology*, 51 (4): 605–622.

Hesmondhalgh, D. and S. Baker (2015), 'Sex, Gender and Work Segregation in the Cultural Industries', *The Sociological Review*, 63 (S1): 23–36.

Leonard, M. (2016), 'Girls at Work: Gendered Identities, Sex Segregation and Employment Experiences in the Music Industries', in J. Warwick and A. Adrian (eds.), *Voicing Girlhood in Popular Music: Performance, Authority, Authenticity*, 37–55, New York: Routledge.

Miller, D.K. (2016), 'Gender and the Artist Archetype: Understanding Gender Inequality in Artistic Careers', *Sociology Compass*, 10 (2): 119–131.

OECD (2015), *Education Indicators in Focus*, March. Available online: http://www.oecd.org/education/skills-beyond-school/EDIF-2015-No-30-ENG.pdf (accessed 7 July 2018).

Pitts, S. (2003), 'What Do Students Learn When We Teach Music? An Investigation of the "Hidden" Curriculum in a University Music Department', *Arts and Humanities in Higher Education*, 2 (3): 281–292.

Strong, C. and F. Cannizzo (2017), *Australian Women Screen Composers: Career Barriers and Pathways: Research Report*, Melbourne, Australia: RMIT University. Available online: http://apraamcos.com.au/about-us/industry-research/australian-women-screen-composers/ (accessed 5 October 2018).

Tobias, E.S. (2014), 'Solo, Multitrack, Mute? Producing and Performing (Gender) in a Popular Music Classroom', *Visions of Research in Music Education*, 25. Available online: http://www.rider.edu/~vrme (accessed 14 June 2018).

Wittel, A. (2001), 'Toward a Network Sociality', *Theory, Culture & Society*, 18 (6): 51–76.

Zhukov, K. (2006), 'Gender Issues in Instrumental Music Teaching in Australian Conservatoriums', *Research Studies in Music Education*, 26: 22–36.

Part Two

Current Practice

6

Gender, Policy and Popular Music in Australia: 'I Think the Main Obstacles Are Men and Older Men'

Maura Edmond

Same as it ever was

The recent documentary *Her Sound, Her Story* (dir. Michelle Grace Hunder and Claudia Sangiorgi Dalimore 2018) opens with archival footage of a young Kylie Minogue reflecting on her experiences as a woman in the Australian music industry. The original interview is from *Sisters Are Doin' It for Themselves*, a 1994 documentary produced by celebrated Australian musician Lindy Morrison. The original video, made for an educational series on the business of the music industry, remains an all-too-rare example of an explicitly feminist Australian music documentary, and even-more-rare, one that traverses indiscriminately across a range of local scenes and genres. But despite the calibre of the musicians featured in Morrison's documentary – including some of the biggest names (then and still) in the Australian music industry – there appears to have been little interest in the final video beyond its release as an educational resource. It received no wider screenings on local public broadcasters or at film festivals and remains available only on VHS in a couple of Australian libraries. That the collaborators behind *Her Sound, Her Story* have profiled the footage in their own recent documentary on the same topic is both exciting and frustrating. While it's terrific to rediscover this material, now twenty-five years old, it is also confronting to take stock of just how little has changed in the intervening decades. In Morrison's original documentary, Kylie Minogue – by then already a seven-year veteran of the industry having released five studio albums and a greatest hits compilation – describes having to constantly prove herself because she is young, female and blonde. Minogue joins other Australian pop and rock stars, including Christine Anu, Wendy Matthews, Tina Arena, Ruby Hunter, Betty McQuade and Lindy Morrison herself, all of whom describe similar issues. Men totally dominate the industry – the bands, the road crew, the record labels. Women don't receive comparable recognition for what they do. Women making music are seen as exceptional or a novelty. Women are discriminated against because they are 'too hot' or 'not hot enough'. And women of colour experience other intersecting prejudices. Those same sentiments from Morrison's 1994 documentary are echoed almost verbatim in a series of new interviews for *Her Sound, Her Story*, undertaken with a wide range of contemporary Australian musicians, a great many of whom would have grown up watching the likes of Kylie and Tina from a very young age. Same as it ever was.

If there is one quality that haunts discussions of the gender gap in Australian arts and culture more than any other, it is this one: a gnawing, inescapable sense of déjà vu. Since the late 1970s, a range of government agencies and industry organizations have attempted to understand and remedy a serious gender gap that encompasses the breadth of Australia's creative and cultural industries. The earliest of these reports include research into women's involvement in the film and broadcast industries, such as *Women Working in the Australian Mass Media* (1976), *Women in Australian Film Production* (Ryan et al. 1983), and large-scale studies such as the Australia Council funded *Women in the Arts* report (1983). During the 1990s and 2000s, there was negligible policy discussion of women's participation in arts and culture and a dismantling of special interest women's funds. After a long hiatus, and in keeping with a wider resurgence of popular feminist discourse, there has recently been a series of new reports that have revisited these themes. These include *Women in Theatre* (Lally and Miller 2012), *Women in the Victorian Contemporary Music Industry* (2015), *Gender Matters* (2015), *Skipping a Beat* (Cooper et al. 2017) and *Turning Pointe* (Westle 2018). Written variously by academics, government agencies and professional industry organizations, the reports adopt a range of approaches to documenting the problem and use different indices to measure inequality, including income levels, overall proportion of the workforce, level of seniority relative to education background, etc. Despite the methodological differences, however, the key obstacles they identify remain remarkably consistent.

Having now read over many of these reports for a research project examining the history of Australia's cultural gender gap (see Edmond and McGowan 2017), what has become clear is their predictability. If you were to select a policy report on gender inequality from just about any Australian creative field and from any point in time over the previous forty years, its contents would be much the same. It would say words to the effect that women are well represented at the level of audiences, students and early career practitioners, but with each hurdle towards success, recognition and something approximating a sustainable career, their numbers dwindle dramatically and entirely disproportionately. It would also identify a set of explanations for this gender gap which are just as consistent: motherhood; boys' club; confidence gaps; a lack of women in leadership positions; segregation along lines of gender with women overrepresented in traditionally feminized roles and widely missing from the better paid and more career sustaining technical and leadership roles; and for at least some of the women surveyed, sexist and hostile working environments where they've experienced harassment, intimidation and assault.

The consistency of these reports, in terms of both their findings and their broad recommendations, would suggest that the problem of gender inequality within Australia's arts and cultural industries, from a policy perspective at least, is relatively well understood and that the real difficulty lies in developing the right initiatives and programs to help remedy the gap. Viewed collectively and longitudinally, however, the reports reveal that over the course of nearly forty years of public policy interventions, Australia has struggled to close the cultural gender gap, and in many creative fields the situation has deteriorated. So, while the data produced by these studies allows us to measure the scale of the problem at different points in time (though more successfully for some creative sectors than others), translating those findings into effective, longer term change has proved extremely elusive.

In the following chapter I explore in more detail some of the patterns we can observe in terms of both women's inequality in creative work, and in policy research and interventions into that inequality, paying attention to recent developments surrounding women in the Australian music industry. In particular, I argue there are recurring problems in the design and framing of gender equality policy, including a tendency to return to the same types of interventions and recommendations again and again. As government agencies and professional industry organizations slowly begin to revise how they address the issue, there are also some important differences emerging between cultural sectors in terms of policy coherence and commitment. Alongside more formal efforts to remedy the cultural gender gap, this chapter also considers examples of popular and subcultural feminist responses that have developed at arm's length from centralized policy and in doing so, I argue, challenge some of the more problematic policy discourses on gender equality in the arts and cultural industries.

Starting from a very low base

The status of women working in the media has been the subject of policy research in Australia since the mid-1970s, emerging out of the work of the Women's Media Action Group at the ABC and catalyzed by the UNESCO International Women's Year in 1975. There were reports produced first on women in film and broadcasting, followed in the early 1980s by extensive studies of women in the visual and performing arts (*Women Working in the Australian Mass Media* 1976; Ryan et al. 1983; *Women in the Arts* 1983). By comparison, there has been relatively little policy research into women's participation in the Australian music industry. Until recently, the most detailed study was the Australia Council's *Women in the Arts* report from 1983, which observed major similarities across artforms in terms of gender inequality but singled out music, and popular music in particular, as especially problematic. In a breakdown of the gendering of different jobs (senior, administrative, technical, managerial, creative), the report noted that men dominated senior managerial positions across all areas, from orchestras to the recording industries, but in the case of popular music, 'the rock music industry is dominated by men in all fields' (*Women in the Arts* 1983: 82). In the intervening thirty years, however, there has been very little research into gender inequality in the Australian music industry. As the *Skipping a Beat* report observes, 'there is a lack of expansive, representative and current data' (Cooper et al. 2017: 6).

Three recent reports into the status of women in the Australian music industry have attempted to overcome this lack of data, by aggregating and documenting current inequalities of participation: *Women in the Victorian Contemporary Music Industry* (Music Victoria 2015), *Australian Women Screen Composers: Career Barriers and Pathways* (Strong and Cannizzo 2017) and *Skipping a Beat: Assessing the State of Gender Inequality in the Australian Music Industry* (Cooper et al. 2017). Echoing the findings of *Women in the Arts* from 1983, these new studies suggest that what holds true for women's participation in other creative sectors – there are less women overall in the workforce; dramatically less women in technical roles; less women in senior leadership positions; and a gendered earning gap – is even more true for the music industry. In attempting understand the basis of these inequalities of participation the reports return to familiar ground. They cite caring responsibilities and the career impacts of taking time out for children (which disproportionately affect women) as a major hurdle to women's participation in the music industry. In keeping with studies of other creative fields, the reports find that a 'confidence gap' is a significant obstacle for women's music careers. Women in the music industry feel they lack the necessary confidence to succeed and they are perceived, by themselves and by others, to be less willing to put themselves 'out there' (Music Victoria 2015: 2). The reports point to the prevalence of a 'boys' club' mentality in which men give gigs to their immediate networks and friendship circles, resulting in a blokey status quo that is perpetuated and obscured by the informal and 'meritocratic' nature of the industry. Sexual harassment is another key factor that contributes to women's lack of participation. Finally, all the reports point to the absence of women from industry leadership roles. As *Skipping a Beat* notes, women are missing from the overwhelmingly male-dominated boards of key industry agencies like APRA, AMCOS, AMPAL, AIR, and from the ARIA boards, while the state and national music organizations faired only moderately better (Cooper et al. 2017: 8–10). The reports also allude to gendered problems inherent in the casualized, for-the-love-of-it cultural industries more broadly. In Strong and Cannizzo's report, for example, the authors observe that the general health of the industry is a problem for women. Casualized employment conditions, poor remuneration and informal hiring processes disproportionately affect women; moreover, a fragile industry is likely to be more risk averse and more reliant on established networks and 'boys' club' (2017: vii). In this way, the studies indicate how issues of reputation or status inequality play a role in women's ongoing economic inequality, because all the obstacles cited contribute to comparatively fewer paid opportunities for women, precarious and exploitative working conditions, and a pay disparity that undermines women's music careers in the long term. All these findings map closely on to existing policy studies of Australia's cultural gender gap, dating back to the late 1970s.

In lieu of other sustained or direct policy action, these studies by *de facto* constitute a large part of the policy activity on gender inequality in the Australian music industry. Again, this is in keeping with historical trends that can be identified across the breadth of arts and cultural sectors in Australia, in which studies into gender inequality, together with their lists of familiar recommendations, tap into agitation at a grassroots level but rarely result in centralized or top-down policy intervention. In Australian cultural policy discourse,[1] gender equality is most often addressed *indirectly* and *implicitly*, by way of generalized support for concepts of 'diversity', 'inclusion' and 'access' for everyone, 'regardless of cultural background, age, gender or ability, or where they live or what they earn' (*Creative State* 2016: 28). At the level of state and federal government agencies, these vague statements of support for equality of access tend to be very broadly defined (*all Victorians* or *all Australians*), made in reference more to audiences and without clearly determined objectives, especially as they might relate to gender. In the Victorian state government's *Creative State* strategy, for example, 'inclusion and diversity' at the level of programming and participation is one of its key action areas, delivered via partnerships with relevant Indigenous, culturally and linguistically diverse (CALD), and disability agencies. The funding documents for Create NSW claim they are 'committed to improving gender diversity by supporting applications that demonstrate gender equality' but again gender itself is not a 'priority area' (Create NSW 2017: 15). Likewise, the Australia Council's corporate plan identifies gender identity (as well as gendered issues such as parental status and marital status) as aspects of diversity, but they are not the agency's 'diversity priority areas' (*Corporate Plan* 2017: 19). Moreover, these generalized statements of support for inclusivity are inevitably in tension with the entrenched 'excellence' and more recently 'creative industries' paradigms, which otherwise completely dominate Australia's cultural policy discourse and which – with their celebrations of established canonical masters and inculcations to (child-less, care-free) agility, flexibility and entrepreneurialism – contribute to worsening inequalities of participation.[2]

While the rhetoric of diversity and inclusivity is widespread in contemporary Australian cultural policy, there has been much less in the way of direct and explicit initiatives to address the gender gap. To date the most ambitious and high-profile example has been the Gender Matters platform organized by the national screen funding agency Screen Australia. The report and ensuing taskforce emerged after a long-overdue auditing of Australia's screen sector, which revealed that just 16 per cent of feature films were directed by women – a figure that had struggled to improve substantially since the 1970s and was down from a high of 22 per cent in 1992, the time of the last major study of its kind (Cox and Laura 1992: 10; *Gender Matters* 2015: 5–6). In addition to a temporary boost in funding specifically for 'storytelling by women', the Gender Matters Taskforce made funding criteria changes to include gender diversity as part of overall assessment. They also set a target for having 50 per cent of projects funded by the agency to have at least 50 per cent women in key creative roles (writer, producer, director), a target which the agency met (over a three-year average) in mid-2018. In approximation, that amounts to seeking to raise the figure for women's participation from 16 per cent of feature directors to 25 per cent of key creatives, which is a comparatively soft target when compared with the oft-cited 50 per cent quota for all funded production set by the Swedish Film Institute Foundation, and only a modest improvement on Australia's historical benchmarks. Nonetheless, with its explicit efforts to address gender inequality, clearly stated objectives and targets, and leadership by a national funding agency, the Gender Matters Taskforce is exceptional in the landscape of Australian cultural policy. Much more commonly, direct and explicit policy action on gender inequality consists of unpredictable and ad-hoc support for discrete, short-lived initiatives. In the case of women in contemporary music, this has included funding for grassroots feminist organizations which seek to influence talent booking, festival programming and wider industry 'boys' club' norms (such as the Melbourne-based LISTEN collective) and education programs aimed at increasing participation by young women and girls (such as the Girls Rock! camps or The Push's SQUAD program). Most numerously, it incorporates professional mentoring, skill development, networking and related confidence initiatives. Examples include, Music Victoria's 'You Can't Be What You Can't See' activities, and 'Women in Music' mentorship programs organized by Australia's music rights organization APRA AMCOS, and by Queensland's music industry development association QMusic. Most recently, there have been new initiatives aimed at challenging the cultures that enable sexual assault and gender-based harassment to proliferate in live music venues, driven in no small part by grassroots advocacy.[3]

Despite the renewed interest in gender inequality in the arts and cultural industries, including a string of headline-generating studies produced by major agencies and industry organizations, more explicit, centralized and sustained efforts to address that inequality, such as the Gender Matters taskforce, remain a rarity. Notable among the initiatives that do exist, is their emphasis on women's lack of confidence – expressed in the form confidence-building, leadership development, professional development, mentoring and networking schemes. Within popular culture at large, women and girls are routinely identified as lacking in confidence. Rosalind Gill and Shani Orgad (2015) call this 'confidence cult(ure)', a by-the-boot-straps neoliberal expression of post-feminism that can be found everywhere in the rhetoric of confidence, self-esteem, bossy girls, girl-power and *leaning-in*, and which is strikingly similar across a range of different domains, from the beauty industries to the corporate ladder to pop music. The problem, as Gill and Orgad (2015) argue, is that this discourse proposes that women have an inevitable 'shortage' of confidence, one that can be self-corrected through proper application of self-improvement programs. In doing so, it encourages women to see themselves as 'part of the problem' which goes hand in hand with 'a turning away from any account of structural inequalities or of the way in which contemporary culture may impact upon women's sense of self' (Gill and Orgad 2015: 333). In the realm of cultural policy, a lack of confidence is seen as one of and sometimes *the* main factor behind gender inequality. A lack of confidence is ascribed to women both externally by the industry, and individually, evident in the many qualitative responses from women artists who identify themselves as needing or wanting more confidence. This lack of confidence is in turn diagnosed as a major obstacle to women's equal participation in creative fields and it has become the focus of all manner of corrective initiatives and programs. Women artists are constantly petitioned to *lean in* more, as demonstrated by the language of Music Victoria's 'You can't be what you can't see' initiative, which encouraged women to 'look within' to 'achieve their potential' (Music Victoria 2016). The issue of 'confidence gaps' is also implicated in other oft-cited obstacles to gender equality – motherhood, leadership, boys' clubs and earning gaps. There are observations that women lose confidence and drive after taking time out for parenting, that women do not apply for leadership roles thinking they need to be more qualified than male applicants do, they don't apply for grants, they don't ask for enough money, they don't put themselves 'out there', they don't 'network' sufficiently, and so on. This confidence talk is troubling for many reasons, not least of which because of the ways it reinforces more intractable beliefs about women and creative success.

'Why do I have to even think about this shit'?

In February 2017, the only female performer on the bill of Sydney's Days Like This Festival had to cancel due to scheduling conflicts, leaving behind an entirely all-male line-up of comically homogenous electro doppelgangers in matching black t-shirts. Australia's dance music festivals (and EDM scenes more generally) have been particularly bad when it comes to representation of women musicians (McCormack 2016). But across genres, Australian music festivals struggle to reach anything close to gender parity. One of the best performers, Laneway Festival, still hovers above 60 per cent all-male acts (McCormack 2017). The producers of Days Like This at least expressed regret over the absence of women from their program, but all too often festival producers retreat to familiar obfuscations: taste and meritocracy. In January 2018 the multi-city Falls Festival was criticized mid-set by all-women Australian band Camp Cope by way of their song 'The Opener', changing the lyrics to include an explicit dig at the absence of women from festival line-ups and the tendency to feature women-led bands only as quota-filling 'openers' for bigger acts. The response from the Falls Festival programmers was typical of the music industry at large. In a statement to the press, they said that while they have 'a very conscious and strong agenda to book female talent, it isn't always available to us at that headline level' (in Griffiths 2018). According to the programmers there was a dearth of women-led headline-worthy acts and so the festival was instead committed to enacting a 'long term strategy' that seeks 'to nurture and grow the future pool of female headline options' (in Griffiths 2018). In other words, the problem wasn't that the festival was in any way reluctant to program women, simply that there weren't enough good ones. Without a viable pool of high-calibre women-led musical acts from which to program, the festival claimed instead to focus on 'mentoring', 'cultivating' and 'nurturing' female acts, ignoring all the ways that profiling women musicians as main stage acts serves mentoring, cultivating and nurturing functions. Likewise, the promoter of an all-male line-up for the farewell gig at the closing of a popular student bar in Canberra earned a social media lashing when he responded to criticism by suggesting that diversity 'box ticking' was an affront to talent and taste. 'Why do I have too [sic] even think about this shit?' he lamented, the acts were chosen because they were good and he liked them, 'not for what's between their members legs' (in Pianegonda 2017).

In each case, the producers and programmers deny structural injustice or prejudice. That's a real problem sure, they concede, but it exists elsewhere, somewhere less tolerant and more nakedly bigoted than the world of indie music festivals and student union bars. What is so troubling about these examples, and there are many others just like them, is the way in which defensive responses to feminist criticism of women's exclusion from festival line-ups (and industry more generally) mirrors the discourse of

Australian cultural policy. According to which, there is a lack of women artists overall and a lack of confident women putting themselves 'out there', and as a result there is a lack of women artists who are sufficiently capable of the commercial and critical appeal necessary to be deemed 'headline worthy'. There is now a growing and increasingly vocal recognition, especially among Australian women artists, critics and activists, that these explanations and many of the 'pragmatic' recommendations they solicit from policy spheres, are no longer tenable.

One important group to organize around these issues is LISTEN, a Melbourne-based feminist collective that aims to improve the profile and experience of women and gender non-conforming (GNC) artists in Australian music. LISTEN emerged spontaneously in 2014, in the aftermath of a widely shared Facebook post by Melbourne musician Evelyn Morris (who performs under the moniker Pikelet), in which she criticized how women musicians were treated in a newly released book about recent Australian underground music by a local author (Morris 2014). Morris and many other women musicians had actively participated in the scene, a fact Morris felt had been minimized by the book. Objecting to the masculinization of the nascent history of Australia's 2000s underground music scene Morris (2014) wrote: 'I'm gonna publish a book called tastes of Melbourne women underground. So tired of male back-patting and exclusion of anything vaguely "feminine" in subculture'. The great irony of the situation, as Morris pointed out at the time, was that the underground, at least historically and theoretically, is anti-establishment in its prioritizing of amateurism over professionalism and diversity over homogeneity. One would expect it to be more welcoming to women and less slavish to canonical norms.

As discussed in detail in an interview with Catherine Strong (with Morris 2016: 112), Morris explained that 'I had been feeling a pretty impossible-to-put-my-finger-on kind of lack of power for many years'. That feeling resulted in a creative 'gas lighting', which Morris identifies as a major source of a lack of confidence and drive, both for herself and among other women musicians. A constant and entirely disproportionate lack of recognition made them 'feel crazy' and contributed to a sense of hopelessness and inertia (Strong with Morris 2016: 112–113). LISTEN now exists in the form of a diverse range of activities that challenge the masculinzation of local music cultures. There have been events, gigs, conferences, regular appearances on industry panels, and curation of social media discussion, all of which seek to celebrate the work that women and GNC artists are already doing, and to keep a series of feminist agendas in plain view. LISTEN has sought to profile and compile diverse lists of women and GNC people working in the industry in various roles, making it harder to claim, as so often happens, that the problem was not a reluctance to engage female talent but *there was only one and she was unavailable*. LISTEN has also made policy in-roads in several areas, most visibly with the Victorian Government's establishment of a taskforce to address the issue of sexual assault and harassment in live music venues, which has been spearheaded by representatives from LISTEN and another local advocacy group, Save Live Australian Music (SLAM). The taskforce has sought to address the issue of assault and harassment in spaces, actively acknowledging the ways in which inertia on this issue impedes the equal participation of women as both consumers and creators. In wide community consultation with female musicians, broadcasters and academics, the taskforce developed best practice guidelines for venues, culminating in a pilot program to train staff and security in how to identify sexual harassment and assault. Emerging before the #MeToo movement went viral, LISTEN played a direct role in putting sexual assault and harassment back squarely on the policy agenda following nearly a twenty-year hiatus in which such themes were almost entirely absent from the language of government-led cultural policy research or recommendations. Setting aside obvious reasons why the development of anti-sexual-assault guidelines for music venues is a good thing, this work is significant for the way in which it foregrounds the ongoing need for feminist action in the very creative scenes and spaces that most like to imagine themselves as culturally and politically progressive.

Another high-profile popular response to women's lack of representation in the music industry has been the By the Numbers reports produced by Triple J's news program *Hack* as part of the national youth broadcaster's annual Girls to the Front programming to coincide with International Women's Day. First published in 2016, the reports have become progressively larger and more ambitious, drawing on more complex historical data (McCormack 2016, 2017, 2018). The articles touch on several issues discussed elsewhere in policy reports, notably they document the lack of women in influential decision-making roles in the industry, which is manifestly evident in a gender imbalance on industry boards, among A&R reps, record label management, or behind the desks at radio stations. Over the three years, however, the reports have increasingly homed in on data about top performing singles, awards, Hall of Fame inductions, festival line-ups, and airplay on the commercial, community and public broadcasters. In 2018, for example, they examined ten years of playlist data, noting that:

> The data over ten years is relatively consistent: male artists always make up the bulk, if not majority, of the top 100 most-played songs. Solo-female artists or all-female acts are severely underrepresented: on average, they tend to make up about 28 per cent of the most-played songs. (McCormack 2018)

The *Hack* series belongs to a broader growth in data-based journalism and storytelling, and it is one of several similar investigations into gender inequality in the music industries elsewhere in the world (see Mitchum and Garcia-Olano 2018). This also echoes the approach to data reporting and analysis being undertaken in other creative fields in Australia, such as the annual Stella Count organized by The Stella Prize which looks at women's participation in Australian literature, and The Countess reports on women's participation in Australian visual arts. Like the Stella Count and the Countess reports, By The Numbers focuses on questions of popularity, celebration, recognition and canonization of women artists. In doing so, they provide a much more granular account of the intersection of taste and structural inequality, an area which official policy studies and responses have typically avoided. Again and again the reports demonstrate that wins in the areas more likely to be examined by policy research (leadership roles, industry boards, grant recipients) bely clear losses where it really matters – critical and popular recognition. As Elvis Richardson (2016) observes in The Countess report, 'The closer an artist gets to money, prestige and power, the more likely they are to be male'. These studies encourage a reflexive scrutiny of deeply ingrained (and gendered) taste hierarchies that are largely overlooked by official policy research, but which are essential for achieving lasting change.

Launched in time for International Women's Day in 2018, an Australian Instagram account began posting doctored posters showing Australian festival line-up announcements with the names of all the male-only acts removed. Aptly called LineupsWithoutMales, the account recalls the feminist activism of visual arts activists the Guerrilla Girls but reinvented for the social media era. Like the Guerrilla Girls, LineupsWithoutMales uses a combination of droll humour and facts to convey a simple point. What remains of the posters is perhaps the best visual demonstration of women's status in the Australian music industry. As Catherine Strong (2016: 10) wrote of an earlier UK incarnation of the same device, 'The expanses of empty space that remained at the end of this exercise spoke eloquent volumes about the continued marginalization of women in the music industry'. The standard formatting of the music festival poster is a textbook study in the visual communication of hierarchy, with the most valuable acts (commercially and critically) in the largest font at the peak of a pyramid, with lesser acts listed below in smaller font. Any music fan is versed in this language and the release of festival posters are invariably met with debates about font size and placement. In the case of LineupsWithoutMales, what remains is usually a scattering of band names in small font at the bottom of the poster, and in the case of some festivals, there is nothing left at all. Accounts like LineupsWithoutMales and others like it, neatly and memorably demonstrate what LISTEN has captured qualitatively or what Hack's By the Numbers has demonstrated quantitatively, that according to contemporary aesthetic hierarchies, women musicians are still largely invisible.

In addition to the policy and official research into Australia's cultural gender gap, there exists a wide range of popular and grassroots feminist critique. These activities are likewise seeking to understand why so few women achieve equivalent levels of success, celebration and recognition. Instead of identifying 'obstacles to participation', however, they point to the problems that exist in acknowledging and celebrating the work that women artists are already making. The problem is less to do with the impact of a gender imbalance at the level of 'industry leaders' or 'key decision makers', but rather a gender imbalance evident in the choices we all make about which musicians are most critically lauded, most played, most requested, most reviewed, most booked, most taught in classes, and most celebrated in TV docos, coffee table history books or state library exhibitions. *Skipping a Beat* calls these 'other measures of success', beyond the traditional measures of earning gaps and career development (Cooper et al. 2017: 6). But I would argue that these 'other' measures of success – recognition and validation by way of awards, airplay, festival profile and canonization – are in fact much more common-sense and everyday indicators of women's participation in the music industries.

'I think the main obstacles are men and older men'

Christine Anu looks a little perplexed, as if she's worried she might have been given a trick question. Tina Arena just seems exasperated. Both have been asked to comment on the obstacles facing women in the music industry for Lindy Morrison's original 1994 documentary. 'I think the main obstacles are men and older men', says Anu, while Arena argues that, 'I think the thing people were fearful of were women gaining a little too much power'. The interviews have been included in 2018's *Her Sound, Her Story*, and Arena and Anu's sentiments are echoed by a good many of the contemporary interviewees. Their answers indulge in a simple frankness that is in keeping with the initiatives described above, but which has been largely absent from official policy responses to the same broad question: why do women artists continue to be significantly under-represented in Australia's creative and cultural sectors?

Romanticized as non-hierarchical, open, progressive, and even radical, subversive and counter-cultural, the arts and cultural industries are also in many ways stubbornly conservative and resistant to change when it comes to questions of equality in creative labour. This, as others have argued at length, is the great paradox of the creative and cultural industries (Conor et al. 2015; Harvey and Shepherd 2017; Taylor and O'Brien 2017; Brook et al. 2018). While they love to imagine themselves as egalitarian meritocracies where passion, talent and tenacity are all one really needs to succeed, these industries are in fact 'marked by stark, persistent and in many cases worsening inequalities relating to gender, race and ethnicity, class, age and disability' (Conor et al. 2015: 1). Moreover, according to Taylor and O'Brien (2017: 43), 'those who are the most highly paid, and most likely to recruit and elevate the next generation–believe most strongly in the meritocratic account of the sector, and are most sceptical of the role of social reproduction'.

Over a nearly forty-year period and across the sweep of creative and cultural industries, official responses to Australia's cultural gender-gap have time and time again identified the same key obstacles – motherhood, boys' clubs, confidence gaps, earning gaps and leadership gaps (Edmond and McGowan 2017). When gender inequality is addressed explicitly, rather than tacitly through generalized diversity and inclusivity talk, it is overwhelmingly in the form of ad hoc funding for short-lived initiatives. And viewed collectively, those initiatives are predictable and often problematic. There is a focus on efforts to compensate for career interruption from caring, such as with adjusted assessment criteria or small grants aimed at supporting women resuming their practice after time out for parenting. There are concerted efforts to get women into industry leadership positions, which runs the risk of further entrenching the feminization of facilitation and bureaucratic support roles while doing little to improve the representation or recognition of women artists in Australian culture. Most especially and most numerously, there are networking, mentoring, skill-building and professional development initiatives which seek to improve women's perceived lack of confidence. Each of these schemes can be valuable, even transformative for the individual artists involved. But whatever small, individual or short-term changes these initiatives may have achieved, there is a real possibility that they contribute to the persistence or worsening of the very issues they seek to remedy.

The pervasiveness of confidence discourses as a solution to Australia's cultural gender gap needs especially careful and ongoing scrutiny. The arts and cultural industries are fields of practice which – more than any other field – rely on seemingly inscrutable concepts like taste, merit, vision, passion, excellence, quality and artistry. At the same time that we are told again and again that women lack confidence, we are told in dozens of other ways that women lack talent and tenacity. In tandem, the effect is to minimize and obscure the role of more systemic forms of sexism with the net result being more self-doubt, more inertia, not less. The popular music industry in Australia is one of the least well-studied industries when it comes to matters of policy research into gender inequality. In their efforts to move beyond lack-based explanations of inequality and to focus instead on challenging ingrained gendered value regimes and taste hierarchies, LISTEN, By The Numbers, *Her Sound, Her Story*, the recent Women in Music awards, and other equivalent projects in adjacent creative scenes, are slowly reframing the conversation in new and necessary ways. Now we need to make sure we're finally listening.

Notes

1. Sam De Boise (2017) has observed very similar patterns in UK national responses to gender inequality in music, noting vague statements of support for the idea of greater diversity and equality, but with little in the way of specific objectives or performance goals.
2. For more detail on these policy contexts in Australia, see for example Ben Eltham (2016) on the 'excellence' paradigm in Australian cultural policy and Justin O'Connor's (2016) overview of the impact of Creative Industries discourse on Australian cultural policy. See also Rosalind Gil's (2014) writing on gender and the neoliberal subjectivities of Creative and Cultural Industries discourse.
3. See Shane Homan (2011 and 2013) for more on Australian live music policy and regulation. See Bianca Fileborn (2016) for more on Australian live music policy and sexual harassment in music venues.

References

Brooke, O., D. O'Brien and M. Taylor (2018), *Panic! Social Class, Taste and Inequalities in the Creative Industries*. Available online: http://createlondon.org/wp-content/uploads/2018/04/Panic-Social-Class-Taste-and-Inequalities-in-the-Creative-Industries1.pdf (accessed 29 May 2018).

Conor, B., R. Gill and S. Taylor (2015), 'Gender and Creative Labour', *The Sociological Review*, 63 (S1): 1–22.

Cooper, R., A. Coles and S. Hanna-Osborne (2017), *Skipping a Beat: Assessing the State of Gender Equality in the Australian Music Industry*, Sydney: University of Sydney Business School.

Corporate Plan 2018–2020 (2017), Sydney: Australia Council for the Arts. Available online: http://www.australiacouncil.gov.au/workspace/uploads/files/australia-council-corporate-pl-5b90cae755631.pdf (accessed 29 May 2018).

Cox, E. and S. Laura (1992), *'What Do I Wear for a Hurricane?': Women in Australian Film, Television, Video and Radio Industries: A Report*, Sydney: Australian Film Commission.

Create NSW (2017), 'Information for Applicants'. Available online: https://www.create.nsw.gov.au/wp-content/uploads/2017/04/ACDP-information-for-applicants.pdf (accessed 23 August 2019).

Creative State: Victoria's First Creative Industries Strategy 2016–2020 (2016), Melbourne: Creative Victoria. Available online: https://creative.vic.gov.au/__data/assets/pdf_file/0005/110948/creativestate-4.pdf (accessed 30 May 2018).

De Boise, S. (2017), 'Gender Inequalities and Higher Music Education: Comparing the UK and Sweden', *British Journal of Music Education*, 35 (1): 23–41.

Edmond, M. and J. McGowan (2017), '"We Need More Mediocre Women!" Australian Cultural Policy and the Gender Gap', *Overland*, 229 (Summer): 81–87. Available online: https://overland.org.au/previous-issues/issue-229/essay-maura-edmond-and-jasmine-mcgowan/ (accessed 30 May 2018).

Eltham, B. (2016), 'When the Goal Posts Move', *Platform Papers*, 48. Sydney: Currency House.

Fileborn, B. (2016), *Reclaiming the Night-Time Economy: Unwanted Sexual Attention in Pubs and Clubs*, New York: Palgrave Macmillan.

Gender Matters: Women in the Australian Screen Industry (2015), Sydney: Screen Australia.

Gill, R. (2014), 'Unspeakable Inequalities: Post Feminism, Entrepreneurial Subjectivity, and the Repudiation of Sexism among Cultural Workers', *Social Politics: International Studies in Gender, State and Society*, 21 (4): 509–528.

Gill, R. and S. Orgad (2015), 'The Confidence Cult(ure)', *Australian Feminist Studies*, 30 (86): 324–344.

Griffiths, N. (2018), 'Falls Organisers Respond to Camp Cope Calling Out Festival for Lack of Female Acts', *The Music*, 3 January. Available online: http://themusic.com.au/news/all/2018/01/03/falls-organisers-respond-to-camp-cope-calling-out-festival-for-lack-of-female-acts/ (accessed 29 May 2018).

Harvey, A. and T. Shepherd (2017), 'When Passion Isn't Enough: Gender, Affect and Credibility in Digital Games Design', *International Journal of Cultural Studies*, 20 (5): 492–508.

Homan, S. (2011), '"I Tote and I Vote": Australian Live Music and Cultural Policy', *Arts Marketing: An International Journal*, 1 (2): 96–107.

Homan, S. (2013), 'From Coombs to Crean: Popular Music and Cultural Policy in Australia', *International Journal of Cultural Policy*, 19 (3): 382–398.

Lally, E. and S. Miller (2012), *Women in Theatre: A Research Report and Action Plan for the Australia Council for the Arts*, Surry Hills, NSW: Australia Council for the Arts.

McCormack, A. (2016), 'By the Numbers: Women in the Music Industry', *triple j Hack*, 8 March. Available online: http://www.abc.net.au/triplej/programs/hack/girls-to-the-front/7223798 (accessed 23 August 2019).

McCormack, A. (2017), 'By the Numbers: The Gender Gap in the Australian Music Industry', *triple j Hack*, 7 March. Available online: http://www.abc.net.au/triplej/programs/hack/by-the-numbers-the-gender-gap-in-the-australian-music-industry/8328952 (accessed 30 May 2018).

McCormack, A. (2018), 'By the Numbers: The Gender Gap in the Australian Music Industry', *triple j Hack*, 8 March. Available online: http://www.abc.net.au/triplej/programs/hack/by-the-numbers-2018/9524084 (accessed 30 May 2018).

Mitchum, R. and D. Garcia-Olano (2018), 'Tracking the Gender Balance of This Year's Music Festival Lineups', *Pitchfork*, 1 May. Available online: https://pitchfork.com/features/festival-report/tracking-the-gender-balance-of-this-years-music-festival-lineups/ (accessed 29 May 2018).

Morris, E. (2014), 'Noise in My Head'. Available online: http://www.listenlistenlisten.org/noise-head/ (accessed 4 February 2019).

Music Victoria (2016), 'Our Work with Confidence'. Available online: https://www.musicvictoria.com.au/about/gender-diversity/confidence (accessed 29 May 2018).

O'Connor, J. (2016), 'After the Creative Industries', *Platform Papers*, 47. Sydney: Currency House.

Pianegonda, E. (2017), 'ANU Bar's Final Show: Regurgitator Drops Out after Promoter's Response to All-Male Line-Up Backlash', *ABC Online*, 11 April. Available online: http://www.abc.net.au/news/2017-04-11/anu-bar-all-male-line-up-sparks-fierce-online-debate/8433816 (accessed 29 May 2018).

Richardson, E. (2016), *The Countess Report*. Available online: http://thecountessreport.com.au/The%20Countess%20Report.FINAL.pdf (accessed 30 May 2018).

Ryan, P., M. Eliot and G. Appleton (1983), *Women in Australian Film Production*, North Ryde, NSW: Women's Film Fund of the Australian Film Commission, and the Research and Survey Unit, Australian Film and Television School.

Selected Case Studies of Women Working in the Australian Mass Media: Background Paper to the UNESCO 'Women in the Media' Seminar and the 'Women Media Workers' Seminar (1976), North Ryde, NSW: Australian Film and Television School.

Strong, C. (2016), 'Gender, Popular Music and Australian Identity: Introduction to Special Issue', *Journal of World Popular Music*, 3 (1): 10–16.

Strong, C. with E. Morris (2016), '"Spark and Cultivate": LISTEN and Grassroots Feminist Activism in the Melbourne Music Scene', *Journal of World Popular Music*, 3 (1): 108–124.

Strong, C. and F. Cannizzo (2017), *Australian Women Screen Composers: Career Barriers and Pathways*, Melbourne, VIC: RMIT University.

Taylor, M. and D. O'Brien (2017), '"Culture Is a Meritocracy": Why Creative Workers' Attitudes May Reinforce Social Inequality', *Sociological Research Online*, 22 (4): 27–47.

Westle, A. (2018), *Turning Pointe: Gender Equality in Australian Dance*. Delving into Dance. Available online: https://www.delvingintodance.com/turning-pointe (accessed 29 May 2018).

Women in the Arts: A Study by the Research Advisory Group of the Women and Arts Project, Sydney, December 1982 (1983), North Sydney, NSW: Australia Council.

Women in the Victorian Contemporary Music Industry (2015), Melbourne: Music Victoria.

Filmography

Her Sound, Her Story (2018), [Film] Dir. Michelle Grace Hunder and Claudia Sangiorgi Dalimore, Australia.

Sisters Are Doin' It for Themselves: Women in the Contemporary Music Industry [alternative title: *Australian Women in Rock & Pop Music*] (1994), [VHS] Prod. Lindy Morrison, Greg Ferguson. Dir. Greg Ferguson. *Basic Music Industry Skills* [Series], Australia: Aus Music.

7

Setting the Stage for Sexual Assault: The Dynamics of Gender, Culture, Space and Sexual Violence at Live Music Events

Bianca Fileborn, Phillip Wadds and Ash Barnes

Introduction

It's twenty minutes before the start of the next performance and the mass migration of fans between the main stage area and other performance/festival sites is well underway. It's dark and we are attempting to navigate the sea of heavily intoxicated, rain drenched, and often belligerent fans of a popular rock/punk band that have just played, as we shuffle slowly into the space to see the indie pop group next on the line-up. It is quite a case study in fan friction and sub-cultural tension. To start, the lack of ordered crowd movement into and out of the main stage makes it very difficult to move between sites without coming into contact with throngs of revelers. In this case, the flow of fans out of the site was much heavier than those moving in and the natural landscape (going up into the site, and down out of it) made it a particularly confronting challenge. That the groups involved in these movements were so diametrically opposed only heightened the risk of negative interactions, be they sexual, violent or otherwise. (Wadds, field excerpt)

Despite growing global attention to gender-based violence in all its forms, there has been a notable silence regarding sexual violence that occurs in live music spaces. To date, despite a groundswell of action, debate and commentary driven by artists, media and grassroots activists about the prevalence of sexual violence at gigs and festivals, no scholarly work has examined sexual violence within live music scenes. Within an Australian context, there has been considerable media reporting on high-profile incidents of sexual assault and harassment occurring at live music events (see Dmytryschchak 2016; Lewis 2017), with similar experiences documented internationally (e.g. Davies 2017; *The Guardian* 2017). In response to this problem – and the anecdotally common experience of men harassing and groping women at events – several grassroots and government campaigns have emerged internationally, including the Australian 'It Takes One' campaign, and UK-based 'Safe Gigs for Women' and 'Girls Against' (Moran 2017).

In light of this growing momentum, it is timely to examine how and why sexual harassment and assault occur within live music scenes. Clearly, this issue is not isolated or unique to specific settings, but emerging anecdotal evidence does suggest such experiences are common, if not pervasive, at music events. In this chapter, we aim to unpack and explore some of the key issues underpinning this phenomenon and the way they influence experiences of sexual violence in sites of live music. In doing so, we draw on emerging findings from a project on sexual harassment and assault at Australian music festivals (being conducted by Fileborn and Wadds), and research on physical and sexual violence in the Australian punk scene (Barnes 2017).

Defining sexual violence

Before moving on to a discussion of gender and sexuality in the music industry, it is important to first define what it is we mean when we refer to sexual assault and harassment. A broad and inclusive approach is taken here to conceptualizing 'sexual violence'. Our approach is influenced by Kelly's (1988) continuum model, which frames sexual violence as encompassing *all* forms of intrusion, harassment and violence that were experienced as such, privileging and centring victim-survivors' lived experiences. This recognizes the potential for all forms of sexual intrusion, harassment and violence to be harmful, regardless of how seemingly 'minor' or 'trivial' they are constructed as being. It views diverse iterations of sexual violence as inter-related, and acknowledges how these forms of violence work together as a *lived process* in the lives of (particularly) women and LGBTQ people. It is important to note that sexual violence is socially and culturally situated (Gavey 2005; Fileborn 2016), and that this reflects the need to examine how and why sexual violence plays out in specific socio-cultural locations. Drawing on Nicola Gavey's (2005) work, the following section examines how aspects of the music scene provide the 'cultural scaffolding' that enables sexual violence to occur.

'No clit in the pit': Gender and sexualities in an unequal music scene

Recent Australian research has provided evidence of pervasive and systemic gender inequality across virtually all aspects of the music industry (Cooper, Coles and Hanna-Osborne 2017). Women and gender-diverse people are under-represented (particularly in roles with higher levels of power and influence), paid less, and are afforded less social and cultural capital than their cis-gender male counterparts (see also, Strong 2011, 2014; Music Victoria 2015). Evidence of inequality is further documented in relation to radio airtime, where songs by women are played less than those by men, and festival line-ups, which are consistently male-dominated (Cooper, Coles and Hanna-Osborne

2017). As Cooper et al. put it, 'male dominance is seen in the key decision-making roles that shape industry norms, values and practices' (2017: 3). Music listeners themselves often rationalize and excuse these inequalities on the basis of musical taste, yet as Frith (2017) emphasizes, individual 'taste' stems from social conditioning and market manipulation, with men within the industry most likely to possess the requisite social and cultural capital necessary to dictate what constitutes 'good taste'.

Gender inequality is fundamentally intertwined with sexual violence (VicHealth 2011; Wall 2014). This inequality is located within differential access to power and resources, social and cultural norms that systematically devalue women and gender-diverse people, and rigid norms around what it means to be a 'man' or a 'woman', to name but a few examples (Wall 2014). The patterns of gender inequality within the Australian music industry documented here thus mirror the conditions in which sexual violence may flourish.

Gender norms and power

Given that gendered norms and expectations play a role in forming the 'cultural scaffolding' against which sexual violence occurs, it is apt to consider the dominant gender norms within the Australian music scene, and the ways in which these may contribute towards sexual violence. In doing so, it is important to firstly note that the Australian music scene is an increasingly heterogeneous and diverse one. There is no singular way in which gender is 'done' within these scenes. Likewise, the dominant norms that we discuss here can be, and are, contested and subverted. In fact, the carnivalesque, liminal nature of many live music settings often opens up opportunities for gender to be 'done' differently, creating spaces for play (although, as Bannister (2006) cautions, there is simultaneously a danger in positioning the music scene as a space for 'play' whilst disconnecting *who* can take up such opportunities from the social, historical and political context of the scene). Nonetheless, it is fair to say that particular iterations of masculinity and femininity continue to be valourized within the majority of such spaces.

The Australian live music scene is a (white, cis, heterosexual, working and middle-class) masculine one. It is both dominated by men, as our previous discussion illuminated, and symbolically coded as a 'masculine' endeavour (Strong 2011, 2014). Within the scene, men – whether fans or artists – are framed as knowledgeable, masterful, authentic and credible (Davies 2001; Bannister 2006; Strong 2011, 2014). As Strong (2014: 150) observes, 'the gendering of music reinforces the wider social hierarchies between men and women' – it both reflects and actively reinforces the gender inequalities underpinning sexual violence. Numerous authors have observed the homosociality inherent in the production and consumption of music within a range of music scene contexts: they are practices engaged in, by, and for other men, with women having to adhere to the masculine 'rules of the game' in order to participate (examples of this can be found in the work of Davies 2001; Bannister 2006; and Haenfler 2006 amongst others). These practices function to mark the boundaries of inclusion and belonging within the music scene, with women located towards the bottom of the hierarchy if not excluded entirely (Davies 2001). That is, women's knowledge, practices and experiences are systematically devalued and 'othered' within the scene.

The subcultural norms of music spaces

In discussing gendered norms, it is important to examine how these emerge within different music subcultures, and Barnes' (2017) work on punk, alternative and hard-core subcultures provides an important and insightful case study. The punk scene, for example, affords women some scope to play with gender identity and expression, yet they still experience the restrictiveness of a predominantly masculine culture. As Leblanc (1999: 6) emphasizes, punk gives women a platform to protest and to be heard, yet they simultaneously come up against the same pressures and limitations on women as the mainstream culture that punks (supposedly) oppose. Women are encouraged to perform in bands within the scene, yet are not viewed as 'authentic' in comparison to their male counterparts. Whilst 'alternative' subcultures encourage the inclusion of female performers, it is common to witness audience members attempting to delegitimize their performances by telling female vocalists to 'dress hotter' or to expose themselves (Barnes 2017).

Space is closely linked to how individual and collective identity is expressed, and subcultural groups may use space as a type of social resistance, where members physically and spatially draw the symbolic line between 'us' and 'them' (Ensminger 2013). The moshpit is one such space in which identity construction, performance and embodied resistance unfolds in hardcore and punk scenes. Fans use the moshpit as a physical display of devotion to the music, each other and the culture more broadly. Band members encourage audience participation as much as possible and collapse physical boundaries between performer and fan (Ensminger 2013: 2). Close bodily contact is encouraged, contrasting the 'usual' norms of socially acceptable behaviour. This includes members often being cramped chest to back, drenched with others' bodily fluids of spit and sweat.

Moshpits are also sites of gender performance, power and resistance. Within moshpits women may be rejected from contributing due to male fears that they would not be able to 'hold their own' within the chaotic crowd. As a result, the term 'no clit in the pit' continues to feature in the lexicon of punk and hard-core subcultural groups (Barnes 2017). Haenfler (2006: 142) observed that women who enter moshpits are often either protected by concerned men or left alone to uphold the masculine standard of being 'one of the boys'. As a result, women meet each other with hostility and the atmosphere of 'equality' continues. Although dominant constructions of subcultures position them as spaces for individuals to subvert the dominant standards of fashion, behaviour and lifestyles, it is questionable to what extent this is actually achieved (see also Ensminger 2013). Indeed, our discussion here suggests that punk and hard-core scenes may work to (re)produce and reinforce dominant norms of masculinity and femininity as much as it destabilizes or unsettles them.

Whilst women's experiences within male-dominated spaces are shaped and limited by masculine norms, these norms also affect men. Authors such as Riches (2014) have argued that men use the moshpit as a temporary release from the uncertainties and anxieties of masculinity and homosocial interactions. Yet, men also sexually violate other men within this space, but the same gender dynamics and pressures mean that such incidents are typically laughed off as a 'joke' (Barnes 2017). This includes male performers who are subjected to sexual assault on stage but feel they cannot share their experiences due to a culture that refuses to acknowledge vulnerabilities or believe that men can be assaulted by both men and women. Ambrose (2010: 33) further highlights this type of nonchalance towards sexual touching, arguing that moshpits operate as a countercultural space, where young people come to terms with their sexuality. Sexual touching is subsequently seen as an inescapable side effect of the moshpit, with such attitudes serving to normalize and excuse sexual violence that occurs within these spaces.

Musical tunes, sexual undertones: The sexualization of music events

In discussing the cultural scaffolding of sexual violence in the music industry, we must likewise examine the sexual norms or 'scripts' that predominate within this cultural context and the way these intertwine with the gendered norms we have already begun to discuss. To a certain extent, overt sexual interaction can be less acceptable in music scenes compared to other subsets of licensed venues and entertainment spaces (particularly commercial nightclubs). Authors such as Hutton (2006) and Hunt, Maloney and Evans (2010), for example, have observed that within the dance and rave scenes overt sexual interaction is less acceptable or normative: the focus of these scenes is on dancing. Although there is a lack of comparable research in other live music spaces, it stands to reason that similar norms may be in operation, where the primary reason for attending is to watch an artist play. However, that is not to say that these spaces are not sexual ones, rather that engaging in sexual interaction is not the core attraction. Likewise, as Hutton (2006) observes of dance scenes, overt sexual interaction and harassment may be replaced with more subtle interactions.

Festivals are perhaps somewhat different to live music venues in this respect. They are less contained temporally and spatially. With gigs, patrons turn up to watch a specific band, perhaps have a few drinks with friends, and then move on to the next venue or home. Festivals, in comparison, are more fluid and diverse. While many patrons of course attend for the music, there may be gaps in the day when there are no bands of interest. Others may attend for the 'spectacle' of the event or to participate in the scene, rather than to see any particular band. For camping festivals in particular, there may be hours to fill in between music sets, while the presence of tents and camping sites provides ready access to private spaces for both consensual and non-consensual sexual interaction.

Much like gendered performance in the music scene, sexual expression in these spaces is diverse and fluid. The extent to which overt sexual interaction and sexualized performance is tolerated (and the *types* of expression tolerated) no doubt shifts dramatically across sub-cultural scenes, as our earlier discussion on moshpits began to intimate (see also Fileborn 2016). For instance, overt sexual interaction at a rock gig might not be normative, but the stereotype that women try to 'hook up' with members of the band afterwards is. This 'groupie' stereotype simultaneously functions to devalue or de-legitimize women as 'serious' fans, whilst bolstering the suitably 'masculine' status of male musicians. Male rock stars, Davies notes, use 'groupies' 'as an acceptable part of the "rebellious" rock and roll lifestyle whereby men prove their masculinity and freedom from tedious conventional morality by exploiting and abusing women' (2001: 315). Men in bands may be positioned as 'sexy', 'rock gods' or 'tortured romantic artists' (see Davies 2001) while still being taken seriously as musicians – sexual prowess provides a means of achieving hegemonic masculinity in this context. In contrast, women in the scene – whether artists or fans – tend to be valued solely on their 'sex appeal' (Davies 2001; Hatton and Trautner 2011; Strong 2014: 153), or are treated with suspicion that they have used their sexuality to further their career or status within the industry (Davies 2001). Sexuality is also used as a means of discrediting women fans of 'serious' music, 'with their fandom explained by sexual attraction to a male musician' (Davies 2001: 313).

These stereotypes provide part of the 'cultural scaffolding' (Gavey 2005) creating the conditions for sexual violence to unfold, and are often drawn on to excuse sexual violence when it occurs within the live music scene. While many of these sexual interactions may well occur consensually, these stereotypes can be readily drawn on to dismiss or discredit experiences of sexual violence within the music scene. Indeed, there are numerous examples of those within the music industry drawing on their position to gain access to women. Notoriously, John Zimmerman used his position as the manager of a popular Australian band to gain access to young (often underage) women. For example, Zimmerman would offer young women free tickets or entice them with the possibility of meeting members of the band in order to subsequently sexually offend against them, though he also drew on a range of other offending techniques (see Bluett-Boyd et al. 2013).

Having too many and not caring enough: Alcohol, drugs and the 'cultural scaffolding' of sexual violence

Alcohol and drug consumption represent another component of the 'cultural scaffolding' underpinning sexual violence, and are likewise implicated in the performance of gender and sexuality. As with gender and sexual norms, drug and alcohol consumption practices shift across sub-cultural groups. Subcultures may abstain from consumption altogether, as with 'straight edge' hardcore cultures, while others find comfort through collective binge drinking and violent behaviour (Barnes 2017). These behaviours occur within music spaces, culturally designated as 'liminal zones', where people may engage in deviant practices. This creates a 'cover' and conduit for people to legitimize behaviours or forms of consumption designated as 'deviant' within other socio-cultural contexts (Ravenscroft and Mattecci 2003: 1). This provides a practice through which the severity of people's actions and their crimes are excused if offenders appear to have 'lost control' of themselves through intoxication (Fileborn 2016; Barnes 2017). This diffusion of responsibility steeps across music scenes, which tend to deny the significant trauma members feel when they have been sexually violated.

The relationship between alcohol and drug consumption and sexual violence is complex and multidimensional, but has been corroborated by considerable research. Statistically, research has found that approximately half of sexual assault cases involve drinking by the victim, perpetrator or both, prior to the offence (Abbey et al. 2001; Ullman 2003; Ullman and Najdowski 2010). Other research has examined and found strong evidence of the deliberate use of drugs and/or alcohol in the facilitation of sexual assault (Testa et al. 2003; Beynon et al. 2008); the opportunistic perpetration of sexual assault against intoxicated victim-survivors (Littleton, Grills-Taquechel and Axsom 2009); and the role of drugs and alcohol in increasing perpetrator confidence, excusing their behaviour, and delegitimizing victim narratives and recollection (Wall and Quadara 2014). Further studies have established the role of alcohol in physical and cognitive impairment that may lead to poor decision making (Fromme, D'Amico and Katz 1999; Giancola 2013); the promotion of risk-taking behaviour in relation to sex (Tapert et al. 2001; Cooper 2002); the reduction of impulse control (Fillmore and Weafer 2004); and the relationship between alcohol intoxication and increased male concern with the projection of personal power (Tomsen 1997; Graham and Wells 2003). Cultural norms regarding women who consume alcohol tend to position these women as 'promiscuous' or more sexually available and interested than they actually are (Abbey and Harnish 1995). The summary of this extensive body of research is that alcohol and drug consumption is an independent risk factor in the experience of sexual assault (Pope and Shouldice 2001), making people more 'at risk' as potential victim-survivors, and more likely to 'take risks' as perpetrators.

In relation to live music events and festivals, there is solid evidence that these spaces feature higher levels of drug and alcohol consumption than comparable rates in corresponding age-matched cohorts from the general community (Erickson et al. 1996; Fileborn, Wadds and Tomsen forthcoming; Lim et al. 2008; Australian Institute of Health and Welfare 2017). While research varies in terms of the cultural drivers shaping consumption practices at these events, ranging from claims of purely hedonistic cultures of 'determined' drinking (Measham 2006) to forms of 'controlled intoxication' (Martinus et al. 2010), there is strong evidence that high levels of drug and alcohol consumption have become normalized in live music and festival cultures (Duff 2003). In fact, evidence from research recently undertaken by two of the authors of this chapter (see Fileborn, Wadds and Tomsen 2019), indicates that, from a convenience sample of 500 festival patrons, 99 per cent of participants frequently consume alcohol at such events, while 47.8 per cent regularly consume drugs. Festival patrons surveyed also indicated that they drink more in a typical drinking session at festivals than they would in a typical drinking session outside of festival events (72.3 per cent typically consume five or more standard alcoholic drinks in general when drinking, while 81.7 per cent drink five or more alcoholic drinks in a typical session when drinking at festivals. When considering very high levels of alcohol consumption (ten or more drinks in a session), respondents again were significantly more likely to consume ten or more alcoholic drinks at a festival as opposed to outside of festivals (46.7 per cent indicated they drink ten or more drinks at festivals, while 18.7 per cent indicated they typically drink ten or more drinks outside festivals). The intoxication of patrons at events has myriad effects on the experience and opportunities for sexual violence as discussed above, but much of this risk profile is heightened or exacerbated by the generally permissive culture of such spaces that encourages, endorses or obfuscates violence. Such violence frequently plays out in settings that further promote violent or anti-social behaviour, including high levels of crowding, and poor or limited levels of formal and natural surveillance.

Space, design and the dynamics of sexual violence

It's officially New Year's Day (early am) and after an hour of listening to the headline act and supporting DJs, we decided to join the growing throng of people leaving the main stage area and making their way back to the campsite. The air is thick with dust and, combined with the ambient lighting that lines the main walkways of the festival ground, has given the air an alien feel. It has also significantly reduced visibility in an already dark space. The issue of darkness becomes a bigger issue when you leave the main festival area and enter the camp sites. While those closest to the main entrances benefit from a number of large light towers, the further you get from the gates, the poorer the lighting becomes. Given we were late in arriving, our position at the very back of the campsite is almost completely unlit apart from the random dots of light emanating from the few private parties that were still cranking. (Wadds, field excerpt)

As outlined in the previous sections of this chapter, live music events, and music festivals in particular, are key sites of both physical and (sub) cultural convergence. Here, large groups of diverse and often identifiable fan groups, each belonging to and having unique experiences with the subcultural norms and unwritten codes of conduct of live music events, are drawn into communal spaces where there is often a dynamic and pernicious interplay between culture, gender and sexual violence. Adding to issues of crime, deviance and conflict in such settings is the sense of carnival that is a key attraction of attending music events. Here, there exists a culture of transgressive resistance to the restrictive and increasingly regulated routines of everyday life that often plays out in acts of gross hedonism (Presdee 2000). In these liminal and transgressive sites (see Ensminger 2013) there are many spatial features that are particularly conducive to sexual assault and harassment. As can be seen from the above field excerpt, the built design and nature of festival spaces often plays a role in generating and/or exacerbating opportunities for sexual violence. While it is beyond the scope of this chapter to explore in detail all of the ways in which music spaces can shape unwanted sexual interactions, there are a number of key characteristics that we will focus on here, including limited natural surveillance, and the anonymity of patrons.

'Dancing in the dark': Space, light and anonymity

Live music events and music festivals attract large crowds, often reaching into the tens of thousands at major events. The behaviour and management of such large crowds is a key concern of event organizers, police, security and health experts because they tend to be emotionally charged and unpredictable (Earl 2008). In relation to sexual violence, the anonymity, deindividuation and lack of consistently effective natural and formal surveillance in crowded spaces can facilitate perpetrators to engage in assaultive behaviour (Fileborn 2016; Barnes 2017). In observational research conducted by Fileborn and Wadds (see Fileborn, Wadds and Tomsen 2019) – and as highlighted in our earlier discussion – moshpit and crowded performance spaces were consistently the key sites of tension and conflict. The density and constant movement of crowds in darkness increases the anonymity of patrons, providing the opportunity for unwanted sexual interaction to occur. Overlaid with this issue are the peak levels of intoxication that tend to be a feature of the night-time hours.

The difficulty of policing such densely packed crowds in areas of poor lighting and limited surveillance further encourages perpetrators as it is very hard to locate, identify and pursue those responsible for sexual violence in these settings (see also Fileborn 2016). Similarly, the difficulty of surveillance within the crowd environment allows offenders to become anonymous and escape responsibility for their actions (Barnes 2017). Event security, while often strategically placed at venue locations with good sight lines and access to friction points, usually has large areas to survey and limited means of quickly accessing anywhere but the most sparsely populated spaces. In response to these issues, and growing concern over sexual assaults in crowds, NSW Police have recently publicized new strategies where plain clothed and uniformed officers join the moshpit to try to be closer to the source of much sexual violence (Bevin 2017). While it is unknown how successful this approach was in preventing or apprehending offenders, the reality is that without major cultural change, perpetrators will likely continue to use these crowded spaces to engage in sexual violence.

Another particular feature and attraction of many music festivals is the camping experience. Camping spaces are largely unsupervised, with the scale of campgrounds beyond the capacity of security or police to effectively patrol. This leaves the majority of campsites to be regulated by informal modes of surveillance, with friends and other festival-goers often becoming the sole guardians of these spaces. Given that festivals are sites of frequent consensual sexual interaction, the likelihood of bystander intervention in anything but the most obvious sexual assault or act of harassment is reduced. Again, these conditions are amplified at night, when surveillance is even more difficult and where opportunities to exploit high levels of patron intoxication creates vulnerabilities and opportunities for sexual violence.

Previous literature on bystander intervention models suggests that barriers to intervention may be heightened in music spaces, particularly in crowded spaces such as the moshpit. For example, Latane and Darley (1970) explain that bystanders must overcome specific social and psychological barriers before they can intervene effectively. These include recognizing a crime is taking place and to interpret it as an emergency (or incident requiring a response), take responsibility for being a bystander who intervenes, decide how to act and to finally act. Crowd formations can make all forms of bodily touching appear as ambiguous, normative, or 'unavoidable' consequences of the space. This in turn makes recognizing and intervening in sexual assault or harassment difficult – for instance, because it may be difficult to determine if unwanted touch was intentional, or merely a result of the crowded space. Bystanders may also be distracted, given they are there to focus on the music and not to observe the safety of their friends or other revellers. Current literature suggests that crowded music spaces may also impede the use of effective bystander intervention strategies. For example, Moschella, Bennet and Banyard (2016: 4) suggest that effective bystander strategies can include talking directly to the perpetrator, distracting them from the situation and removing the victim from harm. However, live music events and their crowds are continuously moving, which can create a physical barrier to intervening and removing the victim, while loud music makes discussion impossible (Barnes 2017).

Conclusion

In this chapter we set out to examine how and why sexual violence occurs within live music spaces. Drawing on Gavey's concept of the 'cultural scaffolding' of sexual violence, we asked what features within the music scene might enable sexual violence, while simultaneously excusing and minimizing this violence when it does occur. Our examination of research concerning the music industry broadly, as well as our own work on sexual violence in live music scenes, points to a complex interplay of structural inequality, social and cultural norms (particularly regarding gender, sexuality and drug/alcohol consumption), and the physical space and design of performance environments, particularly music festivals and gigs. In many respects, live music scenes can bring together a 'perfect storm' of factors implicated in the perpetration and normalization of sexual violence.

Research on gender inequality, gender and sexual norms in the Australian music scene depicts a cultural context in which victim-survivor voices and experiences are systematically devalued, delegitimized and 'othered'. The structural and cultural factors that underpin sexual violence form the core of the norms, values and structural elements of the Australian music industry. These systems arguably function to normalize sexual violence, and to provide excuses for such violence when it occurs, while at the same time devaluing victim-survivor narratives and experiences such that they are less likely to be believed if and when they speak out. While the norms and values of music scenes are diverse and fluid, these scenes remain male-dominated even within supposedly 'alternative' subcultural spaces. The spatial design and behavioural norms of music scenes ensure that close bodily contact and physical touch is a normal, if not unavoidable, part of the live music experience. In live music spaces, perpetrators can readily draw on aspects of the environment to deny, minimize or excuse their behaviour, while the likelihood of bystander intervention is greatly reduced. The collective and normalized high-level consumption of alcohol and drugs provides another tool for perpetrators in enacting and excusing sexual violence. In short, it is evident that numerous elements of the music scene can be called upon to downplay or deny victim-survivor experiences of sexual violence, and to facilitate and subsequently excuse and minimize sexual offending.

References

Abbey, A. and R. Harnish (1995), 'Perception of Sexual Intent: The Role of Gender, Alcohol Consumption, and Rape Supportive Attitudes', *Sex Roles*, 32 (5/6): 297–313.

Abbey, A., T. Zawacki, P.O. Buck, A.M. Clinton and P. McAuslan (2001), 'Alcohol and Sexual Assault', *Alcohol Research & Health*, 25 (1): 43–51.

Ambrose, J. (2010), *The Violent World of Moshpit Culture*, London: Omnibus Press.

Australian Institute of Health and Welfare (2017), 'National Drug Strategy Household Survey 2016: Detailed Findings', *Drug Statistics Series No. 31*. Cat. no. PHE 214. Canberra: AIHW.

Bannister, M. (2006), 'Loaded: Indie Guitar Rock, Canonism, White Masculinities', *Popular Music*, 25 (1): 77–95.

Barnes, A. (2017), *Bodies in the Pit: An Analysis of Bodily Integrity within the Australian Punk Scene*. Unpublished Honours Thesis. School of Social Sciences, University of Tasmania.

Bevin, E. (2017), 'Falls Festival: Plain-Clothed Police in Mosh Pit in Effort to Stop Assaults', *ABC News Online*, 23 December. Available online: http://www.abc.net.au/news/2017-12-23/falls-festival-warning-on-sex-assault/9283028 (accessed 12 April 2018).

Beynon, C.M., C. McVeigh, J. McVeigh, C. Leavey and M.A. Bellis (2008), 'The Involvement of Drugs and Alcohol in Drug-Facilitated Sexual Assault: A Systematic Review of the Evidence', *Trauma, Violence, & Abuse*, 9 (3): 178–188.

Bluett-Boyd, N., B. Fileborn, A. Quadara and S. Moore (2013), 'The Role of Emerging Communication Technologies in Experiences of Sexual Violence. A New Legal Frontier?', *Research Report No. 23*. Melbourne: Australian Institute of Family Studies.

Cooper, M.L. (2002), 'Alcohol Use and Risky Sexual Behavior among College Students and Youth: Evaluating the Evidence', *Journal of Studies on Alcohol*, (supplement (14): 101–117.

Cooper, R., A. Coles and S. Hanna-Osborne (2017), *Skipping a Beat: Assessing the State of Gender Equality in the Australian Music Industry*, Sydney: University of Sydney Business School.

Davies, H. (2001), 'All Rock and Roll Is Homosocial: The Representation of Women in the British Rock Music Press', *Popular Music*, 20 (3): 301–319.

Davies, H. (2017), 'Are Music Festivals Doing Enough to Tackle Sexual Assault?', *The Guardian*, 25 July. Available online: https://www.theguardian.com/lifeandstyle/2017/jul/25/music-festivals-sexual-assault-rape-safe (accessed 12 April 2018).

Dmytryschchak, G. (2016), 'Man Charged with Urinating on Woman at Spiderbait Gig', *The Age*, 19 November. Available online: https://www.theage.com.au/national/victoria/man-charged-with-urinating-on-woman-at-spiderbait-gig-20161119-gst72h.html (accessed 8 March 2018).

Duff C. (2003), 'Drugs and Youth Cultures: Is Australia Experiencing the 'Normalization' of Adolescent Drug Use?', *Journal of Youth Studies*, 6 (4): 433–446.

Earl, C. (2008), 'Crowds at Outdoor Music Festivals: An Examination of Crowd Psychology and Its Implications for the Environmental Health Practitioner', *Environmental Health*, 8 (1): 34.

Ensminger, D. (2013), 'Slamdance in the No Time Zone: Punk as a Repertoire for Liminality', *Liminalities: A Journal of Performance Studies*, 9 (3): 1–13.

Erickson, T.B., S.E. Aks, M. Koenigsberg, E.B. Bunney, B. Schurgin and P. Levy (1996), 'Drug Use Patterns at Major Rock Concert Events', *Annals of Emergency Medicine*, 28 (1): 22–26.

Fileborn, B. (2016), *Reclaiming the Night-Time Economy: Unwanted Sexual Attention in Pubs and Clubs*, London and New York: Palgrave Macmillan.

Fileborn, B., Wadds, P. and Tomsen, S. (2019) 'Safety, Sexual Harassment and Assault at Australian Music Festivals: Final Report'. Available online: https://www.academia.edu/39795192/Safety_sexual_harassment_and_assault_at_Australian_music_festivals_final_report (accessed 7 July 2019).

Fillmore, M.T. and J. Weafer (2004), 'Alcohol Impairment of Behavior in Men and Women', *Addiction*, 99 (10): 1237–1246.

Frith, S. (2017), *Taking Popular Music Seriously: Selected Essays*, London and New York: Routledge.

Fromme, K., E.J. D'Amico and E.C. Katz (1999), 'Intoxicated Sexual Risk Taking: An Expectancy or Cognitive Impairment Explanation?', *Journal of Studies on Alcohol*, 60 (1): 54–63.

Gavey, N. (2005), *Just Sex? The Cultural Scaffolding of Rape*, London & New York: Routledge.

Giancola, P.R. (2013), 'Alcohol and Aggression: Theories and Mechanisms', in M. McMurran (ed.), *Alcohol-Related Violence: Prevention and Treatment* (1st edition), 35–59, Chichester, UK: John Wiley & Sons.

Graham, K. and S. Wells (2003), '"Somebody's Gonna Get Their Head Kicked in Tonight!" Aggression among Young Males in Bars – A Question of Values?', *British Journal of Criminology*, 43 (3): 546–566.

The Guardian (2017), 'Sweden's Bravalla Music Festival Cancelled Next Year After Sex Attacks', *The Guardian*, 4 July. Available online: https://www.theguardian.com/world/2017/jul/03/swedens-bravalla-music-festival-cancelled-next-year-after-sexattacks (accessed 8 March 2018).

Haenfler, R. (2006), *Straight Edge: Hardcore Punk, Clean Living Youth, and Social Change*, New Brunswick: Rutgers University Press.

Hatton, E. and M. N. Trautner (2011), 'Equal Opportunity Objectification? The Sexualisation of Men and Women on the Cover of *Rolling Stone*', *Sexuality & Culture*, 15 (3): 256–278.

Hunt, G., M. Moloney and K. Evans (2010), *Youth, Drugs and Nightlife*, London & New York: Routledge.

Hutton, F. (2006), *Risky Pleasures? Club Cultures and Feminine Identities*, Hampshire: Ashgate.

Kelly, L. (1988), *Surviving Sexual Violence*, Cambridge: Polity Press.

Latane, B. and J. Darley (1970), *The Unresponsive Bystander: Why Doesn't He Help?*, New York: Appleton Century Crofts.

Leblanc, L. (1999), *Pretty in Punk: Girls' Gender Resistance in a Boys' Subculture*, Brunswick: Rutgers University Press.

Lewis, M. (2017), 'The Growing Epidemic of Sexual Harassment at Aussie Music Festivals', *SBS*, 26 October. Available online: https://www.sbs.com.au/news/the-feed/the-growing-epidemic-of-sexual-harassment-at-aussie-music-festivals (accessed 12 April 2018).

Lim M.S.C., M.E., Hellard, J.S., Hocking and C.K. Aitken (2008), 'A Cross-Sectional Survey of Young People Attending a Music Festival: Associations between Drug Use and Musical Preference', *Drug and Alcohol Review*, 27 (4): 439–441.

Littleton, H., A. Grills-Taquechel and D. Axsom (2009), 'Impaired and Incapacitated Rape Victims: Assault Characteristics and Post-Assault Experiences', *Violence and Victims*, 24 (4): 439–457.

Martinus, T., J. McAlaney, L.J. McLaughlin and H. Smith (2010), 'Outdoor Music Festivals: Cacophonous Consumption or Melodious Moderation?', *Drugs: Education, Prevention and Policy*, 17 (6): 795–807.

Measham, F. (2006), 'The New Policy Mix: Alcohol, Harm Minimisation, and Determined Drunkenness in Contemporary Society', *International Journal of Drug Policy*, 17 (4): 258–268.

Moran, R. (2017), 'Laneway Launches Hotline to Combat Abuse and Harassment at Music Festivals', *Sydney Morning Herald*, 26 January. Available online: https://www.smh.com.au/entertainment/music/laneway-launches-hotline-to-combat-abuse-and-harassment-at-music-festivals-20170126-gtyvfp.html (accessed 12 April 2018).

Moschella, E.A., S. Bennett and V.L. Banyard (2016), 'Beyond the Situational Model: Bystander Action Consequences to Intervening in Situations Involving Sexual Violence', *Journal of Interpersonal Violence*, online first.

Music Victoria (2015), *Women in the Victorian Contemporary Music Industry*, Melbourne: Music Victoria.

Pope, E. and M. Shouldice (2001), 'Drugs and Sexual Assault: A Review', *Trauma, Violence, & Abuse*, 2 (1): 51–55.

Presdee, M. (2000), *Cultural Criminology and the Carnival of Crime*, London: Routledge.

Ravenscroft, N. and X. Matteucci (2003), 'The Festival as Carnivalesque: Social Governance and Control at Pamplona's San Fermin Fiesta', *Tourism Culture & Communication*, 4 (1): 1–15.

Riches, G. (2014), 'Brothers of Metal! Heavy Metal Masculinities, Moshpit Practices and Homosociality', in S. Roberts (ed.), *Debating Modern Masculinities: Change, Continuity, Crisis?*, 88–105, London: Palgrave Macmillan.

Strong, C. (2011), 'Grunge, Riot Grrrl and the Forgetting of Women in Popular Culture', *The Journal of Popular Culture*, 44 (2): 398–416.

Strong, C. (2014), 'All the Girls in Town: The Missing Women of Australian Rock, Cultural Memory and Coverage of the Death of Chrissy Amphlett', *Perfect Beat*, 15 (2): 149–166.

Tapert, S.F., G.A. Aarons, G.R. Sedlar and S.A. Brown (2001), 'Adolescent Substance Use and Sexual Risk-Taking Behavior', *Journal of Adolescent Health*, 28 (3): 181–189.

Testa, M., J.A. Livingston, C. VanZile-Tamsen and M.R. Frone (2003), 'The Role of Women's Substance Use in Vulnerability to Forcible and Incapacitated Rape', *Journal of Studies on Alcohol*, 64 (6): 756–764.

Tomsen, S. (1997), 'A Top Night: Social Protest, Masculinity and the Culture of Drinking Violence', *The British Journal of Criminology*, 37 (1): 90–102.

Ullman, S.E. (2003), 'A Critical Review of Field Studies on the Link of Alcohol and Adult Sexual Assault in Women', *Aggression and Violent Behavior: A Review Journal*, 8 (5): 471–486.

Ullman, S.E. and C.J. Najdowski (2010), 'Understanding Alcohol-Related Sexual Assaults: Characteristics and Consequences', *Violence and Victims*, 25 (1): 29–44.

VicHealth (2011), *Preventing Violence against Women in Australia Research Summary*, Melbourne: VicHealth.

Wall, L. (2014), 'Gender Equality and Violence against Women. What's the Connection?', *ACSSA Research Summary No. 7*, Melbourne: Australian Institute of Family Studies.

Wall, L. and A. Quadara (2014), 'Under the Influence? Considering the Role of Alcohol and Sexual Assault in Social Contexts', *ACSSA Issues No. 18*, Melbourne: Australian Institute of Family Studies.

8

South-West England Open Mics: Gender Politics and Pints?

Sharon Martin

Introduction

This chapter examines issues of gender through the people, practices and places of pub-based open mics in the counties of Somerset and Dorset (UK). This study identifies patterns in the participation of women at these events and explores the reasons behind them, suggesting strategies for change offered by a similar model: community performance events. Beyond the immediate world of open mics, I consider these gender politics in relation to wider gender inequalities within music, in particular songwriting and performance. This research is also rooted in my own experience as a performer at pub open mic events largely dominated by men. Reflecting on my own experience, this research considers the compromises that women have to make to actively participate in open mic settings, the unspoken assumptions of normative masculinity, the extent to which women have a minority status, and to which open mics could be considered as another example of a 'boys' club' within the industry. Within this chapter, I therefore ask why are pub open mics so imbalanced and what is the relationship between gender, space and place in relation to this?

Open mics, pubs and gender

The open mic night is an under-researched area within popular music, and there is a gap in the literature regarding the relationship between open mics and gender politics. This chapter aims to go some way towards addressing this gap and exploring the gendering of space through the experiences of women at pub-based open mics and community performance nights. During an open mic, performers – amateur or professional – play a short set to an audience which is often made up largely of other performers. Within this research all the performances were musical, although other types of open mics, such as comedy, exist. Open mics are often run by an individual who provides the PA and may also act as a host. Performers may use an open mic night as an opportunity to test out new material, gain experience and meet other musicians.

'Community performance nights' share many characteristics with open mics, but are not based in pubs, run instead in places such as village halls and community cafes. This term was used by the organizers to describe the village events included within this study.

Open mics are particularly significant as they provide grassroots opportunities for musical performance and songwriting development. They are 'an integral and developmental step in the biographies of many popular musicians' (Aldredge 2013: 5), and provide opportunities for networking, support, mentoring, the chance to be part of a scene, and a sense of belonging for the aspiring musician and songwriter. Aldredge (2013: 5) suggests that 'the open mic also represents a new kind of social and cultural space where musical knowledge and identities are the focus'. However, open mics take place within a context of wider gender inequality. As Connell and Gibson state (2003: 208), and as is demonstrated extensively elsewhere in this volume, '[g]ender relations infuse all levels of musical activity'. The setting and roles, physical constraints, and the culture of place and performance of open mics are all shaped by gender politics within the wider setting of the music industry. Aldredge's (2013: 119) study of open mic events in New York found women's participation rates to be between 20 and 30 per cent. The culture of open mics values men in performance in a way that excludes women from participating in this important first stage of their development. The gendering of entry spaces impacts upon individuals' attempts to begin a musical career. The open mic is therefore not 'an innocent backdrop to position, it is filled with politics and ideology', intricately intertwined with issues of gender politics and relating to career development (Connell and Gibson 2003: 209). This chapter examines the gendering of this space.

Pubs are the location for the majority of open mic nights in Somerset and Dorset. Brabazon, researching music scenes in the US and UK, argued that pubs are 'the incubators, nurseries and archives of popular music' (2012: 66). However, the pub is 'a socially significant site for gendered identity formation' (Leyshon 2008: 269), and both these places and the music within them are 'framed as masculine' (Brabazon 2012: 67). The gendering of pubs for grassroots songwriting and performance is significant. Access to, and comfort within, these places contribute to the visibility of women as role models, shaping the environment where women songwriters first connect with an audience. As a researcher and musician, participant and observer, insider and outsider, it is possible to gain a reflexive insight into the gender politics of open mics and their relationship to space and culture. As Burnard argues 'the politics of creativities and practices in music and music performance, like claims of creative ownership and claims of authority, can be institutionally bound up in the place and space that authorise the practice' (2015: 201). This research engaged with two very different types of space that had a direct and gendered impact on the experiences of performers. Particularly significant was the extent to which the change of environment and venue led to a change in the participation of women. Within a similar geographical locality there was a marked difference between pub open mics and community performance nights; indeed, women performers in pub open mics were largely notable by their absence. Space and place impacted on women's experience of performance, embodiment, the culture of the venues and their levels of confidence, and these themes – alongside masculine domination and the gendered division of labour – will be discussed in this chapter.

The theoretical approach in this chapter utilizes the work of Bourdieu as a frame through which to examine the gender politics of performance nights. As Reay (2015: xvii) notes, Bourdieu's *Masculine Domination* (2001) 'demands a recognition of power, struggle and hierarchy'. Additionally, Bourdieu's (1977) notion of *habitus* offers a useful means through which to explore the specific context of the pub open mic and the engagement of women and men as performers. The gendered nature of cultural capital within the place of performance helps to explain why fewer women participate in pub open mic events as this shapes practice. As Maton (2008: 51) explains 'the physical and social spaces we occupy are (like the habitus) structured, and it is the relation between these two structures that gives rise to practices'. The pub open mic is a space shaped by what is normatively and unconsciously masculine and the gendered nature of this space shapes the actions and performances within.

Feminist theories and debates also frame this research. In particular, feminist engagements with space and place, and the ways in which individuals perform their identity within these, are used to contextualize my findings. As Johnson (2008: 570) asserts '"gender" becomes a relational contested, differentiated, place-based and performative category. Place too becomes imbricated and mutually constituted by a range of social and spatial relations'. My analysis of the performance of gender within the open mic event is informed by the work of Judith Butler and Angela McRobbie in particular. Within this chapter, therefore, gender is viewed as a performance between bodies and discourses (Butler 1990) and the space of the open mic is considered to be a platform upon which women negotiate femininity and sexuality (McRobbie 2008). My analysis of the masculine domination of musical performance builds on the insights of Rebecca Finkel et al. (2017). This chapter examines how 'women do not have equal access to creative work, are not equally rewarded … [they] are subject to occupational segregation … and hegemonic masculinity continues to be reproduced' (Finkel et al. 2017: 282). In relation to my own research, my comparison of pub open mic nights and community performance nights highlights narratives and practices that contest the norm of hegemonic power relations.

Gaining access to performances and experiences

This study is informed by participant observation at open mic and community performances from 27th March to 28th April 2017 in the counties of Somerset and Dorset. In order to explore the reasons behind the stark gender imbalance at open mics, I undertook thirty semi-structured interviews. I also carried out a short demographic survey of the participants at the open mic and community performance nights. This methodology produced data about the performers and the organization and culture of the events themselves. I attended six evenings in total, in rural villages and towns; three were pub open mic events (two in Somerset and one in Dorset) and three were community performance nights (one town performance night and two village performance nights). This research is therefore a non-representative snapshot of performance in Somerset and Dorset.

This research was prompted by my experience as a woman, songwriter and musician. I started writing songs after receiving a ukulele for my fortieth birthday. I first performed my songs at a pub open mic, and so these events have had a significant impact on my creative development and experience of performance. This reflection upon my own practice was important to my work as a researcher; personal experience can provide additional insight into the culture being studied (Ellis and Bochner 2000: 740). Indeed, 'Bourdieu validates, and even requires, close involvement of the authorial subject with his or her objects of study' (Dylan Smith 2015: 62). Being a performer and playing the violin facilitated my access to my interviewees as I had performed with some of them, enabling me to gain and demonstrate cultural capital (Reay 2015: xviii). The interviews took place away from the performance areas in informal and more private settings such as the kitchen which, alongside the semi-structured nature of the interviews, enabled more conversational interaction. Whilst I had an insider identity – which I had to negotiate alongside my own involvement with the dominant practices in these performance spaces – I critically questioned my own assumptions, the research process challenging my perception of the events.

I employed opportunity sampling, a technique that suited the nature of the scene under study and my own engagement within it. Interviews were recorded using a digital recording device alongside note-taking, and all interviewees gave their informed consent. In addition to performers themselves, I also interviewed a woman singer-songwriter whom I contacted at university who was interested in the research and who had experience of open mic environments and performance. Two of the interviewees were also the organizers and hosts of the pub open mics and the community performance night, the latter of which took place by phone due to time constraints on the night itself. Pseudonyms were used throughout the research to ensure confidentiality. Due to the noticeable gender imbalance and the desire to provide a space for women to speak about their experiences at open mic nights, the decision was also made to focus primarily on women's responses in this chapter. These provided rich data and vivid accounts of gender inequality in open mic performance.

The importance of place: Findings and discussion

Setting the scene

The two Somerset pub-based open mics took place in the same setting, a traditional pub where a small group of men sat on barstools watching, and the rest of the audience present were also performers. A small performance area faced the bar where the musicians performed between the speakers and window seat. This space, as identified by Leyshon in his research, was 'clearly coded and territorialized' (2008: 275). The host was a man who sat adjacent to the performers introducing acts, controlling the PA and deciding who played and for how long, loosely based on time of arrival. He acted as a musical gatekeeper, allowing access to the musical performance. Just as O'Shea (2008: 57) noted that men's employment as leaders in traditional Irish music-making sessions gave them legitimacy and authority, so, it could be argued, does the position of men as open mic hosts. The Dorset pub open mic, at a larger dark and wood-panelled venue, was run by the same host as the Somerset pub open mics. Again, the audience sat near the performance area and was mostly made up of performers. Audience and performers were predominantly men.

In comparison, the town community performance night took place in a community café. There were hot drinks and cakes available and the audience sat around little tables lit by candlelight and watched performers intently and in silence on a stage festooned with fairy lights. The night was organized by a musical collective, the running order decided by the woman hosting and introducing the acts. The two village community performance nights were organized by a woman and held in a beautiful high-ceilinged village hall lit with coloured lights. The audience sat round little tables buzzing with chatter during the performances. The running order was decided seemingly at random by the man hosting the event. There was constant activity around the hall during performances as there was a swap shop, a donation-based bar selling local beer and cider, and a stall selling locally produced food. The functions of this audience were different. Less attention was paid to performances than at the town performance night, and, as one of my interviewees commented, this seemed to give women performers more confidence to perform. Children were part of this, laughing, running around, dancing and crawling under the tables. These nights offered something akin to the kitchen sessions described by O'Shea (2008) in her study of women performers of traditional Irish music, with sessions in traditionally feminine spaces (such as the kitchen) as providing an opportunity to practice performance and develop musical friendships in an alternative space to the pub, also the main space for the performance of traditional Irish music (ibid: 60).

Masculine domination and the pub

The pub is a common location of open mics in the UK, yet it is not an easy environment for a woman to negotiate or perform in. This can be seen in the breakdown of performers at different events, shown in Table 8.1, which shows that open mics in pubs feature far fewer women performers than men. In addition to this, I encountered only two other women at pub open nights; a mother and daughter. The much higher numbers of women performing at and attending community nights tell us that women are more involved in these types of events, and the difference here suggests that there is something about the environment of the pub open mic that discourages them.

The pub is not a neutral environment or safe space and has to be navigated in terms of gender, class, ethnicity and sexuality. It 'remains a space in which men's needs and tastes predominate and women do not feel "at home"' (O'Shea 2008: 59). This is evidenced by the extent to which men predominated in performance at pub-based

Table 8.1 Performance Settings and Gender Percentages

Venue	No. of performances per event	Gender % Women: Men
Somerset pub open mic	10	10: 90
Dorset pub open mic	12	8: 92
Somerset pub open mic 2	8	37: 63
Community performance night – village 1	11	45: 55
Community performance night – town	10	40: 60
Community performance night – village 2	11	45: 55

open mics during my research, and data from interviewees, such as Leslie (audience member), who referred to the pub as an environment still dominated by men. This space is 'a socially significant site for gendered identity formation' (Leyshon 2008: 269). Women need to be part of the open mic informal performance circuit to challenge existing gender politics and to improve their chances of equality within the wider music industry, as networks are crucial to gendered power relations in music (Reimer 2016: 1034). However, Leyshon argues that within the pub context 'visible conviviality masks an underlying sociality of social exclusion' (2008: 284). Andrea (singer-songwriter and songwriting student) stated there is always 'competition for open mic slots' and as Campbell identifies in her research, 'male drinking practices … persist because they are a site of male power and legitimacy … rural pubs can actually operate as a key site where hegemonic forms of masculinity are constructed, reproduced and successfully defended' (2000: 563).

Women's exclusion is enacted in a number of ways. While Lucy (performer and music student) commented about the pub open mic audience that 'the second they see a woman they take even less notice', many other interviewees discussed 'leering men' (see also Leyshon 2008: 297). Debbie (singer-songwriter) stated that 'you feel a little bit under threat sometimes, feel a bit like I have been leered at, chatted up … you learn to deal with it and brush it off'. The women interviewed were aware of the relationship between place, space and embodiment and their sexualization and objectification. Lucy, for example, stated that clothing choices affected how she was listened to in a pub setting: 'you have to dress up to make the audience take notice'. The place and space of performance and the audience of men were sometimes identified as uncomfortable for the women interviewed, requiring additional emotional labour by them (Monaghan 2019). As Amy (musician and music leader) stated, '[pubs have a] culture of beer and shouting and raucousness'. Some of the interviewees were aware of their objectification during performance and this produced tensions and contradictions, as Debbie articulates: 'you tell guys what they want to hear sometimes just to gloss over what you think they are really getting at'. As O Shea argues, in order to negotiate the masculine space of the pub, women use 'assertive and defensive actions both resisting and complying with patriarchal social control' (2008: 60). However, such engagements were further complicated by notions of ageing and sexuality:

[When I started performing] I could do myself up in an attractive way, I was a relatively young woman [mid 20's] and I was blonde … I knew how to put on makeup and sexualise myself as a performer … now that I am getting older [late 30's] I'm aware I look different to how I used to …, and I've got all these narratives in my head, and I don't want to look as mutton dressed as lamb and all that sort of thing. (Andrea)

These findings echo Bourdieu's (2001: 66) assertion that:

Masculine domination has the effect of keeping (women) in a permanent state of bodily insecurity, or more precisely of symbolic dependence. They exist first through and for the gaze of others … what is called 'femininity' is often nothing other than a form of indulgence towards real or supposed male expectations.

The place and space of performance shape the performance of femininity, and the gender representation within open mics themselves, which is reflected by the wider structural inequality present within the music industry. Thus space and place can reinforce masculine domination and, as Born and Devine identified in music classrooms (2016: 17), pub open mics are discursively, atmospherically and spatially masculine. In contrast community performance nights could offer a space less shaped by masculine domination.

Table 8.2 Gender and Preferred Instrument of Interviewees

Instrument	Women	Men
Guitar	2	13
Voice	8	0
Drum	1	1
Ukulele	1	1
Bass	0	1
Piano	0	1
Accordion	1	0
Total	13	17

N.B. When more than one instrument was named the first was included.

The gendered nature of music making and performance

As Waksman (2001), Dibben (2002) and Monaghan (2019) have noted in their own work, songwriting and the playing of particular instruments are gendered practices. This is vividly demonstrated in Table 8.2 – out of seventeen men in this study, thirteen played the guitar, and eight out of thirteen women considered themselves to be primarily singers. As the following section illustrates, this perceived reliance on voice rather than instrumental skill or song writing abilities translated as a reduction of cultural capital compared to men performers. In particular, the guitar, and its masculinity as an instrument, was commented on by men and women interviewees. Lucy for example says 'There is a masculinity thing about playing the guitar and it is the thing that they (men) own'. The potential impact of this on women's participation is noted by Heidi's (singer-songwriter) description of pub open mic nights as 'only male performers, only men playing guitar and they were singing and no variation and I think that's quite a barrier'. Furthermore, due to the creative subject being viewed as a man (Mayhew 2004: 150), the musical engagement and skills of men are valued more highly than those of women. Lucy illustrates how this has played out in relation to band dynamics:

> If anyone offers a performance opportunity it is as a lesser, pretty singer to have in the background ... one of them (my friend) is an amazing jazz guitarist, writes all her own songs in a jazz band and men will only ever comment on her voice ... They completely ignore any instrumental ability when they are talking to you or any chance that you would have an equal status in the band as them.

Penny (a full-time music student), spoke about the ways in which this gendered valuing of men guitarists and songwriters in the open mic context also translated into a right to speak and a gendered valuing of voice:

> I think it's connections, it's trying to befriend some male musicians ... and usually because it's quite male dominated ... a male voice will usually have a little bit more weight. So you're only as good as your male fanship is.

The singing of original songs in a pub open mic setting confers more cultural capital on the men who participate in the event. The open mic setting and space normalizes the relationship between men and songwriting, and the gendered division of labour. Consequently, women may be, as Jessie states, 'intimidated to perform'. Debbie (singer-songwriter) defines songwriting as 'traditionally male orientated ... it doesn't occur to as many girls that they could be doing it'. She also describes songwriting as 'part of the image of being a rebellious teenager'(for men). To quote Jessie, open mics are 'often middle-aged men singing about their problems'. The invisibility of successful and valued women songwriters leads to a lack of role models and this absence could reinforce a cycle of gendered inequality and the relative invisibility of women. As Jessie comments, 'girls don't feel yeah I could do that too'. In explaining the lack of visible women songwriters on the open mic stage, Jessie thought that songwriting 'maybe feels a bit more personal to women ... a song might be something you don't want other people to hear'. Every woman interviewed during this research referred to the significance of role models and/or the importance of music at home whilst growing up. Role models are significant in encouraging participation in music performance, yet the pub as a place does not empower women to take part.

Space, place and confidence

Place can shape levels of confidence. Every woman interviewed referred to confidence as a barrier for women in performance. Mary (musician) stated that 'boys are encouraged to be confident and take the lead'. Amy agrees: 'you need to be a strong and confident person particularly a female to stand up at a mic ... and feel confident enough that you've got something to offer'. This was echoed by Heidi, who said 'women worry more about how they sound, men are much more they'll give it a go and they don't care if they mess up. I think women probably don't dare ... there is a lack of confidence perhaps'. This relationship between confidence and gender was also identified by Bartmann (2017) when she examined its impact on performance and assessment for popular music students. One response from thirteen-year-old Clare (performer and musician) at a community performance night highlighted the internalization of masculine domination. When asked why fewer women perform she replied 'women are a bit more closed, introverted and selfish ... scared, anxious and self-conscious'. Another response from Lucy, again at a community performance night, made me reflect on my own nervousness when performing:

> You see a woman of a similar age (we had referred to a middle-aged man performing previously) and she is shaking so much she can hardly play the guitar even though she sounds really good. Her guitar playing is decent compared to most of the blokes there ... I've always wondered why that is.

This nervousness could in part be explained by women performers' lack of cultural capital, their habitus and the place of performance. Each element must be disrupted in order to challenge normative masculinity, to address issues of women's confidence, and to ensure that women enjoy performance and are therefore more likely to continue to participate. This lack of confidence has been addressed by initiatives like Girls Rock (a not-for-profit organization who run all-girl rock camps around the world), who found that encouraging girls to take up more space improved their self-confidence and body image scores (Girls Rock London 2018). In relation to the performance and self-consciousness of girls, Baker and Cohen (2008) suggest that women-only spaces are conducive to skill development and confidence building amongst the girls in their study on community-based music activities. Similar recommendations could be used for the open mic context.

As Table 8.1 demonstrates, community performance nights clearly attracted a more balanced ratio of performers and audience in relation to gender, pointing to the significance of place and space. The organizers had created a space that empowered more women to take part. As Bloustien argues, change is possible when girls and women take an active part in creating and controlling spaces in the public sphere (2016: 239). It is significant that the organizers of both community performance nights were women. Within these roles, they set up expected behaviours for the nights, disrupted dominant power structures, acted as role models, and produced an alternative space. In contrast, the physical and spatial characteristics of the pub open mic reinforced a gendered division of labour. The pub environment, and the timing of events, usually from nine to eleven-thirty pm, meant children were unable to be present and there was no childcare available, limiting the participation of primary caregivers (see also O'Shea 2008: 58). These issues were also identified by the interviewees. This contrasted with the practical and cultural aspects of community performance nights which operated within a different cultural paradigm, where toys were available with the aim of widening participation and encouraging children's attendance. As Sarah (the community performance night organizer) said 'I knew all the kids were playing … and dressed up in swap shop clothes … everyone is really open to children, (they) crawl under tables so the parents can relax and enjoy the night'. Heidi commented that:

> the place has a big impact, the first time I performed was here, and it's a very easy going, friendly, welcoming place. I felt very supported and very encouraged. Singing (at another setting) was more nerve-wracking because people are sitting there listening, there's a difference whether people are chatting whether they're focusing on you or not. I feel much more relaxed performing here.

Heidi's experience reflects the organizer of the village community performance nights' intention to encourage informality, which was commented on by several of the women interviewed, and identified as a reason for their willingness to perform at these nights as opposed to pub open mics. Furthermore, the women I spoke to also attributed their increasing confidence to this change in environment. The place, its culture and organization and role models contributed to higher participation rates of women at community performance nights.

Conclusion

Whilst all the performance settings examined in this research were gendered, the inequalities were more marked at pub open mic nights. The lack of women participating at pub open mic nights represents one challenge preventing the transition from amateur to professional music making and reflects the gender imbalance in gigs and festivals more widely (Savage 2018). It is evident that pub open mics reward men with more cultural capital. The space of the pub reinforces masculinity and values the culture of men, thus prioritizing a masculine habitus. Gender as a performative act is shaped by the site of its performance and pubs shape both this performance and the creation of gendered identities (Butler 1988: 526). This means that place and space have a significant impact on women's self-confidence, their visibility, and their access to the music industry. The place and space of performance are factors in determining the opportunities that women have to define themselves as musicians and songwriters. To increase inclusivity for women in music it is therefore important to critically examine these places and spaces, even those that are traditionally the domain of amateur music-making.

The functions and cultural norms of the pub-based open mic nights and community performance nights were distinctive, demonstrating that there is a relationship between the physical environment, the gendered culture of place and gendered power relationships. The swap shop, locally produced food and family-friendly nature of the community performance nights help to explain the differences in culture, the greater participation of women as performers and greater inclusivity of these events. It is apparent that alternatives to the 'traditional' pub open mic can encourage women to participate and are thus a strategy for change. In a similar way to Girls Rock, they could remove barriers and dismantle oppressive norms (Marsh 2018: 98). Another strategy for change is the redesigning of spaces of performance with positive thinking about cultural and gendered expectations. As Sarah, the organizer explains, conscious planning to change the norms and values within a space can work: 'we moved the bar from the kitchen area and put the bar into the main area so that that created a social space in the music area ... we purposefully did that'. The way in which the space was consciously laid out impacted on the culture and women's participation rates at the community performance nights. In addition, the community performance nights provide insight into practical steps that can be taken to make open mic and performance nights more accessible to women. The timing of events, their location, the provision of childcare and/or of family-friendly facilities, and different settings, for example would all have an impact. Beyond the provision of comfortable spaces for women, there is also a clear need for role models and the increased visibility of women in music performance and as songwriters to engender change. Women and men need to acknowledge inequalities and take individual and institutional measures to address them. Open mics and community performance nights operate within gendered places and can reinforce gendered power relationships. Gatekeepers to open mic and performance night cultures need to positively frame 'their' spaces as inclusive to attract more diverse participation. This would benefit women and men because, as Blair Petterson argues, 'gender equality isn't a women's problem, nor are the benefits of a more gender-balanced world limited to women' (2016: 3). Firstly recognizing and secondly challenging the gendered nature of spaces is important. These events represent an informal and early performance circuit which plays a central role in musician and singer-songwriter development.

References

Aldredge, M. (2013), *Singer-Songwriters and Musical Open Mics*, Burlington, VT: Ashgate.

Baker, S. and B. Cohen (2008), 'From Snuggling and Snogging to Sampling and Scratching: Girls' Nonparticipation in Community-Based Music Activities', *Youth and Society*, 39 (3), 16–339.

Bartmann, D. (2017), Turning Passion into a Career: A Wise Choice? Effects of Studying Popular Music Performance on Intrinsic Motivation. University of Westminster. 26 May 2017.

Blair Pettersson, L. (2016), 'Next Steps for Gender Equality in the Music Industry'. Available online: http://www.lucyblairpettersson.com/2016/04/25/gender-equality-in-music-the-next-steps/ (accessed 20 April 2017).

Bloustien, G. (2016), 'God Is a DJ: Girls, Music and Performance and Negotiating Space', in C. Mitchell and C. Rentschler (eds.), *Girlhood and the Politics of Place*, 228–244, New York: Berghahn.

Bourdieu, P. (1977), *Outline of a Theory of Practice*, Cambridge: Cambridge University Press.

Bourdieu, P. (2001), *Masculine Domination*, Cambridge: Polity Press.

Born, G. and K. Devine (2016), 'Gender, Creativity and Education in Digital Musics and Sound Art', *Contemporary Music Review*, 35 (1): 1–20.

Brabazon, T. (2012), *Popular Music: Topics, Trends and Trajectories*, London: Sage.

Burnard, P. (2015), 'Working with Bourdieu's Cultural Analysis and Legacy: Alignments and Allegiances in Developing Career Creativities', in P. Burnard, T. Hofvander and J. Söderman (eds.), *Bourdieu and the Sociology of Music Education*, 193–209, Farnham: Ashgate.

Butler, J. (1990), *Gender Trouble: Feminism and the Subversion of Identity*, Abingdon: Routledge.

Butler, J. (1988), 'Performative Acts and Gender Constitution: An Essay in Phenomenology and Feminist Theory', *Theatre Journal*, 40 (4): 519–531.

Campbell, H. (2000), 'The Glass Phallus: Pub(lic) Masculinity and Drinking in Rural New Zealand', *Rural Sociology*, 65 (4): 562–581.

Connell, J. and C. Gibson (2003), *Sound Tracks Popular Music, Identity and Place*, Abingdon: Routledge.

Dibben, N. (2002), 'Gender, Identity and Music', in McDonald, R et al. (eds.), *Musical Identities*, 117–134, Oxford: Oxford University Press.

Dylan Smith, G. (2015), 'Masculine Domination in Private-Sector Popular Music Performance Education in England', in P. Burnard, T. Hofvander and J. Söderman (eds.), *Bourdieu and the Sociology of Music Education*, 61–78, Farnham: Ashgate.

Ellis, C. and A. Bochner (2000), 'Autoethnography, Personal Narrative, Reflexivity: Researcher as Subject', in N. Denzin and Y. Lincoln (eds.), *The Handbook of Qualitative Research*, 2nd edn, 733–768, California: Sage.

Finkel, R., D. Jones, K. Sang and D.S. Russell (2017), 'Diversifying the Creative: Creative Work, Creative Industries, Creative Identities', *Organization*, 24 (3): 281–288.

Girls Rock London (2018), *Girls Rock London*, Available online: http://www.girlsrocklondon.com/ (accessed 20 October 2018).

Johnson, L. (2008), 'Re-Placing Gender? Reflections on 15 Years of Gender, Place and Culture', *Gender Place and Culture*, 15 (6): 561–574.

Leyshon, M. (2008), 'We're Stuck in the Corners: Young Women, Embodiment and Drinking in the Countryside', *Drugs: Education, Prevention and Policy*, 15 (3): 267–289.

Marsh, C. (2018), 'When She Plays We Hear the Revolution: Girls Rock Regina – A Feminist Intervention', *IASPM@Journal*, 8 (1): 89–102.

Maton, K. (2008), 'Habitus', in M. Grenfell (ed.), *Bourdieu Key Concepts*, 49–65, London: Acumen.

Mayhew, E. (2004), 'Positioning the Producer: Gender Divisions in Creative Labour and Value', in S. Whitley, A. Bennett and S. Hawkins (eds.), *Music, Space and Place: Popular Music and Cultural Identity*, 149–162, Aldershot: Ashgate.

McRobbie, A. (2008), *The Aftermath of Feminism: Gender, Culture and Social Change*, Los Angeles: Sage.

Monaghan, U. (2019), *One Hundred Stories: Perspectives on Gender and Irish Traditional Music*. National University of Ireland Galway. 9 February 2019.

O'Shea, H. (2008), 'Good Man Mary! Women Musicians and the Fraternity of Irish Traditional Music', *Journal of Gender Studies*, 17 (1): 55–70.

Reay, D. (2015), 'Foreword', in P. Burnard, T. Hofvander and J. Söderman (eds.), *Bourdieu and the Sociology of Music Education*, xvii–xx, Farnham: Ashgate.

Reimer, S. (2016), 'It's Just a Very Male Industry: Gender and Work in UK Design Industries', *Gender, Place and Culture*, 23 (7): 1033–1046.

Savage, M. (2018), 'Music Festivals Pledge 50/50 Gender Equality', *The Guardian*, 26 February. Available online: https://www.bbc.co.uk/news/entertainment-arts-43196414 (accessed 15 February 2019).

Waksman, S. (2001), *Instruments of Desire: The Electric Guitar and the Shaping of Musical Experience*, Cambridge: Harvard University Press.

9

Gender Mainstreaming in the Music Industries: Perspectives from Sweden and the UK

Sam de Boise

Introduction

This chapter focuses on how 'gender mainstreaming' practices have been implemented in the UK and Sweden as a means of reducing gender inequalities in the music industries. Specifically, the chapter looks at the strengths and limitations of this approach in these two contexts. The two have very different legislative and cultural policy structures, which shape different strategies to address issues of access and discrimination within music (see de Boise 2017b). Here, however, I want to focus instead more on the similarities in approaches, rather than contrasting them. In order to do this, data is drawn from nine key stakeholder interviews with representatives from Sweden and the UK working with organizations committed to tackling gender equality in relation to music, as well as existing data and policy documents.

It is important to note that the term 'music industries' (plural) here is used to denote that I am not just interested in the recorded music industry (Negus 1999). Extending the focus to the music indust*ries* implicates chains of distribution, publishing and production (Anderton et al. 2013), as well as music education institutions and live 'scenes' which are transnationally interdependent. I also use the term 'gender inequalit*ies*' (plural) to denote that gender discrimination can occur, and be experienced, in different if related ways, in different aspects of the industries by different gender groups. Whilst literature has largely focused on discrimination against cis-gendered women (with good reason), intersectional differences mean that different groups of women suffer from varying degrees of discrimination which are inextricable from, but not reducible to, each other (Verloo 2006). It is also important to recognize that trans* individuals face discrimination in music spaces on the basis of their gendered expression and identities (Taylor 2013; Pearce and Lohman 2018). Such forms of discrimination may, then, be rendered invisible in judging equality based on the numbers of binary genders. As such, there should be greater consideration as to how definitions of gender equality entailed in mainstreaming may also work to both include and potentially exclude those marginalized on the basis of gender.

Gendering musical labour: Discrimination and access

Academic literature has dealt, at length, with gender inequalities across different music activities related to the music industries. Yet there has been very little written on gender inequalities with a focus on the music industries specifically (this book, thus, marking a timely intervention into existing work on gender and music). Academic research has instead tended to either focus on representations of women in the industries (Leonard 2007; Lieb 2013) or group the music industries with the cultural industries more generally (Hesmondhalgh and Baker 2015; McRobbie 2016). The former do not address the way in which labour structures within the music industries are gendered, whilst the latter overlook some specific dynamics (in contrast to film, literature, fashion or graphic design for instance) which are integral to the music industries' various ecosystems.

Part of the problem in estimating the extent to which the music industries are gendered is the difficulty in generating reliable statistics on who counts as 'working' within them. There is actually very little quantitative research on the extent of the problem of either participation or discrimination (for rare exceptions see Goldin and Rouse 2000; Macarthur 2014; Strong and Cannizzo 2017). In lieu of comprehensive research data, music industries bodies, government agencies and voluntary or charity organizations have produced specific data detailing the extent of gender divisions. From this, we can ascertain that, depending on the country, between 65–90 per cent of senior management positions are occupied by male-identifying individuals (PRS 2016; McCormack 2017; Musiksverige 2017) and there are quantitative skews across different music-related professions (CCIL 2011). The majority of funding for music projects, too, has often gone to men (Kulturrådet 2009; Arts Council England 2015) and the majority of acts booked to play festivals or concerts, often irrespective of genre, are also male-identifying (Jämställd Festival 2016; KVAST 2016; Women in Music 2016; female:pressure 2017). Men are also more likely to make up a significantly higher proportion of *paid* songwriters (STIM 2016; Smith et al. 2018). This does not reflect the 'total' number of musicians or interest in music by gender. Rather it reflects how opportunities, labour and, therefore ultimately resources, are unequally distributed by gender (Cameron 2015).

Crucially, existing academic research has shed light on how such quantitative divides rely on broader processes of gendering musical labour. For instance, various authors have noted how the gendering of technology and instruments influences who receives opportunities to play, or reinforces perceptions about who is capable of playing certain forms of music (Wych 2012; Gavanas and Reitsammer 2013; Gadir 2017). The status and power of different positions within the music industries also affect the likelihood of gendered exclusion and labour segregation (Hesmondhalgh and Baker 2015) and harassment and discrimination affect music industries workers' differentially gendered experiences (Macarthur 2014; Strong and Cannizzo 2017).

Gender mainstreaming in the music industries

Given the persistence of these divisions and experiences, it is clear that change requires both a cultural and a political shift. Gender mainstreaming (GM) is a concept which has been used in other occupational fields in order to tackle similar problems. The concept itself has been understood (and deliberately misunderstood) in a variety of ways (Walby 2005). However, in terms of policy measures, in Europe, it has most often been interpreted from the Council of Europe's (1998: 7–8) initial definition of gender equality, as meaning 'an equal visibility, empowerment and participation of both sexes in all spheres of public and private life'.

GM strategies, more concretely, take a number of different forms from employment or board quotas to conducting gender impact assessments around organizational decisions (Sainsbury and Bergqvist 2009: 228). Most commonly, however, at state and local government level, GM is enacted through conscious attention to recruitment processes, policy decisions and strategic resource allocation. Indeed one of its key rhetorical and practical strengths as a strategy has been to put the discussion of gender equality on the political agenda in a variety of ways and to provide practical, documentable steps to address issues of discrimination and representation (Sainsbury and Bergqvist 2009: 219).

Crucially, GM has, recently, been mentioned in a number of state-level cultural policy initiatives designed to specifically reduce the representational skew on gendered *participation* in 'cultural organizations' and cultural policy across European states (EIGE 2016). Sweden has received special mention in EU recommendation documents for its implementation of gender impact assessments in cultural policy funding decisions since 2006 (EIGE 2016: 14) and the music industries specifically (Musikverket.se 2015; Musiksverige 2017). This GM approach extends also to student recruitment selection procedures within higher education institutions, directly affecting conservatoires (de Boise 2017a), as well as voluntary organizations funded by state or local government entities (de Boise 2017b). In the UK, the Department of Culture Media and Sport (DCMS), has also outlined a commitment to ensuring equality of (binary) genders on the boards of organizations to which it allocates funding (DCMS 2008). Arts Council England (2015) has also conducted a thorough gendered analysis of who receives funding through its streams.

Equally important is that equality and discrimination legislation in both the UK (The Equality Act 2010) and Sweden (Diskrimineringslagan 2008) have been shaped by policy structures operating at a supranational level (The European Commission). These demands have, therefore, filtered down to organizational requirements in how private and non-state entities operate. With regard to music, in the UK, GM initiatives have been implicated in relation to the music industries in several different ways. For example PRS's (2016) *Women make Music* initiative as well as UK Music's (2013) *Equality and Diversity Charter* both draw attention to the need to address quantitative imbalances in musical labour with specific reference to the 2010 Equality Act. In reality, enforcing discrimination legislation is not always effective due to the casualization of labour within the music industries, and especially musicians' labour (see Gadir 2017). However this underscores a political will, to varying degrees, in both places, to increase women's labour market participation and visibility in the music industries and to distribute economic resources 'more equally' amongst musicians on the basis of gender.

Gender mainstreaming in practice

Motivations for mainstreaming

The majority of the interviewees[1] in this study mentioned problems in trying to counteract the argument that women were 'missing' or 'not confident enough' as an explanation for their comparative absence on the live stages or working within the industries. Problems of representation, therefore, were one of the key issues that all the organizations sought to address. For instance, Ruth, who works with promoting women in jazz, and Sue, who runs an all-girl music technology workshop network, both in the UK, commented that:

> ... [in the 1960s] people kept telling me 'there aren't any women jazz musicians are there?' and for years I kept telling people *you've just been watching one!*' ... [in 1986] I'd written to all the likely libraries and colleges in Britain saying 'have you got any material on British women [in jazz], if you have could I see it?' ... Most of them said 'there aren't any women jazz musicians anyway'. (Ruth)
>
> When people ask the question: 'why are there not more women?', people then start speculating ... So when you launch an event and 2 hours later it's full, of names that I've never seen before, I think 'well, people *are* interested'. (Sue)

In Sweden, Helena, who works with a local government organization promoting women as jazz musicians, and Rebecka, who chairs a grassroots organization focused more on promoting women in rock, also noted that:

> I know that on the stages in Sweden there are mostly men. I also know that there are females ... who are musicians. They are going to the schools and they are not on the stages ... we had 60 musicians on stage, on the festival, over 3 days ... you can see it as a manifestation to everyone who says 'we want to book women but there are none'. (Helena)
>
> it can be hard for women in bands to be taken seriously. To get time onstage ... [we're] both helping the ones who are there as well as show 'hey, this works – we *have* representation'. (Rebecka)

Persistent references to 'missing women' indicate a problem more broadly with changing exclusionary cultures, often including an insistence that current representation reflects some form of 'natural' state of consumer demand. To this end, Nina – who works with allocating funding to women musicians at the national level in the UK – actually commented that a male-identified industry executive explicitly stated that audiences were not as interested in women musicians as a means of defending his own choices for gender imbalances in booking policies. Yet she went on to note that:

> There is this other really difficult reality which is that one of the biggest groups of consumers are teenage girls who love boybands, for example, and so it's ... we're

all perpetuating the status quo in different ways I suppose ... [but] when we first launched the scheme, the interesting point was that: what do you mean? There's Adele, there's Björk, there's loads of women in music! There's more women than men. (Nina)

Decisions on what music to market (as well as consumer responses) are clearly shaped by gendered assumptions. For instance, Donze (2017) highlights that promoters 'anticipate' audience preferences but that they tend to gear their selections more towards male-identified listeners who often have different preferences from female-identified listeners. Similarly, Lieb (2013) notes how executives working in the industries tend to promote narrow definitions of femininity based on their own gendered assumptions of what sells. These data, therefore, suggest active resistance from (largely male-identified) music industry executives towards changing their practice, due to a reliance on the 'missing women' argument and a belief that the industries reflect rather than co-construct consumer demand.

Conceptualizing equality: '50/50' and 'balance'

Given that market actors see themselves as reflecting gendered patterns in either tastes or labour supply, it is clear that a gendered perspective needs to be more firmly integrated into decision making at all levels. Gender equality, according to funders working at the national level, here was primarily conceptualized in terms of counting numbers of men and women or, as Helena summarized, 'the easiest, the first step, I think is to count heads ... Because then you realise how it looks'. This initial exercise of 'counting heads', again, is broadly in line with strategies to mainstream gender through appeals to quantitative representation through 'balanced' binary genders (Walby 2005; Verloo 2006; Sainsbury and Bergqvist 2009; de los Reyes 2016). With regards to these organizations' work, GM was most often concerned with monitoring the number of applications people of binary genders were making, or how many musicians or other industry workers were employed or booked to play:

> ... we want the projects [people apply for funding for] to be 50/50 ... [it's about] numbers – how many. (Sofia)
>
> [we] started off counting how many pieces [by women] are actually played by the orchestras in Sweden each year. (Anna)
>
> [Jämställd Festival – a non-state organisation] have, systematically, put pressure on the biggest festivals in Sweden to book equally and that is 50/50 it's not 80/20 it's not 75/25 you know, it's not good until it's 50/50. (Elin)

Whilst this approach was perhaps more commonly mentioned in Sweden, given the legal requirement placed on organizations funded by state or local government actors to adhere to GM agendas (see de Boise 2017b), this was also echoed by organizations in the UK:

> At the point when it becomes normal to have *half* of the lineup as women, that would be a success. (Cara)
>
> [our project] is all about trying to have a *50/50 balance* of men and women involved in the debate. (Nina) (emphasis added)

The notion of gender mainstreaming as 'balance' has also been a theme in policy initiatives and lobbying strategies. PRS, which lobbies for composers' royalties and performance rights in the UK, also recently introduced the Europe-wide *Keychange* initiative, with financing from the European Commission. This project was explained as ' ... a pioneering international initiative which empowers women to transform the future of music and encourages festivals to achieve a 50:50 gender *balance* by 2022' (Keychange.eu 2018: emphasis added). Similarly, the Swedish Performing Arts Agency (Musikverket) launched an initiative that ran between 2011 and 2014 specifically targeted towards ensuring 'a more gender-equal *balance* in Swedish music life' (Musikverket.se 2015: 3, emphasis added). Here, in both Sweden and the UK 'balance' is understood largely in terms of quantitative representation of binary genders. This means being attentive to the ways in which structural factors impact both on equality of opportunity (working with promoters or organizations to change their policies) as well as outcomes (how many women and men are booked). Yet, despite a focus on providing opportunities for women, it is clear that equality is also seen as affording the same opportunities to women *and* men rather than 'privileging women'.

Importantly, most of the discussions as to what gender equality meant, in interviews, focused specifically on performers rather than workers within the music industries on the whole. This reflects a broader preoccupation in much of public debate as a matter of who is 'visible'. However there was limited focus on other types of industry occupation and discussions of women's 'empowerment' and 'leadership' as key to GM approaches. For instance, Helena and Sofia both drew specific attention to the need to have women in leadership positions, whilst other interviewees focused on the visibility of sound technicians and music producers:

> men work with other men and if there is a gig somewhere and you want to have somebody in you call your friend who is a man too, so the networking is important. So I think that's important to strengthen the networks for women. (Helena)
>
> [We started a] development program for Swedish, female leaders and many of them who did that program are now the sort of, at the forefront ... we [now] have this strong network of other female leaders. (Sofia)

This recognizes that homosocial networks within the industries themselves work to reproduce representational inequalities (Cameron 2015). Given that 'men work with other men', promoting women was thus seen to be a means of breaking homosocial patterns of dominance. This was explained specifically through the notion that women leaders' power and/or influence would 'trickle down' on two grounds: firstly, that women were more aware of the particular situation of other women labourers within the music industries; and secondly that women were more likely to promote music made by women once they were within positions of power.

The limitations of mainstreaming-only approaches

Intersectionality

Whilst GM approaches have been important interventions, it is equally important to stress that there are particular limitations to the approach outlined here. As Crenshaw's (1989) concept of intersectionality demonstrated, gender discrimination legislation in the United States tended to be separated from racial and/or ethnic discrimination legislation. Thus, the particular situation of women of colour was not covered by either, leaving women of colour relatively more vulnerable than either men of colour or white women. As Verloo has shown, in her discussion of intersectionality, GM policies in EU legislation, particularly, run into difficulties when trying to theorize the intersections of race and gender given that there is a tendency to conflate the two and ignore the overlapping dynamics. She argues that:

> The fact that inequalities are dissimilar means that such 'equality' mainstreaming cannot be a simple adaptation of current tools of gender mainstreaming … Moreover, the fact that multiple inequalities are not independent means that such 'equality' mainstreaming cannot be a simple extrapolation of gender mainstreaming. (Verloo 2006: 222)

In fact, the impact of gender mainstreaming on black and minority ethnic (BAME) women in Sweden, in other employment areas, has received particular criticism precisely on the grounds that GM approaches, understood largely in terms of 'counting' binary genders, has often failed to provide support for women of colour because '50/50 representation' promotes women from largely economically privileged backgrounds (de los Reyes 2016).

Sweden does not routinely generate statistical data on racial or ethnic classifications. This makes it difficult to ascertain the scope and extent of BAME women's underrepresentation. Yet, in the UK, a recent report has detailed that whilst women made up 42 per cent of workers in music and performing arts, only 4.8 per cent identified as BAME (Brook et al. 2018: 22). UK Music's (2017) Equality and Diversity survey, too, identified that only 15.5 per cent of the music industries' workforce identified as BAME. Yet whilst women only made up 30 per cent of senior executive positions, BAME individuals made up only 11 per cent. Conservatoires UK admissions data also shows that *no* Black British domiciled applicants were admitted to any conservatoire between 2011 and 2013 (de Boise 2017a: 12) with numbers of applications extremely low. However, whereas Sweden does not collect data on race and ethnicity, the UK does not provide interlocking data on race, ethnicity and gender. As such it is not clear the extent to which BAME women, specifically, are impacted by both gendered *and* racial discrimination within music institutions. An awareness of intersectionality was more frequently spontaneously mentioned during interviewees in the UK than Sweden, owing largely to Britain's colonial legacy and the activism of feminists of colour since the 1970s. Yet the lack of intersectional statistical data on ethnicity or race makes it difficult to ascertain the scale of overlapping forms of marginalization.

In addition, gender identity should be taken into consideration when advocating for gender equality, in that people who do not identify with the gender they were assigned at birth experience different forms of exclusion and discrimination which are not addressed by counting numbers of binary genders. In the interviews, whilst most of the organizations which regarded themselves as women-only were inclusive of trans* women, it was clear not all had even considered the question of self-definition and gender diversity, even those with a remit over strategic funding. Furthermore, there were problems in that, even if spaces were nominally inclusive of trans* women, trans men and non-binary individuals were perhaps excluded from these concerns altogether, despite also suffering from gender discrimination:

> At the moment we say it's for people who address themselves as women, and today when there are many people who don't feel conformed to like one gender that it's not very good way to put it. (Rebecka)
>
> It's a problem because a trans* man has 'grown up female' and ... at some point what [our policy seems to be] saying is, 'if you don't identify as a woman, that means you can't come to group' [... that] they have to self-declare and 'move out'. (Sue)

This is a difficult issue given that, as with race and ethnicity, there are critical ethical implications with creating databases on gender identity and/or expression. Yet the desire to count, or to focus largely on issues of representation and resources amongst binary genders, belies a broader issue in the way in which the concept of GM frames our understandings of gender equality more generally. Indeed, the problem of trans* discrimination and recognition may actively be hampered by a focus on GM in terms of representation (Hines 2013).

Representation, resilience and aesthetics

Critiques of GM in relation to political implementation have been varied. Particularly, some have suggested that, despite its merits, GM reduces gender equality to a variety of techniques rather than focusing on the ethical reasons for working towards equality (Sainsbury and Bergqvist 2009). In this way, GM often becomes an end-in-itself rather than a means to affect structural change. In the worst cases, a narrow understanding of gender equality understood as quantitative balance can be used to promote a de-politicized notion of 'balance' rather than a concerted attempt to fight against historical inequalities. With respect to music, this can clearly be seen in the UCAS

Conservatoires (UK) report whereby the proportionately lower acceptance rate for women is explained thus:

> The acceptance rate is higher for men because around the same number of men and women are accepted to undergraduate courses, but the number of men applying is much lower than the number of women applying. (UCAS Conservatoires 2015: 23)

This assertion is broadly in line with the notion of equality as balance between binary sexes. Yet, a focus only on the numbers of men and women clearly misses the initial political will and history behind GM which aimed to recognize that women are marginalized by implicit forms of bias, sexism and structural discrimination. Instead, by equating balance with numbers of binary genders, this removes the impetus to think critically about equality in a way which works against structural critiques of gendered privilege.

According to my interviewees, a focus on improving representation was also commonly based on two problematic assumptions: 1) that 'toughening up' women* or trans* individuals would 'correct' problems of representation. This ignored the gender bias in selection and recruitment procedures as well as the discriminatory foundations on which certain traditions were built; and 2) that aesthetic practices related to or performed by cis-men were already assumed to be *a priori* better and therefore something to aspire to emulate. Thus, as Anna noted, 'if you don't teach the musicians that will be playing in our orchestras, in the future, this kind of thinking or awareness then you won't succeed ... then perhaps the figure 50/50 isn't the *most* important thing'.

These two problems are related but distinct. The first relates to the idea that 'masculinizing' particular practices in order to make women 'more competitive' solves the problem of inequality. As Fraser (2013) has argued, this is a cornerstone of the way in which feminist arguments for self-determination have been co-opted in the structuring of neoliberal subjectivities. The idea that 'empowerment' means 'competition at the expense of others' becomes a way of disciplining women's labour to the demands of precarious labour markets which are inherently inegalitarian (see Foster 2016).

Importantly, in direct contrast to the notion that power 'trickles down', by focusing largely on women in leadership, there was an admission that women in positions of power occasionally did little to promote other women, leading to little change in patriarchal occupational cultures:

> It's also very strange because it's like in politics or in any other things, like if you succeed as a minority, you don't want to go back, you don't want to talk about it because *you* have succeeded. (Helena)

This individualistic conception of equality resonates with broader critiques of 'liberal feminism' as a sustainable path for transformation. As James (2015) has observed, discourses of 'resilience' and 'overcoming' are an important part of the aesthetic appeal and branding of white, middle class women pop musicians as feminist. However, this works to discipline particular neoliberal feminist subjectivities and fragment collective solidarity, whilst doing little to transform the structural inequalities which privilege cis-gendered men in the first place (see Gavanas and Reitsammer 2013); in short it places the burden of transformation on those who are already marginalized. Thus, as Nina was careful to note, 'I'm in two minds. I can understand entirely why a talented, female songwriter doesn't want to talk about being a woman all the time. And because they are successful, they're the go to interviewee for every subject on it, you know?'

The second problem points to the issue of how formulations of aesthetic critique, even within popular music (Kruse 2002), are frequently gendered rather than objectively given (Battersby 1989; Macarthur 2002). Thus, a focus only on representation as the 'end point' serves to leave the assumption that certain aesthetic expressions or practices, which have been more commonly associated with 'masculinity', are *de-facto* of greater value (McClary 1991: 9–10), entirely intact. This is a problem that, as observed by one respondent:

> ... it's seen as 'better' if girls start to do everything that guys do and I don't, I'm not sure if that's the solution because I know that female musicians can be criticised like 'it's just like girls standing singing, playing guitar' it's not so – you know – 'cool' or whatever ... It's not better because it's loud or fierce, you know [laughs]? Every expression should be worth the same – that is a problem I think. (Elin)

This is an issue with gender mainstreaming more generally in that: 'traditional equal opportunity policies are inherently limited because they mean that women can only gain equality with men if they are able to perform to the standards set by men' (Walby 2005: 326). Whilst the idea that certain musical aesthetics are 'set by men' is problematic, the idea of representation as a goal in-and-of-itself, therefore, negates more fundamental concerns over the relationship between gendered aesthetics and value judgements of musical practice; in short, the tendency is often to focus on getting women into 'high-status' musical spaces or careers rather than to re-focus discussions of status and value on areas and spaces where women* and trans* individuals are already visible. Crucially, in attempts to get women into areas where they are underrepresented, this constructs 'feminine/femme' practices as *a priori* 'deficient' or 'lacking' (Macarthur 2010) instead of broadening an appreciation of aesthetics' relationship to gender. As such, mainstreaming, understood in terms of representational 'absence' or 'lack', has implications for how the conditions attached to resource allocation are shaped by patriarchal frameworks.

Conclusion

There are clear indications that industry executives, conservatoires and state organizations are reluctant to be the drivers of radical change with respect to equality in the music industries; whether by actively working against homosocial, patriarchal networks or through broadening aesthetic choices and recognizing implicit gender biases. It is therefore important to recognize that intervention at state or policy level is one of the ways to bring about meaningful change, either in response to, or as support for, more activist measures and initiatives.

Gender mainstreaming, understood as a set of techniques and practical considerations to affect such changes, in response to broader legislative changes, has almost definitely led to improvements in terms of representation within these two contexts. Furthermore, whilst existing initiatives and public campaigns have been more focused on the number and visibility of musicians and performers there have been limited attempts to affect gendered labour imbalances within the industries themselves, particularly with regards to the number of people in leadership positions.

However, as this chapter has argued, GM within the music industries has tended to focus *only* on representation conceived in terms of balance between binary genders. As such, this ignores both intersectional and more aesthetic concerns. In addition, the notion that women executives' power will 'trickle down' by focusing primarily on leadership does not always tally with experience. These echo broader critiques of GM in other fields such as politics, education and tertiary sector industries whereby a few individuals, often from more privileged backgrounds, are promoted and used as 'proof' against the persistence of inequalities.

In noting the limitations of GM, this chapter does not intend to criticize the individuals responsible for implementing GM decisions and strategies, given that they, too, are constrained by particular political and policy frameworks and expectations. Nor do I want to suggest that GM should be abandoned. Crucially, however, the idea of GM through a notion of 50/50 representation and balance may actively work against the very feminist aims behind political will to mainstream gender. It should be emphasized instead that both focus on representation and a broader intersectional critique of gendered labour concerns (including aesthetic reception) within the music industries need to be addressed in tandem.

Note

1. In line with national ethics guidelines, respondents have been assigned pseudonyms in order to protect their anonymity. Furthermore, respondents provided both recorded verbal and written consent to be interviewed and were informed of the project's aims and scope, as well as their right to anonymity, in advance of the interviews.

References

Anderton, C., A. Dubber and M. James (2013), *Understanding the Music Industries*, London: Sage.

Arts Council England (2015), 'Equality, Diversity & the Creative Case: A Data Report'. Available online: http://www.artscouncil.org.uk/sites/default/files/download-file/

Equality_Diversity_and_the_Creative_Case_A_data_report_2012-2015.pdf (accessed 12 December 2016).

Battersby, C. (1989), *Gender and Genius: Towards a Feminist Aesthetics*, London: The Women's Press Ltd.

Brook, O., D. O'Brien and M. Taylor (2018), 'Panic! Social Class, Taste and Inequalities in the Creative Industries'. Available online: http://createlondon.org/wp-content/uploads/2018/04/Panic-Social-Class-Taste-and-Inequalities-in-the-Creative-Industries1.pdf (accessed 17 April 2018).

Cameron, S. (2015), *Music in the Marketplace: A Social Economics Approach*, Abingdon: Routledge.

CCIL (2011), *The Music Blueprint: An Analysis of the Skills Needs of the Music Sector in the UK*, London: Creative and Cultural Industries Ltd.

Council of Europe (1998), *Gender Mainstreaming: Conceptual Framework, Methodology and Presentation of Good Practices*, Strasbourg: Council of Europe. EG-S-MS. (98) 2 rev.

Crenshaw, K. (1989), 'Demarginalizing the Intersection of Race and Sex: A Black Feminist Critique of Antidiscrimination Doctrine, Feminist Theory and Antiracist Politics', *University of Chicago Legal Forum*, 14: 538–554.

DCMS (2008), 'DCMS Equality Scheme'. Available online: https://www.gov.uk/government/uploads/system/uploads/attachment_data/file/77334/DCMSEqualityScheme20072010.pdf (accessed 3 March 2017).

de Boise, S. (2017a), 'Gender Inequalities and Higher Music Education: Comparing the UK and Sweden', *British Journal of Music Education* [online first], 1–19 DOI: 10.1017/S0265051717000134.

de Boise, S. (2017b), 'Tackling Gender Inequalities in Music: A Comparative Study of Policy Responses in the UK and Sweden', *International Journal of Cultural Policy* [online first] DOI: http://dx.doi.org/10.1080/10286632.2017.1341497.

de Los Reyes, P. (2016), 'When Feminism Became Gender Equality and Anti-Racism Turned into Diversity Management', in L. Martinsson, G. Griffin and K.G. Nygren (eds.), *Challenging the Myth of Gender Equality in Sweden*, Bristol: Policy Press.

'Diskrimineringslagan' (*Discrimination Act*). *Legislation.Gov.Sweden*, 2008. Available online: https://www.government.se/information-material/2015/09/discrimination-act-2008567/ (accessed 14 July 2019).

Donze, P.L. (2017), 'Gender and Popular Culture: A Comparison of Promoter and Listener Preferences for Popular Music Artists', *Sociological Perspectives*, 60 (2): 338–354.

EIGE (2016), 'Gender in Culture'. Available online: http://eige.europa.eu/sites/default/files/documents/ti_pubpdf_mh0216894enn_pdfweb_20170124111005.pdf (accessed 17 August 2017).

'Equality Act 2010'. *Legislation.Gov.Uk*, 2010. Available online: http://www.legislation.gov.uk/ukpga/2010/15/contents (accessed 23 August 2019).

female:pressure (2017), 'Facts 2017 – Results.' Available online: https://femalepressure.wordpress.com/facts/facts-2017-results/ (accessed 12 January 2018).

Foster, D. (2016), *Lean Out*, London: Repeater.

Fraser, N. (2013), *The Fortunes of Feminism: From State Managed Capitalism to Neoliberal Crisis*, London: Verso.

Gadir, T. (2017), 'Forty-Seven DJs, Four Women: Meritocracy, Talent and Postfeminist Politics', *Dancecult: Journal of Electronic Dance Music Culture*, 9 (1): 50–72.

Gavanas, A. and R. Reitsammer (2013), 'DJ Technologies, Social Networks, and Gendered Trajectories in European DJ Cultures', in *DJ Culture in the Mix: Power, Technology, and Social Change in Electronic Dance Music*, 51–78, London: Bloomsbury.

Goldin, C. and C. Rouse (2000), 'Orchestrating Impartiality: The Impact of "Blind" Auditions on Female Musicians', *The American Economic Review*, 90 (4): 715–741.

Hesmondhalgh, D. and S. Baker (2015), 'Sex, Gender and Work Segregation in the Cultural Industries', *The Sociological Review*, 63: 23–36.

Hines, S. (2013), *Gender Diversity, Recognition and Citizenship*, Basingstoke: Palgrave Macmillan.

James, R. (2015), *Resilience & Melancholy: Pop Music, Feminism, Neoliberalism*, Alresford: Zero Books.

Jämställd Festival (2016), Available online: http://jamstalldfestival.se/ (accessed 10 January 2016).

Keychange.eu (2018), 'Keychange: PRS Foundation'. Available online: http://keychange.eu/ (accessed 17 April 2018).

Kruse, H. (2002), 'Abandoning the Absolute: Transcendence and Gender in Popular Music Discourse', in S. Jones (ed.), *Pop Music and the Press*, 134–155, Philadelphia, PA: Temple University Press.

Kulturrådet (2009), 'På Väg Mot Jämställd Scenkonst', Available online: http://www.kulturradet.se/Documents/publikationer/2009/pa_vag_mot_jamstalld.pdf (accessed 1 March 2016).

KVAST (2016), 'Repertoargenomgången 2014/15.' Available online: http://kvast.org/repertoarstatistik-201415/ (accessed 15 October 2016).

Leonard, M. (2007), *Gender in the Music Industry: Rock Discourse and Girl Power*, Aldershot: Ashgate.

Lieb, K.J. (2013), *Gender, Branding, and the Modern Music Industry: The Social Construction of Female Popular Music Stars*, London: Routledge.

Macarthur, S. (2002), *Feminist Aesthetics in Music*, London: Greenwood Press.

Macarthur, S. (2010), *Towards a Twenty-First-Century Feminist Politics of Music*, Farnham: Ashgate.

Macarthur, S. (2014), 'The Woman Composer, New Music and Neoliberalism', *Musicology Australia*, 36 (1): 36–52.

McClary, S. (1991), *Feminine Endings: Music, Gender and Sexuality*, Minneapolis: University of Minnesota Press.

McCormack, A. (2017), 'By the Numbers: The Gender Gap in the Australian Music Industry'. Available online: http://www.abc.net.au/triplej/programs/hack/by-the-numbers-the-gender-gap-in-the-australian-music-industry/8328952 (accessed 12 July 2017).

McRobbie, A. (2016), *Be Creative: Making a Living in the New Culture Industries*, Cambridge: Polity.

Musiksverige (2017), 'Jämställdhet I Musikbranschen'. Available online: https://www.musiksverige.org/blogg/2017/10/25/jmstlldhet-i-musikbranschen (accessed 25 January 2018).

Musikverket.se (2015), 'För Ett Jämställt Musikliv'. Available online: http://musikverket.se/jamstalldhet/ (accessed 31 August 2015).

Negus, K. (1999), *Producing Pop: Culture and Conflict in the Popular Music Industry*, London: Arnold.

Pearce, R. and K. Lohman (2018), 'De/Constructing Diy Identities in a Trans Music Scene', *Sexualities* [Online First] DOI: 10.1177/1363460717740276.

PRS (2016), 'Background to Women Make Music'. Available online: http://www.prsformusicfoundation.com/funding/women-make-music-2/background-to-women-make-music (accessed 5 May 2016).

Sainsbury, D. and C. Bergqvist (2009), 'The Promise and Pitfalls of Gender Mainstreaming', *International Feminist Journal of Politics*, 11 (2): 216–234.

Smith, S., M. Choueiti and K. Pieper (2018), *Inclusion in the Recording Studio? Gender and Race/Ethnicity of Artists, Songwriters & Producers across 600 Popular Songs from 2012–2017*, Annenberg Inclusion Initiative: University of Southern California.

STIM (2016), *STIM Annual Report 2015*, Svenska Tonsättares Internationella Byrå.

Strong, C. and F. Cannizzo (2017), *Australian Women Screen Composers: Career Barriers and Pathways*, Melbourne: RMIT.

Taylor, J. (2013), 'Claiming Queer Territory in the Study of Subcultures and Popular Music', *Sociology Compass*, 7 (3): 194–207.

UCAS Conservatoires (2015), 'End of Cycle Report 2014'. Available online: https://www.ucas.com/sites/default/files/ucasconservatoires_eoc2014.pdf (accessed 5 September 2015).

UK Music (2013), 'UK Music – Equality & Diversity'. Available online: http://www.ukmusic.org/equality-diversity/ (accessed 27 October 2016).

UK Music (2017), 'UK Music Diversity Survey'. Available online: http://www.ukmusic.org/equality-diversity/uk-music-diversity-survey-results/ (accessed 1 May 2017).

Verloo, M. (2006), 'Multiple Inequalities, Intersectionality and the European Union', *European Journal of Women's Studies*, 13 (3): 211–228.

Walby, S. (2005), 'Gender Mainstreaming: Productive Tensions in Theory and Practice', *International Studies in Gender, State and Society*, 12 (3): 321–343.

Women in Music (2016), 'BBC Proms Survey'. Available online: http://www.womeninmusic.org.uk/proms-survey.htm (accessed 12 December 2016).

Wych, G. (2012), 'Gender and Instrument Associations, Stereotypes and Stratification, a Literature Review', *National Association for Music Education*, 30 (2): 22–31.

10

The Gatekeeper Gap: Searching for Solutions to the UK's Ongoing Gender Imbalance in Music Creation

Emma Hooper

Introduction

In March 2018, a small furore erupted in the commercial music industry. David Byrne released an album called *American Utopia* on which he proudly presented collaborations with twenty-five other musicians (Beaumont-Thomas 2018). The work's title, whether meant to be ironic or not, could not help but highlight the album's problem and add fuel to the backlash-fire: all twenty-five collaborators (as well as Byrne himself, of course) were male. The album could just as well have been called *Music Industry Utopia*, as, though the public was quick to notice and critique, the pattern it presented is far from unique. We know now, firmly and without argument, that the music industry is overwhelmingly male. In the UK, for instance, we've had it brought to our attention in terms of festival line-ups (Sherlock and Bradshaw 2017), earning disparity (Jones 2018), live venue bookings (BBC News 2017) and in myriad other situations and statistics. What's notable about the Byrne situation, however, is that it highlights a particular disparity that, increasingly, is looking to be a, if not *the*, key factor in much of the industry's gender imbalance. It's highly unlikely, given his quick response (Beaumont-Thomas 2018) and previous output that Byrne consciously set out to exclude women from his contributors list. It therefore serves as an excellent example of an industry force that is mostly hidden, statistically-obscure, and often unconscious: the power of gatekeepers' informal connections, or networks.

Collaboration in its many forms, and the network connections it depends upon, are an inarguably essential part of any musician's career (see Watson 2008; Crossley 2009). It is therefore troubling that '[t]hese informal social networks often advantage men. Social networks in artistic fields can resemble "old boys' clubs" where information, resources, and opportunities circulate through men's friendship networks and remain less accessible to women' (Miller 2016). They're also so deeply entwined in the social and other non-measured or unregulated areas of one's life and experience that drawing a firm line between what (and who) 'counts' and what (and who) doesn't, in terms of how these relationships function personally and professionally, can be incredibly difficult, as can, therefore, spotting areas of bias or formally measuring or accounting for its impact.

The 'old boys' club' and selection bias (conscious and un-) is not unique to the music industry. But understanding, challenging and rewriting how these systems work within the music industry at the 'gatekeeper' level, both consciously and unconsciously, and specifically in terms of the promotion and *presentation* of creative content creators (i.e. music artists), promises significant potential for impact, and, I'd argue, a novel direction for real, measurable and lasting change. Within this chapter I will analyse two new data sets leading to the conclusion that current gatekeeper practice is indeed a significant cause of gender imbalance in the UK's creative music industry, and will conclude that the introduction of quotas could well be an effective, if controversial, route to lasting change.

What led us here: Methodology

The new data explored and expanded on in this chapter comes from two primary sources, one quantitative and one qualitative. In 2011, promoter and singer-songwriter Nuala Honan and I – a popular music academic, songwriter and performer – co-founded the women-in-music research and action organization, The World Is Listening (based in Bristol). This was a response to a statistic published by the UK's Performing Rights Society (PRS) on their Women Make Music website, stating that only 13 per cent of their members were female (or female-identifying; precise methods of data gathering and labelling will be discussed below). With over 95,000 composer and songwriter members, PRS is the organization that ensures that professional composers and songwriters in the UK are compensated for the use of their work. This statistic, therefore, represented a genre-spanning picture of the overall UK music-maker industry and was a seemingly strong indicator of a particular, gendered imbalance in terms of music creation within the larger scope of UK music industries. Surprised and disappointed by this, we gathered a committee of twelve core members including researchers, musicians and journalists. We sought to delve deeper into the potential causes of and correlations to this gender imbalance in PRS's membership by seeking out related demographic data beyond gender, including breakdowns of membership by genre, age, years active and revenue, to see how and if these additional factors correlate to membership gender.

I therefore spearheaded a research partnership between The World Is Listening's research branch and the PRS in 2012, and together we constructed a project to extract, sort, present and analyse data from the PRS membership databases. This represented the first, quantitative branch of our research. The cooperation, effort and data provided by the PRS was invaluable in this first stage: they raked through their intimidatingly vast troves of figures for us, collecting and presenting the member data we requested for the project, and provided some of the primary analysis (including the figures included later on). PRS membership-data is all self-reported, in the form of the initial information provided upon members' registration (and, in the case of dynamic data, such as financial earnings, tacked to that account and tracked accordingly). Due to the potentially inconsistent nature of this type of individual reporting, this data had to be recovered one member at a time 'by hand', as it were. Great care was taken to protect PRS members and their privacy, and all data was anonymized.

There were various singularities about the nature of the study and the data sourced that required unique consideration. Firstly, since it is unknown if member records were lost when transferring to the electronic system, the earliest data we considered was just after this transfer, in 1994. Further, due to a change in PRS's methods of calculating earnings and earning members in 2015, we set this as our end point, therefore confining our study to the period between 1994 and 2015 (twenty-two years). By the end of 2014, PRS's membership had swollen to more than 115,000; however, approximately 40,000 members have earned nothing since 1994. These members will skew any average figures so all member numbers provided in the report are 'earning members; in each year'. On the other hand, members who have passed away but whose works are still earning (for successors) continue to be counted as members.

The genre data is perhaps the least concrete of that gathered, as genres are entered into the system on a free text field by the member and so a wide variety of genres have been identified, and are subjective. Where these are clear they have been allocated to one of a number of standard genre groupings. Where members have specified more than one genre the primary genre has been used. Likewise, the data regarding gender could, at times, be ambiguous, although less so than with genre. Gender has been determined based on Mailing Name where title is held, or based on name; where a name can be unisex, or only an initial has been recorded this has been recorded as unknown. Finally, we were, unfortunately, unable to gather data regarding the age of PRS members (at the time of earning), as there was an issue within the PRS databases whereby a significantly large per cent of members were appearing without any date of birth listed or entered. Seeking out this particular seam of currently missing demographic information will therefore be a priority in further research.

The resulting report left us with the following areas of information (all of which represent PRS membership between the years 1994 and 2015): membership by genre, membership by gender; earnings by genre; earnings by gender; average member earnings by genre; average member earnings by gender; and genre by gender (including 'unknown' gender).

It doesn't get better: Quantitative findings

In 1994, only ten per cent of PRS earning members were female (2,120 female members, 18,392 male). In 2015, twenty-two years later, that number was only marginally higher, at 14 per cent (6,951 female members, 40,516 male) (see Figure 10.1).

This does not, unfortunately, represent a slow but steady movement towards gender parity. If we look at average earnings by gender over this same period (Figure 10.2), we see that in 1994 the Average Female Earnings was just over half that of the Average Male Earnings; this fluctuated to 72 per cent at its closest point in 2002 (Average Female Earnings in 1994: £1,775.32, male: £3,162.88. In 2002, female: £3,257.56 and male: £4,800.76). By 2015 the Female Average Earnings had dropped to approximately half of the Average Male Earnings again (female: £2,479.54 and male: £5,006.97).

The data we gathered regarding genre was somewhat inconclusive, as – due to both the self-reported nature of this information, and the rather subjective nature of musical genre categorization – 'unknown genre' is a significantly large enough primary category for both female and male (and unknown gender) to make findings skewed and unclear. Although they certainly contain a number of unique interesting points worthy of their own study, nowhere did we find a strong demographic correlation that could direct us towards the specific nature of the imbalance in the UK music-making industry. Not

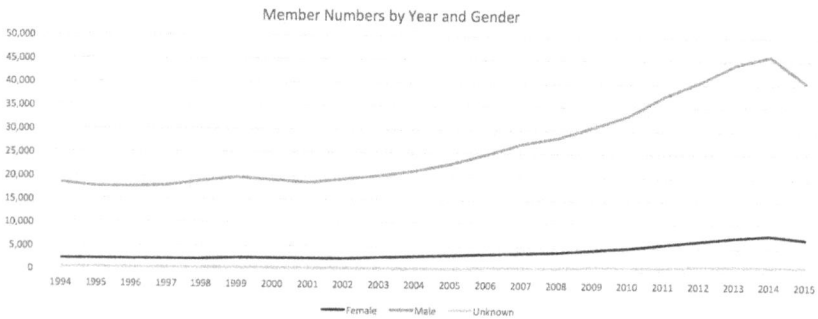

Figure 10.1 PRS Membership Numbers by Gender, 1994–2015.

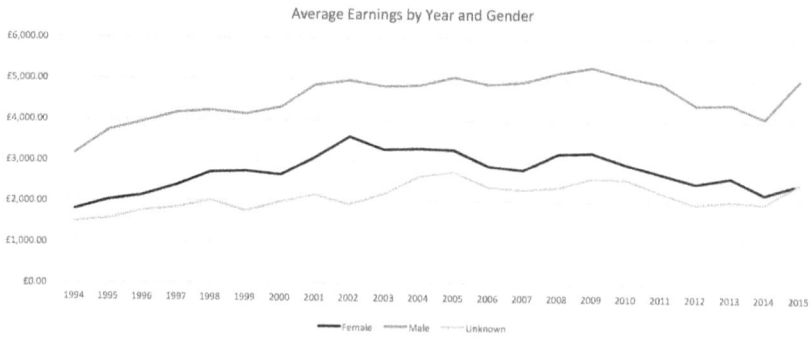

Figure 10.2 PRS Average Earnings by Year and Gender, 1994–2015.

pointing towards any particular quick-fix demographic correlation, our data implies an imbalance spread fairly consistently across membership, earning and genre, and is, therefore, a seemingly strong indicator of an ongoing gendered imbalance writ deep and spread broad within the UK music-creation industries. Other, equally depressing data revealing similar stagnation, though in different formats (i.e. album sales, charts and festival line-ups) can be found in the BPI annual reports (BPI 2017), Music Ally resources (Music Ally 2018) or a quick glance over festival programs over the last few years (Sherlock and Bradshaw 2017).

Interviews

Having learned as much as we could, at present, from the PRS data, The World Is Listening then refocused the project onto the collection of qualitative data, hoping to shed light on more nuanced elements of the imbalance through personal accounts and narratives. In collaboration with Bristol Community Radio (BCFM), and Larmer Tree and Shambala festivals, The World Is Listening members Jazlyn Pinckney, Nuala Honan, Jasmine Ketiboah-Foley and Sarah-Jane Dobner conducted (and recorded) a series of interviews with female music-makers regarding their experience in the industry. Apart from a couple of initial ice-breaker questions, these interviews were intentionally structured to be as open as possible, to allow interviewees the opportunity to steer the conversation in directions they found most pertinent and allow details and stories to flow naturally. All interviews were recorded live on site at the festivals.

Of the dozens of interviews conducted, we filtered down to the thirteen most clear and coherent (four from Shambala 2016 and nine from 2017) where a satisfyingly varied set of voices was still represented. The World Is Listening researchers Sarah-Jane Dobner and I then conducted a structured analysis of this interview set to identify and rank common/recurring themes. The potentially limiting factor of both Shambala and Larmer Tree festivals representing specific, non-universal music events within the larger UK industry (both English, both relatively 'southern', and both catering to a left-leaning, younger audience) was acknowledged, and an attempt was made to nevertheless include as much demographic variety as possible within the interviewee sets, with interviewees ranging from London-based political punk groups, to traditional musicians of Iranian descent, to local singer-songwriters, to Scottish DJs. With this 'cluster sampling' approach (Denscombe 2007) the hope was to extrapolate patterns that apply to other UK festival artists and beyond, to the wider music industry.

The most common/recurring themes we found were: collaboration with other artists; creative expression; and barriers in the music industry. Perhaps surprisingly, objectification and body image was one of the very least common themes, cropping up only six times total across all interviews, as opposed to collaboration's thirty-three mentions. Delving further into context it soon became clear that two of these most-prominent themes, collaboration and industry barriers, were connected to the same general cause of career frustration and obstacles in interviewees: Gatekeepers. The most frustration and, sometimes, despair, in terms of interviewees' careers pointed back that way again and again, as in this representative quote, from a 2016 festival artist interview: 'Who's that person who's going to get me the radio interview I need? If they don't get it, how am I going to go forward?' (female folk performer, Shambala Festival). Or, from a 2017 artist interview, 'I just gave up; I had no way in' (female singer-songwriter, Shambala Festival).

From here we turned our attention to a new, and currently ongoing stage of interviews and secondary research, focusing on gatekeepers, looking to identify why and how these 'cultural intermediaries' (Bourdieu 1984) and their practices could be both the cause and the solution to the problem of gender balance in the UK's creative music industry. Thus far we have conducted 'gatekeeper' interviews with directors of three 'medium-sized' UK festivals (capacities of between 1,000 and 25,000), one festival stage-manager, two regular venue promoter/bookers (urban), one radio programmer and the creative director of one independent label (all anonymized by request). Although this second, gatekeeper-centric interview stage of The World Is Listening's data collection is still in its infancy, those interviews we have completed, combined with our earlier findings and information gleaned from secondary research, have highlighted some distinct, and troubling, patterns in UK music industry gatekeeper behaviour, as well as possible directions for positive change.

A bit of context

What is particularly disheartening, and remarkable, about the seeming stagnation of gender progress in the creative music industry as shown in our PRS data, is that it is news to no one. That is to say, long before 2015, the industry experienced a sharp rise in awareness of the issue, inspiring and fostering scores of initiatives endeavouring towards more gender balance in the UK music industry, including numerous targeted organizations, endeavours and specially cordoned-off pots of funding, for example the PRS's own Women Make Music fund, Music Week's Women in Music Awards, the Women in Music UK organization, myriad focus-on-female-composers or female rockers or female producers media features, and many, many more. Nevertheless, things seem to be improving at a very minimal rate, if at all, and these endeavours can, at times, even seem to have the opposite effect of that intended, as in the instance of an anonymous festival programmer who claimed he'd 'done his bit' after having booked two all-female awareness events, despite the overall gender balance at his festival sitting below 30 per cent (male festival booker, 2017).

It is here, with this festival programmer, and others like him (including the ones who are 'her's) that the stickiest problem sits. It's all very well to say, 'You go girl(s), you can do it!' when, in reality, those who hold the key to this change aren't the girls and women involved, no matter how motivated and skilled, but the industry gatekeepers, whose decisions and patterns of behaviour are based on a number of entrenched biases and traditions that no amount of brilliantly empowered 'female DJs' or 'female drummers' on their own can shake. We therefore need to turn our attention towards these music industry gatekeepers and their practices as both a key problem, and an opportunity for hope in the movement towards a more gender equal creative music industry.

Gatekeepers: Who, exactly, are they?

As a subclass of Bourdieu's 'new petit bourgeois' (1984), music industry gatekeepers as we are defining them here come in numerous forms, with a variety of official roles, levels of status and levels of direct connection to content creators themselves. However, at the heart of it, they all do the same basic job of: 'manag[ing] the interface at which artistic creations are transformed into marketable products and ... play[ing] a critical role in determining what products eventually reach audiences' (Foster, Borgatti and Jones 2011: 248). Or, in the words of one of our interviewees, they 'filter out the shit' (Male promoter, 2017). They are venue managers and radio DJs, festival programmers and label A&R bods; they might be Gary from the pub who books local bands for Friday nights (see Martin in this volume) or a board member deciding on programming for the televised Proms, or David Byrne, an industry veteran, deciding which newcomers to feature on his latest collaborative album. Bourdieu famously describes them as 'need merchants, sellers of symbolic goods and services who always sell themselves as models and as guarantors of the value of their products, who sell so well because they believe in what they sell' (1984), while Foster et al. offer a further, more succinct definition: '[g]atekeepers are brokers who mediate between artists and audiences' (Foster, Borgatti and Jones 2011: 248). Both of these definitions are appropriate to the scope of this chapter; however, I would alter the latter very slightly to emphasize that gatekeepers are those who, very often, mediate not just between artists and audiences, but between artists and *opportunity*.

Despite the highly publicized rise of 'self-made' artists whose stories feature an ascent from nothing with little more than gumption and luck, citing DIY platforms like YouTube (Justin Bieber), open mic nights (Ed Sheeran), or busking on the high street (Tracy Chapman), these situations and stories are overwhelmingly the exception (Watson 2008; Hracs 2015; Lizé 2016), and, often, actually still do depend upon the outstretched hand of a gatekeeper or ten along the way, as with Bieber and Scooter Braun, Sheeran and Jamie Foxx, and Chapman and Brian Koppleman (Harrison 1991; Widdicombe 2012; Lynch 2017). As one of our festival interviewees put it, 'I need all of those people [gatekeepers] to contribute to survive' (Female R&B artist, Shambala Festival, 2017). You can be making the best, most unique musical product in the history of the world, but without the help of gatekeepers, chances are, relatively few people will ever hear it, and any chance of a viable industry career are slim to none (Lizé 2016).

Balancing artistic integrity and risk

While there are a number of factors that gatekeepers must take into consideration when determining which artists to 'let in' or work with (Foster, Borgatti and Jones 2011), generally, it boils down to striking a balance between maintaining some definition of 'artistic integrity' while, at the same time, mitigating risk (De Roeper 2008). The former appeals to the idea that gatekeepers are, the vast majority of the time, looking to promote something 'good' in their own terms and according to their own tastes. As a male festival booker told us, 'obviously I want to book the best, something that sounds, and looks, great. It's not always possible, but that's what I want, and what I'm always trying to do' (2017). The artistic integrity element is at play when, for example, a BBC Radio 6 DJ opts to play the a new demo she loves but that nobody has heard of over a current hit single she knows her audience will respond positively too. While the most obvious iteration of this is in musical or artistic terms, I'm also including elements such as a bent towards novelty, social responsibility or any other factors that play into an individual's 'personal taste'. This would include, therefore, the curation process of one of our gatekeeper interviewees who has committed herself to always playing more than 50 per cent female content-creators on her national radio program.

Hiring and promotion based on artistic integrity within the music business (as with many others), however, is not as benign as it at first appears, and is, in fact, often heavily gendered. In 2006, German researchers Ralf von Appen and André Doehring collected and analysed thirty-eight 'best album of all time' lists, collating theses into one 'meta-list' (von Appen and Doehring 2006). What they found was sociologically remarkable, if not entirely surprising: 95 per cent of the thirty 'best albums of all time' were by white men (all American or British). This is particularly of interest to our gatekeeper study, as von Appen and Doehring conclude, 'any kind of canonization inevitably entails exclusions that can be traced back to the social dispositions of the participants. Accordingly, any canon should be examined and critically questioned as it implies latent claims to power and authority' (ibid: 34). The bias this sort of data represents, therefore, can and does affect gatekeeper decisions regarding what they deem 'good enough' to promote. When our platonic ideal of a great artist is 'implicitly masculine' (Miller 2016: 119), it follows that gatekeepers, despite potential noble intentions, will continue to be working within this system of bias. As one gatekeeper interviewee admitted of colleagues, 'There are people who don't support women. I know that exists' (male venue booker/promoter, 2017). Or, as put to us by another interviewee regarding her industry, 'nobody I know is going to admit to sexism, everyone knows that's not okay, but, still, you take a look at the bands they choose to represent, and count how many women there are ... not many, sometimes none' (female label director, 2017). Miller argues that '[e]valuative bias is particularly problematic for women artists because aesthetic quality is inherently ambiguous ... What appears to be audience preference or innocuous differences in taste can actually be the subtle, systematic favoring of men artists and creative workers' (Miller 2016: 120). This is illustrated by of one of our gatekeeper interviewees, who admitted, 'it can be pretty hard, you know, to find, or think of a lot of "girl-bands" good enough to book' (male venue promoter, 2018). This gatekeeper works in a big, culturally rich city, with a surplus of 'good enough' talent available of both genders; however, having booked predominantly male acts and been surrounded by others booking male acts for most of his career, it's likely any female acts that may make their way through the stickily gendered network onto his radar will still fall outside his model (unconscious though it may be) of what 'good enough' bands look like (and indeed sound like). This problematic pattern is traceable across genres, as numerous other studies have demonstrated (Goldin and Rouse 2000; Bowles, Babcock and Lai 2007; Millar 2008; Cohen 2013). One example of this is the remarkable increase in gender-balanced outcomes when musical auditions are done 'blind' (Goldin and Rouse 2000). Seeing, and therefore knowing the gender (and age and race) of the person making the music you're aesthetically judging can, and very often does, heavily influence how you hear and judge it.

As discussed above, a large part of what gatekeepers do is decide who, i.e. which acts, to 'let in' based on the rather shrouded and immeasurable basis of personal judgement, or aesthetic integrity. In other words: music and musicians they deem 'good'. We now know that the judgement of aesthetic quality is heavily influenced by pervasive, often unconscious gender stereotypes and biases, and that these disadvantage female music makers in ways all the more damaging and dangerous for their relative untraceability. As Miller (2016: 121) notes, '[f]irst, collective understandings of creative genius center a masculine subject. Second, collective evaluations of aesthetic quality systematically favor men over women'.

The second main consideration for gatekeepers is that of mitigating risk, as highlighted by an interviewee: 'I'd love to book only the most amazing acts I can find; I'd love to book only women and minorities, but if I do and then we sell no tickets, well, it's kind of pointless, isn't it?' (male festival director, 2017). Note that the weighing out of the balance between risk and integrity will vary greatly from case to case, though, often, integrity is weighted more heavily in smaller scale operations and risk in larger (Foster, Borgatti and Jones 2011). The 'risk', in this case, is often financial, but can also be in various other terms, for example brand reputation or audience retention. An example of the mitigation of risk element at play was described to us by one of our gatekeeper interviewees as the reason behind an acquaintance of theirs, a Glastonbury 2010 staff member, supporting the booking of The Rolling Stones (i.e. a big, safe name they know will boost ticket sales) despite hating the music (male festival director, 2018).

In a study of rock venue bookers and promoters across the larger Seattle region, Foster et al. (2011: 249) found that a, if not *the*, primary tactic of risk mitigation for gatekeepers looking to book original music producers (aka artists and bands) was their reliance on the large and informal industry social network within which they worked: '[w]e find that talent buyers in markets for novel products maintain arm's length relations with many bands and are embedded in dense communication networks with each other'. The importance of social networks in mitigating the risks involved in musical gatekeeping has also been confirmed in our interviews: 'so often it just boils down to recommendations from people you trust' (male festival booker, 2017), and, again, in numerous local cultural geography studies and observations (Crossley 2009; Cohen, 2013; Hracs 2015). Contrary to the common expectation of a strongly competitive environment where gatekeepers keep their proverbial cards close to their chests, it's been observed that this type of social information sharing is the foundation of how the majority of gatekeeping decisions, including booking, promoting and featuring, are made: 'we compete, yeah, but at the end of the day we need each other; we do trust each other' (male venue promoter, 2017). When much rides on a decision, and the party in question (i.e. the artists) themselves are unknown, gatekeepers are able to mitigate the risk involved by turning to those they know and trust, their own industry and social networks: 'it's scary, booking something you've never seen before. Will they sound as good live as on Soundcloud or whatever? Do audiences like them? Will they turn up on time? Will they even turn up? That's why I either stick with what I know or ask around before booking something else, something new' (male festival stage manager, 2017). The phenomenon at play here is described by Jones et al.'s (1997) conception of 'network governance theory', which 'explain[s] this pattern [of gatekeeper behaviour] because of its prediction that ties among buyers can reduce uncertainty by spreading information about opportunistic actors and producer quality while also diffusing cultural norms and practices' (Foster 2011: 261).

There are two primary reasons why this practice can put female (and other minorities) at a distinct disadvantage. The first is the 'diffusing cultural norms' element. As discussed above in relation to the artistic integrity component of a gatekeeper's function, the cultural norms and practices diffused through such networks privilege existing structures of (often unconscious) bias and demographically-exclusive aesthetic ideals. The second way in which this social and industry connection model can work against female artists is the 'old boys' club' situation discussed earlier. Although gatekeepers might not be overtly trying to book or work with more male acts than female – all but two of our gatekeeper interviewees mentioned being aware of the current imbalance and claimed to be trying to book more female acts – this particular system of risk mitigation is set in these deeply entrenched and unequal patterns. As Ellis-Petersen succinctly noted in a piece for *The Guardian*, 'the problem of a lack of diversity was self-perpetuating, as those in senior positions tended to promote people who were similar to them – mostly white men' (2017). Our interviews revealed the same pattern: 'The people who own the studios, the people running the mixing desk or the people managing the venues or the promoters, they're disproportionally men, so it's not surprising to me [that there is a gender-imbalance in the creative music business]. It makes total sense. It's unfortunate, we have a lot of work to do' (female R&B artist, Shambala Festival, 2017).

This sounds more overtly biased or negative than it actually is; in truth, we are all most likely to have a majority of friends who are 'like us' (Christakis and Fowler 2014), due to numerous causes, many of which are out of our control. This is why the issue is so tricky and difficult. There are no overt 'bad guys' on which to lay the blame, instead, there are bad systems and patterns, which are much more subtle, unconscious and difficult to trace (Millar 2016). This is the issue we see at play with the David Byrne example considered earlier. Byrne didn't set out to exclude female collaborators on *American Utopia*, he was just working within the pool of those he knew to be good and those known to be good by others he trusted. The intent is not (necessarily) gendered, but the networks and patterns almost inescapably are.

These two factors, artistic integrity and risk mitigation, are of fairly non-negotiable importance in gatekeeper's successful navigation (and maintenance) of their roles (De Roeper 2008): '[i]t's hard; it's a continuous balancing act, this [gatekeeping] gig' (female label director, 2017). However, it's also clear that these two factors also both contribute significantly to the stubbornly ongoing issue of the gender imbalance in the music making industry, and need to be addressed in order for us to effect, and see, lasting change.

What next? New strategies, new hope

The patterns illuminated in our interviews and examined above are promising explanations of why the PRS member statistics have retained their unequal gender proportions across demographics after decades of awareness and action. They demonstrate how, often despite awareness and the best intentions, the biased and unequal status quo we've observed persists. The powerful ubiquity of these gatekeeper systems will take more than a handful of bursaries or special edition concerts or magazines to overturn. As noted by a PRS 'Women Make Music' bursary grantee, 'To change a paradigm deeply entrenched in the psyche of established practice will require a monumental overhaul of systematic convention' (PRS 2017a). However, this doesn't mean there are no other, more potentially effective, methods of rectifying the inequality in the creative music business. In other words: there is still hope.

A female label director in our 2017 interviews said 'I'd love for things to be different, to be more balanced [gender-wise]; we all would, in theory, I think ... but short of somebody actually forcing hands, I'm not sure that will ever really happen. Not in my lifetime, anyway' (female label director, 2017). However, in terms of 'forcing hands', something interesting is happening with festivals. There has been a lot of focus on gender balance in festival line-ups over the last few years (Sherlock and Bradshaw 2017; PRS 2017b) and, recently, the big news is of a new PRS Foundation initiative – Keychange – through which eighty-five international music festivals and conferences, including the BBC Proms, have pledged to full 50/50 gender split programs by 2022 at the latest (PRS 2017b) as a new, ongoing, basic standard (see Raine, this volume, for a further discussion of this). This, along with other quota systems and practices of affirmative action, is certainly controversial and brings a host of complexities (Balafoutas, Davis and Sutter 2016); however, this type of approach is quite often effective, as seen in Beaurian and Masclet's recent study regarding affirmative action and gender in hiring decision contexts (2016). This study found that, 'without question, the introduction of quota systems reduces discrimination against women significantly: the employment of females increases' (Beaurian and Masclet 2016: 369). What's more, and notably, they also found that this change occurred 'without negatively impacting overall performance' (ibid: 369), a fear often cited by critics of this type of approach.

Using this same method of immovable, concrete goals and figures, it seems as though the music industry too could potentially escape the 'messy and complicated ... [and] not always amenable to mathematical models' (Crossly 2009: 31) patterns of (most) current gatekeeper practice. Actual changes must come through actual changes to the way things are done, not just, magically, through the desire or awareness of the need for such change. 'I've known about the issue for a long time, and, of course, not been happy with [the situation], but it wasn't until I made actual, firm, rules for myself, making myself commit to playing at least one female band or songwriter for every male one [I played], that I actually was able to beat out my old habits and programming shortcuts' (female Radio Programmer, 2017).

So, what would this 'actual forcing of hands' mean, in practice? I'd argue it means ensuring hardline adherence to these controversial yet effective quotas. It means Spotify playlists, label AR departments, radio DJs and TV, film, and advert music fixers following the example of the Keychange initiative, over a significant period of years. And then, after a significant period of five or ten or twenty years of treading this new ground, the networks will have changed, enlarged, and unconscious gatekeeper bias will have been necessarily over-ridden time and again, until, we can only hope, their traditional, and, as we have seen, flawed methods and networks are rewritten and re-programmed in a more gender-balanced way. 'Keychange? Do I think it could work? Do I approve? I think it's bloody brilliant. I think it's about time' (male festival director, 2018). Of course, music industry inequalities don't end at gender, and this method could arguably be as effective at addressing issues of other currently excluded minorities; this is something worth attending to at more length in future discussions as well.

Like all routes to real change, this would not be without bureaucratic issues and annoyances, or outspoken opponents, but could ultimately, I believe, lead to a more equal, and therefore *better*, music industry, for music makers of any gender, as well as for consumers and, yes, even, gatekeepers, as we allow the best art and artists clear routes to eager, (unbiased) audience ears: 'We've earned our place, in that music, and, in that community' (female Songwriter, Larmer Tree Festival, 2016).

References

Balafoutas, L., B.J. Davis and M. Sutter (2016), 'Affirmative Action or Just Discrimination? A Study on the Endogenous Emergence of Quotas', *Journal of Economic Behavior and Organization*, 127: 87–98.

BBC News (2017), 'Doctor Browns Pub Avoids "Women Singing Rock"', *BBC News*, 8 December. Available online: http://www.bbc.co.uk/news/uk-england-tees-42280212 (accessed 11 May 2018).

Beaumont-Thomas, B. (2018), 'David Byrne Apologises for the Lack of Women on Album with 25 Male Contributors', *The Guardian*, 6 March. Available online: https://www.theguardian.com/music/2018/mar/06/david-byrne-apologises-for-not-collaborating-with-women-on-album-with-25-male-contributors (accessed 11 May 2018).

Beaurain, G. and D. Masclet (2016), 'Does Affirmative Action Reduce Gender Discrimination and Enhance Efficiency? New Experimental Evidence', *European Economic Review*, 90: 350–362.

Bourdieu, P. (1984), *Distinction: A Social Critique of the Judgement of Taste*, Cambridge, USA: Harvard University Press.

Bowles, H.R., L. Babcock and L. Lai (2007), 'Social Incentives for Gender in the Propensity to Initiate Negotiations: Sometimes It Does Hurt to Ask', *Organizational Behavior and Human Decision Processes*, 103: 84–103.

BPI (2017), *2017, All About the Music*, London: BPI Ltd.

Christakis, N.A. and J.H. Fowler (2014), 'Friendship and Natural Selection', *PNAS*, 111 (Supplement 3): 10796–10801.

Cohen, S. (2013), 'Men Making a Scene: Rock Music and the Production of Gender', in S. Whitely (ed.), *Sexing the Groove: Popular Music and Gender*, 17–33, New York: Routledge.

Crossley, N. (2009), 'The Man Whose Web Expanded: Network Dynamics in Manchester's Post/Punk Music Scene 1976–1980', *Poetics*, 37 (1): 24–49.

De Roeper, J. (2008), 'Serving Three Masters: The Cultural Gatekeeper's Dilemma', *Journal of Arts Management, Law & Society*, 38 (1): 51–70.

Denscombe, M. (2007), *The Good Research Guide for Small-Scale Social Research Projects*, New York: Open University Press.

Ellis-Petersen, H. (2017), 'Upper Reaches of Music Industry "a Man's World," Diversity Study Finds', *The Guardian*, 9 January. Available online: https://www.theguardian.com/business/2017/jan/09/upper-reaches-of-music-industry-a-mans-world-diversity-study-finds (accessed 11 May 2018).

Foster, P., S.P. Borgatti and C. Jones (2011), 'Gatekeeper Search and Selection Strategies: Relational and Network Governance in a Cultural Market', *Poetics*, 39 (4): 247–265.

Goldin, C. and C. Rouse (2000), 'Orchestrating Impartiality: The Impact of "Blind" Auditions on Female Musicians', *American Economic Review*, 90 (4): 715–741.

Harrison, J. (1991), 'Persuasion Pays Off for a Talent Scout', *The New York Times*, 20 January: Ll12. Available online: https://www.nytimes.com/1991/01/20/nyregion/persuasion-pays-off-for-a-talent-scout.html (accessed 11 May 2018).

Hracs, B.J. (2015), 'Cultural Intermediaries in the Digital Age: The Case of Independent Musicians and Managers in Toronto', *Regional Studies*, 49 (3): 461–475.

Jones, R. (2018), 'The Music Business's Gender Pay Gap Is Embarrassing and Uncomfortable. It's Time for Change', *Music Business Worldwide*, 4 April. Available online: https://www.musicbusinessworldwide.com/the-music-businesss-gender-pay-gap-is-embarrassing-and-uncomfortable-its-time-for-change/ (accessed 11 May 2018).

Jones, C., W.S. Hesterly and S.P. Borgatti (1997), 'A General Theory of Network Governance: Exchange Conditions and Social Mechanisms', *The Academy of Management Review*, 22 (4): 911–945.

Lizé, W. (2016), 'Artistic Work Intermediaries as Value Producers. Agents, Managers, *Tourneurs* and the Acquisition of Symbolic Capital in Popular Music', *Poetics*, 59: 35–49.

Lynch, J. (2017), 'Jamie Foxx Reveals How He Helped Launch Ed Sheeran's Career', *Business Insider UK*, 26 June. Available online: http://uk.businessinsider.com/jamie-foxx-helped-launch-ed-sheeran-career-couch-open-mic-2017-6 (accessed 11 May 2018).

Millar, B. (2008), 'Selective Hearing: Gender Bias in the Music Preferences of Young Adults', *Psychology of Music*, 36 (4): 429–445.

Miller, D.L. (2016), 'Gender and the Artist Archetype: Understanding Gender Inequality in Artistic Careers', *Sociology Compass*, 10 (2): 119–131.

Music Ally (2018), 'Music Ally'. Available online: www.musically.com (accessed 5 May 2018).

PRS Foundation (2017(a)), *Women Make Music Evaluation 2011–2016*. Available online: http://www.prsformusicfoundation.com/wp-content/uploads/2017/03/PRS-Foundation-Women-Make-Music-evaluation-report-2017-FINAL.pdf (accessed 27 August 2017).

PRS Foundation (2017(b)), *Keychange*. Available online: http://keychange.eu (accessed 4 May 2018).

Sherlock, P. and P. Bradshaw (2017), 'Festivals Dominated by Male Acts, Study Shows, as Glastonbury Begins', *BBC News*, 22 June. Available online: http://www.bbc.co.uk/news/uk-england-40273193 (accessed 11 May 2018).

von Appen, R. and A. Doehring (2006), '"Nevermind the Beatles, Here's Exile 61 and Nico": The Top 100 Records of All Time: A Canon of Pop and Rock Albums from a Sociological and an Aesthetic Perspective', *Popular Music*, 25 (1): 21–39.

Watson, A. (2008), 'Global Music City: Knowledge and Geographical Proximity in London's Recorded Music Industry', *Area*, 40 (1): 12–23.

Widdicombe, L. (2012), 'Teen Titan: The Man Who Made Justin Bieber', *The New Yorker*, 3 September. Available online: https://www.newyorker.com/magazine/2012/09/03/teen-titan (accessed 11 May 2018).

Part Three

Strategies for Change

11

Queer Noise: Sounding the Body of Historical Trauma

Samuel Galloway and Joseph Sannicandro

In the wake of punk rock's Do-It-Yourself (DIY) revolution in the mid-1970s – encompassing everything from independent record production to amateur fashion – a generation of young artists were inspired to pursue a wide variety of styles and genres. Home recording and cassette tape production liberated them from the constraints of the established music industry. In London, a small scene of artists inspired by 'industrial' music pioneers, Throbbing Gristle, pushed past punk's aesthetic of loud and fast guitars, adopting an anti-music approach that embraced the sound of machines and the potential of noise. This fomented a diverse scene that included the whimsical and psychedelic *musique concrète* of Nurse with Wound, the esoteric occult neo-folk of Current 93, the post-industrial avant-pop of Coil, and the 'power electronics' noise of Whitehouse.

Although this newly emerging scene resonated on the periphery of popular music, it was not immune to the constrictive, exclusionary trends of the mainstream. Consisting of Diana Rogerson and Jill Westwood, Fistfuck (1981–1984) was one of the most prominent of the few female groups in the scene. But, while many of their male peers have benefited from newfound exposure in the Internet era – with reunion tours, waves of deluxe reissues and new music – Fistfuck have largely been excluded from critical recuperation. In part, this was because rather than producing studio recordings for sale and circulation, Fistfuck was at its core a scandalizing live act, fusing noise music with (improvisationally consensual) sadomasochistic (s/m) audience-participation performance.

Relegated to footnote status in recent critical histories of the period, and often derided as derivative, Fistfuck continues to occupy a position between noise musicians and performance artists, with BDSM (Bondage and Discipline, Domination and Submission, Sadism and Masochism) as a mediating practice. BDSM later came into use as a catch-all term to describe the myriad erotic practices and relationships that had been previously characterized as 'fetish', a subculture which developed around nightclubs and sex shops, and which drew influence from the writings of de Sade and Masoch, as well as films including Cavani's *The Night Porter* (1974) and Pasolini's *Salò* (1975). This chapter contends that in explicitly fusing noise and s/m, a relationship already latent, but inchoate, in the nascent noise scene, Fistfuck's example allows theorizing noise through queer aesthetic practices of *sounding* the body of historical trauma.

The artistic output of the broader industrial and noise music scene of the early 1980s may seem at best nihilistic and at worst reactionary in its cold abstraction, fascist imagery and pornographic, s/m themes. All of these characteristics, it might go without saying, are *traditionally* coded as very 'masculine' (Reed 2013). When considering industrial music in his *Noise Music: A History*, Paul Hegarty describes the confrontational performances common to the genre as a 'masculine aggressiveness (not restricted to men, but a valorized male attribute)' which 'replaces the (would-be) sexual masculinity of virtuosity', such as the ostentatious guitar solo traditionally associated with rock music, in which soloing up and down the putatively phallic neck of the guitar takes on masturbatory significance (Hegarty 2007: 99).

Such a scene may therefore seem an inhospitable place for a female duo. However, the very fact that the post-punk industrial/noise scene was coded as aggressively masculine tells us something about the culture within and against which Fistfuck staged their performances. Hegarty (2007: 184) further argues that at that time 'male musicians were adopting a "feminine" attribute in refusing skill, or at least in minimizing it'. How did women participate in this 'feminine' refusal of skill, in 'masculine' aggressiveness? Rather than a reversal of tropes, we argue that the induction of audience participation into Fistfuck's s/m noise performances transformed the aesthetic implicit in the genre by actualizing it, bringing into relief the status of the body in noise music.

By resisting the normative diminution of noise, 'an extreme strain of electronic music' (Novak 2015: 128), we are able to recuperate the example of Fistfuck. Specifically, we contend that their contribution offers an historical example that figures then, as now, as a culturally significant and collectively intelligible *sounding* of unreflective attachments to heterosexist capitalism, embodied thresholds of pleasure and pain, and the corporeal inscriptions of historical trauma. In their queer, genre-bending performances, Fistfuck's squealing feedback, screamed invective and s/m performativity cultivated subversively sensual relationships between performer and audience, relationships that played with and tested the power of exposure to vulnerability and precarity to affect meaningful counter-public experiential community.

Fistfuck is an example of artistic production in the face of institutional indifference, and points up the capacity for even neglected artists to leave behind meaningful work under such circumstances. At the same time, however, this means that Fistfuck presents as a partial object, since no video footage of their live s/m-noise music performances exists, an absence which is all the more complicated by the gendered, heterosexist norms of the music industry. Thus, there is a limited archive from which our analysis can draw. By archive, we mean – more than any site, institution or curated collection – the totality of material available to posterity. Fistfuck's *record*, such as it is, presently consists of a contemporaneous live cassette, a vinyl reissue, a dozen-odd black and white photographs and negatives, and a handful of journalistic recollections. To this public record, we add excerpted written responses to interview questions posed via email to Fistfuck's Diana Rogerson and Jill Westwood in preparation for this chapter.[1]

At the same time as we draw on this record, we turn to the thematic and critical resources of queer theory to guide our approach to Fistfuck as a partial object. We do so because queer studies routinely orientates itself around and towards aesthetic and historical objects where the challenge is sustaining attachments to lost, forgotten, maligned or impossible aspirations for publicity under political conditions of worldly impoverishment and social contraction (Butler 2002; Ricco 2002; Love 2007; Muñoz 2009; Freeman 2010; Halberstam 2011; Berlant and Edelman 2013). By the traditional standards of the music industry, there is little value in the poor-quality live audio recordings of Fistfuck that survive. And yet, if what is 'missing' from Fistfuck's archive is a video record of their performances, it is fortuitous that the performances in question enacted scenes of s/m with audience members. We suggest that because the 'missing' s/m is an absent presence in the surviving live audio recordings of Fistfuck, what listeners now hear is a faint echo of what contemporaneous audiences then would have been immersed in, the impact of which continues to resound.

We begin by setting the stage of Fistfuck's historical appearance, their art school training and the fusion of performance art practice with a queer post-punk attitude. We then interrogate Fistfuck's unique hybridization of noise and s/m, arguing in the process that it foregrounds the body as the animate interface of historical trauma which, as such, is capable of magnetizing other bodies together around the perversity of such pain to also be experienced in an idiom of reciprocal relations of pleasure. We conclude by arguing that, despite a lack of recordings, Fistfuck remains relevant as an antecedent to a community of contemporary noise practitioners that has flourished in the intervening decades, who use noise to collectively sound the body of historical trauma.

From art school to fetish club

Diana Rogerson and Jill Westwood created Fistfuck as a scandalizing live performance act that existed at the confluence of art school training, a DIY punk impulse, and the queer subculture of the rubber and leather fetish scene. The deliberate cultivation of an underground scene, the rejection of the fine arts establishment, and an ironic embrace of themes of control put them squarely within broader trends that characterized London's underground of the late 70s and early 80s. Roughly analogous to New York's so-called 'no wave' scene – what Edmund (2016) has characterized as a loose grouping of musicians, filmmakers and artists in downtown Manhattan who rejected virtuosity and disciplined technique in favour of improvisation and amateurism – the artistic foment of Thatcher's London was marked by a similar convergence of forces.

By the 1980s, the hierarchical distinction between 'serious' composers and amateur experimenters was beginning to collapse, especially with the influence of art school students-cum-musicians rising to fame, exemplified by Brian Eno. Understanding Fistfuck's emergence from and influence on this innovative scene requires appreciating the formative forces that were active in the 1970s. The political realities of the 1970s (the oil crisis, 'stagflation', rising tensions over immigration, the decline of traditional working-class sociality, the beginnings of neoliberalism and austerity politics, the ascension of Margaret Thatcher) manifested in obvious ways across a variety of genres, from punk (the Sex Pistols 'Anarchy in the UK') to reggae (I Roy's 'Black Man Time'). The explicitly political content and radical formal experimentation of the music of the 60s and 70s coincided with the availability of affordable consumer recording technologies, alternative media and DIY record production. By contrast, the 1980s are often portrayed as decadent and depoliticized, the training ground for the commercialization witnessed in subsequent years.

At the same time, gendered and sexual minorities cultivated – in the absence of more institutional alternatives – DIY or 'punk' techniques for production and staged less well-documented shows, exhibits and performances (see Frith and Horne 1987; Bayton 1998, and Johnson-Grau 2002). Frith and Horne (1987: 155) remark: 'It is often argued that punk opened a space which allowed women in – with its debunking of "male" technique and expertise, its critique of rock naturalism, its anti-glamour. But the spaces were there because of women's involvement in the first place' [6]. One of the reasons why women were involved at the inception of these scenes is that the means of production allowed wider participation.

However, as Tara Rodgers stresses, readily-circulated 'origin stories tend to normalize hegemonic cultural practices that follow', suggesting the problem of gender inequality is, at least in part, historiographic (2010: 13). Further, as Catherine Strong (2015: 426–427) argues:

> The democratizing promise of punk, whereby anyone could potentially be in a band regardless of musical talent or any other factor, did indeed give women more space to participate in music-making. Their legacy, however, has not been retained in the same way that the contributions of male bands have been.

Strong draws on Lieb (2013) and quotes Assmann (2011), who each remark that even success in more widely-circulated genres like pop does not mitigate against women musicians having shorter careers and, as a result, more rapidly fading from cultural memory because it is deemed as having 'no vital ties to the present and no bearing on identity formation' (Assmann 2011: 127).

A similar narrative has been told regarding the art world by Siona Wilson's *Art Labor, Sex Politics* (2015). Wilson gives an overdue reconsideration of British art and performance of the 1970s, particularly a body of performance work which was directly influential on the musical scenes in question here. In Wilson's telling, the infamous exhibit 'Prostitution', COUM Transmissions' swansong at the London Institute for Contemporary Arts in 1976, and the debut of their rechristening as musicians Throbbing Gristle, stands as a watershed moment and a key reference for the subsequent generation of performers, including Fistfuck.

Rogerson and Westwood, too, are representative of this broader cultural shift towards genre-bending in punk, post-punk and performance art, performing at the liminal imbrication of this queer convergence of influences. Fistfuck blurred the lines of music and performance in a way that has made it difficult for them to be 're-discovered' as so many of their male peers have been in the era of mp3 blogs and deluxe vinyl reissues. In contrast to the prolific output of the DIY culture of the time, the performances of Fistfuck are largely undocumented. No videos are available, commercially or otherwise. This incompleteness stems in part from the fact that the venues available to them – fetish sex clubs, women's art galleries – were not spaces readily conducive to or equipped for video or photographic preservation.

A 1984 split cassette with their peers, Produktion, served as their only contemporaneous release and is comprised of audio from two live performances.[2] Additional live material, recorded in 1982 at Air Gallery in London and Der Putsch in Amsterdam, was released in 2007 in a vinyl edition limited to 150 copies via the boutique label *Welt Am Draht*, priced at fifty-nine euros. The same few photos of Fistfuck performances recur, notably as the cover of that release, and within David Keenan's *England's Hidden Reverse: A Secret History of the Esoteric Underground*, a book which reconstructs the rise of and culture around the musicians Coil, Current 93 and Nurse with Wound. Keenan devotes only a few pages of attention to Fistfuck, generally concentrating on their relationship to their male peers. While Diana Rogerson has since released a number of solo records, including two under the name Chrystal Belle Scrodd in the mid-1980s, these too have been unfairly dismissed by some critics as crypto Nurse with Wound albums, due to the involvement of Rogerson's then-husband Steven Stapleton (Nurse with Wound) in their production.

Even Fistfuck is painted with this brush, despite sounding nothing like Nurse with Wound and having been recorded prior to Rogerson even meeting Stapleton. The online mail-order site Soundohm, for instance, described the *Welt Am Draht* record as such: 'Listing this record as "Nurse with Wound" in the title is not totally wrong as this is a great live performance (1982) of Steven Stapleton's wife Diana Rogerson …' This subordination of Fistfuck's artistic output to the nonexistent contributions of Rogerson's future partner is due, in part, to the fact that Fistfuck's music resists traditional generic tropes that are traditionally coded as 'feminine'. Strong (2015: 426) states the matter clearly: 'Women […] face a greater likelihood of being forgotten if they participate in creating music that has been (or comes over time to be) strongly coded as masculine'. Moreover, Fistfuck's performances, even if they had been well-documented, were not inherently reproducible works. This contributed to Fistfuck's mystique and renown, but also to their historical underappreciation and erasure.

Rogerson and Westwood met at the Sheffield College of Art,[3] where they first encountered punk and experimented with performance art and multimedia practice. Helen Chadwick, one of the first women artists to be nominated for the Turner Prize, was a tutor there. Her work was of particular influence for how it played with gendered binaries in ways that disrupted stereotypical perceptions of the body. Yet, Rogerson recalls 'the only person who seemed at all quirky was Jill Westwood'. Through the filmmaker and conceptual artist Cerith Wyn Evans, Rogerson and Westwood were introduced to a broader network of young British artists. It would be at a screening of work by Wyn Evans and Derek Jarman that Coil[4] would make their live debut, illustrating the imbrication of these underground social networks of artists, filmmakers and musicians, and how important concepts of multimediality were to these aesthetic practices.

Prior to attending the Royal College of Art in London, Westwood, Rogerson and others rented a stall in Kensington Market selling fetish-inspired fashion that paid 'homage to the punk fashion queen Vivienne Westwood and Worlds End'. Their stall tapped into the energy of the emerging fetish nightclub scene and reflected their use of rubber as a clothing and sex material. Westwood notes how they were taken with 'dressing up in rubber garments/costumes' to attend the clubs: 'this opened up another dimension of playing with the interface of life and art. Exploring power roles and experimenting with a dominatrix persona or position. This was in some ways a liberating experience – to challenge the gender stereotypes'. The use of violence in this way by two female artists was all the more poignant, given that violence towards women was dramatically in the spotlight at the time, as serial killer Peter Sutcliffe (known as the Yorkshire Ripper) was convicted in 1981 of murdering women in Sheffield.

Both Rogerson and Westwood produced short films during this period in London. Westwood's films operated in a more surreal terrain, removed from the aesthetic of Fistfuck's performances, while Rogerson's embraced similar subject matter to that of the band. According to Keenan (2003: 108):

> [Rogerson's] most notorious short was *Twisting The Black Threads of My Mental Marionettes*, a harrowing study of masochism that was soundtracked by Stapleton and his friend Geoff Cox. Stapleton has since destroyed the prints but those who saw it – and it was shown publicly around various art cinemas in London – describe it as being a more extreme version of the Fistfuck stageshow, with a lot of sexual humiliation involving hammers, razorblades and cheese graters.

Rogerson describes the film rather more poetically as 'a beautiful ballet of male bodies playing with physical extremes'. Performance art, especially coming out of the radical experimentation of the 1970s (Aktionism, Body Art), was understood to entail an intensive sensory experience that would disrupt and provoke the spectator, and often relied on photographic or video evidence as documentation of a performance.

The name Fistfuck was borrowed from the gay male scene Rogerson and Westwood had become acquainted with through Wyn Evans. Westwood recounts that 'liberated gay sexual practices' served as a point of departure for exploring 'a world of taboo, of some other wild and unknown physical, sexual, intimate, bodily experiences between people – a way of exploding, confronting and questioning usual classifications. Maybe also a pursuit of heightened states of experience through the body'. For Rogerson, too, aesthetic experimentation rhymed with her sense of gendered and sexual embodiment. In her staccato interview responses, she reflects, 'did my thesis on gender ... as a tom boy ... felt I was a gay man trapped in a woman's body ... I shaved my head ... got breast implants ... dressed like a transvestite ... ch[anged] my name to Crystal, and she was a he ... ' (cf. Halberstam 1998). For both Rogerson and Westwood, this period in which Fistfuck was conceived allowed them the opportunity to *live* the experimentation with both domination/control and gender insubordination that would fuel their art.

Another important catalyst for Fistfuck was witnessing Death and Beauty Foundation (Val Denham and Antal Nemeth) perform at the RCA. That performance consisted of a series of improvised encounters between the two performers, wearing makeup and cross-dressing, interacting with each other and the audience, transforming ordinary activities into strange encounters, making sounds from ordinary objects. Westwood highlights this as a pivotal event, describing them as 'Samuel Beckett meets punk'. As we will see momentarily, an aesthetic practice of retuning the sensoriums of audience members to the recurring dissonances of ordinary anticipation proves crucial to Fistfuck's queer s/m-noise performance, as it sought to suspend the normative temporality of punitively progressive historicity to allow attending to what from the past haunts the historical present and, so, conditions collective aspirations for future repair. On this score, it is also salient that Westwood specifically refers to the 1981 Semiotext(e) issue on Polysexuality as an important inspiration for their practice. Here we follow Jennifer Doyle (2006), who emphasizes that queer art is defined by its process, calling into question traditional art historical subject/object relations. This emphasis on queerness as practice results in many artists like Rogerson, Westwood, and Wyn Evans, forging paths that did not strictly coincide with established institutions of dissemination and reproduction.

What is more, while superficially Fistfuck embraced many of the same elements as their predominantly male peers, they did so in such a way as to force men to literally confront their own rhetoric, imagery and desire, often tying up members of the audience, abusing them and humiliating them: pissing on them, knocking them around, subjecting them to aural assault screamed against a background of 'home made tapes' consisting of intense guitar feedback and noise. A telling passage from *England's Hidden Reverse* recalls Fistfuck with characteristic awe:

> They were dubbed by many eyewitnesses as a female Whitehouse. 'Jill Westwood was a fucking superhero as far as I was concerned,' says [John] Gosling [of Zos Kia]. 'She had total bottle. She wasn't scared of anything. She'd get up on stage and do the craziest shit, totally wild performance art. Fistfuck were mental'. (Keenan 2003: 108)

Westwood confirms, stating: 'I think we were inspired by the force and impact of Whitehouse to arrest their audiences. We saw a gap with regard to any female contributions of this kind and we found ourselves drawn towards filling it'. Whitehouse was a pioneering noise group characterized by their 'boy next door' looks juxtaposed with offensive lyrics and an extreme sound. Unlike the legion of Whitehouse imitators, who often uncritically adopted a misogynistic aesthetic for the sake of provocation, Fistfuck's use of these tropes upended the active-passive dichotomy upon which early noise was founded (cf. Keenan 2003; Hegarty 2007; Reed 2013). Westwood herself recalls that their motto was, 'fear is the key'.

Thus, while Whitehouse and others deployed explicitly violent lyrics and pornographic album covers seemingly for the sake of provocation, Fistfuck brought this aesthetic to life through their use of s/m in their performances. And, where punk fashion superficially incorporated bondage gear and wryly flirted with fascist imagery, the role of rubber in Fistfuck's performances was instrumental as much as aesthetic, portending the conscription of audience members into live scenes of BDSM. In both the post-punk and fetish scenes, the lingering trauma and simmering threat of fascism served as a potent trope through which to explore other relations of societal control and domination, as well as the powers of the body to experience historical trauma otherwise, through potentially life-affirming, collective aesthetic practices. Fistfuck's hybridization of noise and s/m hinged on exploiting these tropes towards such ends, *sounding* the body for both its sensitivities to these raw roots and for its capacities to exceed the common-sense bounded limitations of the sensible.

Queer sounding

In one of the few available photographs of Fistfuck's performances, which also serve as the cover art for the 2007 live album, Westwood occupies the stage. She fills it in and sounds it out, performing with mic in hand and clad in a full-body rubber suit, her hooded head cocked back, her pelvis thrust out into our central line of sight, luring our imagination. This photo offers a 'movement-image' of action suspended midstream (Deleuze 2000).

In Amelia Jones's account of 'body art', she suggests that aesthetic work finds its record in the ephemera of a live act, like this photograph, which documents and sustains the 'liveness' of a performance in absentia (Jones 1998). She thus challenges the notion that a spectator's presence grants a more authentic access to the performative work. In dialogue with such accounts, José Esteban Muñoz (2009) works through Giorgio Agamben's concept of potentiality in an effort to queer the absence/presence of aporia. For Muñoz, '[t]he utopian performative charge of [such] image[s] allows one to see the past, the moment *before* the actual performance, the moment of potentiality; and the viewer gains access to the affective particularity of that moment of hope and potential transformation *that is also the temporality of the performance*' (Muñoz 2009: 103, emphasis ours). This queer staging of utopian potentiality implicates the viewer in a collaborative relation made possible precisely by the aesthetic object's partiality: 'the [photo of the] performance, in its incompleteness, lingers and persists, drawing together [a] community of interlocutors' (Muñoz 2009: 106). In so doing, it discloses '[n]ot a nostalgic past but a past that helps us feel a certain structure of feelings, a circuit of queer belonging' (Muñoz 2009: 111).

We propose that both noise and s/m are collaborative exercises in endurance defined by sustaining sensorially intensive durations. Fistfuck's combination of these two practices of arousal makes this commonality apparent. Following Foucault, David Halperin (1995) theorizes s/m as a use of pleasure in the care of the self. For Halperin, s/m radicalizes and proliferates across the body what Leo Bersani, in 'Is the Rectum a Grave?' (2009), theorizes as the self-shattering *jouissance* of anally-receptive sex. What is redemptive on this count of s/m, Elizabeth Freeman (2010) remarks, is its disaggregating impact upon the bodily ego, that it loosens the hold of sovereign subjectivity in the turns of pleasure and pain.

We wish to complicate further this rendering of s/m as a relational care of the self. Westwood characterizes Fistfuck's performances in terms of working through the polarized power-relations between performer and participant that nonetheless enable the fuzziness of intimacy and trust. Westwood would go on to earn a PhD in art therapy and now works in that field, presenting a career arc that suggests one means of fusing art and life quite removed from the violent performances of her past. Rogerson, by contrast, relates her experience with Fistfuck to her past trauma and precarious lifestyle: 'I loved danger ... I lived with a transvestite and nearly got aids [*sic.*] ... I shared needles with addicts ... ' Rogerson's notions of life and art are also intensely blurred. She points out, 'We worked as mattresses [sex-workers] by night as well so we were living the performances'.

Rogerson's evocation of her own history of trauma and abuse is telling. To better understand this aspect of Fistfuck, we follow Freeman further in attending to the historicity of s/m – its emergence as an anachronistic feudal performance at a moment of populist revolution; its post-war repurposing of the accoutrements of fascism and chattel slavery – and, so, its peculiarly sexualized treatment of the body as a receptacle of traumatic history that its rituals re-members (cf. also Sharpe 2010). If there is a 'therapeutic' aspect to sadomasochism it is that, as Freeman (2010: 137) argues, 'however one views s/m, it is inescapably true that the body in sadomasochistic ritual becomes a means of invoking history – personal pasts, collective sufferings, and quotidian forms of injustice – in an idiom of pleasure. This is its scandal and its promise'.

Building on the work of Deleuze (1986, 1991), Freeman proposes s/m as a practice of erotohistoriography that yields a '*suspended temporality*, that is, a temporality of anticipation, poise, readiness ... in short, of attendance' (Freeman 2010: 153, emphasis in original). She focuses on the way s/m is able to revalue historical trauma through practices of pleasure without devaluing the enduring liveness of the pain it referentially incorporates. It is salient in this regard that Rogerson includes reference to personal traumatic history in her recollection of Fistfuck's performances, attesting thereby to the seepage of vulnerability and enjoyment in rituals of repetition and suspension. Indeed, the very practice of s/m 'plays with and literalizes power *as* time' (Freeman 2010: 153).

This attendant temporality creates a 'pause' in putatively progressive historical time, that, like Muñoz's invitation to theorize utopian potentiality, 'does not signal an interval between one thing and another; it is itself a thing, analytically and experientially available, that reveals the ligaments binding the past to the present' (Freeman 2010: 155). Thus, we follow Freeman when she asserts that:

> Despite the centrality of sadomasochism to a paranoid criticism that often seems to insist on a separation between pleasure and analytic rigor, eroticism and historical memory, S/M relentlessly physicalizes the encounter with history

and thereby contributes to a reparative criticism that takes up the materials of a traumatic past and remixes them in the interests of new possibilities for being and knowing. (Freeman 2010: 144)

We wish to extend to Fistfuck's performances these considerations about the utopian potentiality of s/m's queering of embodied senses of historical time by attending to its sonic quality, an aspect of s/m Freeman gestures towards in the title of her chapter, 'Turn the Beat Around', but upon which, unfortunately, she does not elaborate. Indeed, while our supplemental examples thus far have been filmic, the auditory register of Fistfuck's performance is fundamental to the sadomasochistic ritual of their hybrid aesthetics. To further draw out the materiality of the audile components of s/m, we deploy the concept of queer 'sounding'.

We mean 'sounding' as a handy heuristic. While, in nautical contexts sounding explores depth, as in musicology it pings resonance, both invoking a sense of capacity that we do not wish to diminish, we deploy sounding instead in the sense of the queer s/m practice, meaning the inserting of a rounded steel or rubber rod into the urethra. Queer sounding offers an apt way to conceptualize the play with inversion that Rogerson and Westwood were exploring, as its practice emphasizes how inviolable inside becomes the outside surface of contact. Here we follow Deleuze who, when reading Foucault, remarks that 'the outside is not a fixed limit, but a moving matter animated by peristaltic movements, folds and foldings that together make up an inside: they are not something other than the outside, but precisely the inside *of* the outside' (Deleuze 2000: 96–97). The play of sounding with corporeal boundaries points up how the pleasures of activity yield to enduring 'passive' receptivity, as the conceptual phallus is not castrated, but penetrated and, thus, rendered a receptive orifice, a capaciously dilatory sphincter like the anus, vagina, throat, pupil or pore (cf. Dean 2000: 256). Noise *sounds* the labyrinthine ear as one of these elastic folds (Derrida 1985: 11). And yet, in treating not only the ear, but the entire body as a resonant hollow, sounding thus serves as an equalizer that enables mixing two different frequencies of the intensive s/m-noise experience that we will explore in a moment.

While we do not wish to suggest that Rogerson and Westwood were literally sounding audience members at live shows, we *do* wish to accentuate how sounding, as a technique, exemplifies the potentiality that s/m, as a practice, aspires to and plays with. Moreover, the polyvalent resonance of queer sounding allows us to posit a certain homophony between s/m and noise music that, wittingly or not, Fistfuck singularly amplifies. Here we build on Marie Thompson's treatment of noise, especially as she argues that it 'embraces negativity as positive, productive and desirable; as a means of gaining new or alternative sensuous experience' (Thompson 2012: 210). Thompson accentuates how noise music intentionally 'seeks to emulate noise as force'. She argues that '[a]t its most intense, noise music disorganizes the body; it disrupts the organization of the organs. […] Noise music addresses me as matter, rendering the body porous. I can feel it in my lungs, my stomach, my throat; it can turn me inside out' (Thompson 2012: 211).

Noise sounds the body. And, in fact, there are stories of the extreme volume at concerts resulting in vomiting and fainting, most infamously during the early performances of the band Swans (Simpson 2015; cf. Berlant and Warner 1998). Sounding requires an audience, an intimate public to be sounded. 'Our audiences seemed to be accidental', Westwood recalls, but nonetheless open to the experience. 'They all looked a bit shocked but living [sic] the extreme nature of it'.

More pointedly, sounding – both as s/m and noise technique – attests to those tempos, or, better still, durations, of the s/m ritual that are not defined by *beats*, but by expansive microphysical transversals of sensorial thresholds of intensity also attested to by Fistfuck's namesake practice (fistfucking). A beat slowed down simply becomes a record of intensification and passage. Thus, as much as s/m allows participants to collaboratively 'turn the beat around', it is worth remarking that Fistfuck's noise is rarely rhythmic, but defined more by steady waves of unrelenting sound. Instead of beats, it echolalates the tactile contact of bare flesh against rubber. The guitar's feedback often sounds squeaky, frictional, as if the suspended immediacy of s/m's syncopated *beats* are given an acoustically protracted duration and what we hear is the dark sound of passing through a pinprick of potentiality. In this way, Fistfuck's sounding does not dispatch phallogocratic hegemony as over and done with, but rather works through its normative hold on bodies in the historical present by re-membering its potency in a queer idiom of pleasure. Fistfuck's queer sounding densely layers the materiality of temporality and allows us to conceptualize how s/m's tactile beats and noise music's acoustical dilations are interanimating echoes of one another still haunting their live recordings.

Attending to how Fistfuck integrated noise into s/m ritual, and so, conversely, s/m into noise, allows us to see the ways in which their musical act made live the historical traumas of gender subordination in a way that endeavoured a collaborative eroticohistoriography that sounded out the limits of audience members to endure exposure to sexual and corporeal vulnerability. Their shows (and albums, as partial records of these intensities) enabled a counter-public coming together of audience members and performers, where undergoing intensive sounding allowed forging queer circuits of belonging. These are sticky affective circuits that not only sustained the scene then, but which also routed the potentiality for communal sounding into the future, connecting these scenes of gender insubordination and aspirational community to now contemporary artists who are continuing to dilate the noise music scene.

We thus agree with Thompson, who rightly insists that, '[i]t would be problematic to suggest that noise music, as many have previously claimed in the name of the avant-garde, is simply subversive towards musical, and by extension, socio-political codes due to its oppositional status' (Thompson 2012: 217). Halberstam, in *The Queer Art of Failure* (2011), makes a similar intervention relative to queer s/m sex, problematizing straightforward claims to its transgressive and oppositional potential. Sensitive to these critiques, we suggest that Fistfuck's performances were affirmative and affected a space for community building through a shared affective attunement to the suspended temporalities of sounding.

Where the boys had the protection of leather *hides*, Rogerson and Westwood don black rubber body suits that cling tightly, accentuating the body's constitutive vulnerability and exposure, even in prophylaxis. Fistfuck's performance of queer sounding intrusively asserts a claim on counter-public space – the gallery, the 'scene', the stage – that is unabashedly erotic and hardly naïve about gender subordination. That this display was on the surface was also the point, as it sought an intimate publicity that is, 'like punk, a modality of performance that is aesthetically and politically linked to populism and amateurism' (Muñoz 2009: 100).

Sounding the body politic

Remembering the distinct contributions Fistfuck made at the emergence of the noise scene – their hybrid articulation of the performance of noise with s/m audience participation – is important in its own right, as this furnishes posterity with a more complete account of the history of this period. And yet, this incompleteness is in no small measure symptomatic of the gender inequality that relegates women's participation in musical scenes, like noise, to only of minor, supplemental importance. To this extent, then, recovering Fistfuck as we have endeavoured to do is also a matter of correcting the record, an effort that further primes us to perceive differing, often more complex deployments of noise today.

Through the concept of sounding, we have demonstrated the ways in which the ostensibly passive act of listening to noise is reconfigured as the active attendance of embodied receptivity. Rather than fetishize the putatively autonomous, reproducible record, amplifying Fistfuck's subversive practice throws analytic focus on the experiential, relational and social conditions of possibility that enabled their performances, a potentiality that continues to give noise critical edge today. In this way, Rogerson and Westwood were able to confront attachments to not only personal trauma but world-historical gender subordination in a collaborative ritual of sounding the limits of the body as a propaedeutic to dilating the limits of the socio-political imaginary.

Thus, we might understand appeals to Rogerson or Westwood as 'valuable' because of their either maternal or matrimonial roles in an aggressively male-dominated scene precisely as a way of supplementing this anxiously perceived deficiency of exchange-value (e.g. the dearth of 'authenticating' recordings or other documentation of their performances). Through Gayle Rubin's (1975) 'notes on the "political economy" of sex', we see how Fistfuck have been rendered the object of exchange, a traffic in women that produces value by bringing together men. It is against this often unreflective heterosexist, patriarchal capitalism that we contend that the queer practice of sounding through s/m-noise performance provoked precisely an intimate, resounding critique of value in its own right.

When heard in this register, what the live record replays as precisely a failure (in terms of capitalist exchange-value) is nevertheless one that also intentionally presents itself as, at the least, recording the potential opportunity to experience the communal amplitude of the body's sensuous powers. This failure, in other words, succeeded in opening a tenuously reciprocal relation between performer and audience that worked to turn inside-out the terms of bodily exposure and vulnerability by soliciting attention to the historical life of precarity. In this way, we understand Rogerson and Westwood to have been 'filling a gap' in the noise scene, as they duly claim to have done, not simply by virtue of representing women with 'bottle', but also by acting as its performative, immanent critique.

This was a critique that signalled the need for greater female participation in excess of their own contributions. Further, it was an immanent critique of the masculinist prerogative to violence that sounded out, and thus reattuned sensitivity to, common conditions of exposure and vulnerability. Finally, Fistfuck's performances worked to invoke, so as to sound, and thereby temporarily suspend, the propulsion of a historical narrative that writes women out of history, that subordinates them to their male peers, and which polices gender presentation, sexuality, and expressions of minoritarian power and community. Taken together, Fistfuck thus suggest one way in which 'the aesthetic fuels the political imagination', intrusively dilating spaces of appearance to allow for collaborative expressions of and experiences in dissonance to proliferate on the body, and the body politic (Muñoz 2009: 106).

Excavating and attending to the historical example of Fistfuck sensitizes us to more recent, more nuanced and complex uses of noise music to sound, and in this way re-member, a panoply of live, often intersecting traumatic histories. In this regard, one way to gauge the continuing resonance of Fistfuck is attested to by the relatively high proportion of female, queer, and trans artists in the contemporary noise scene. Thus, where Rogerson had to make it a point of pride that 'even within outsiders I was an outsider', today there is a thriving, if underground, scene inflected by the absent presence of Fistfuck's ground-breaking intervention.

Pharmakon's disconcerting noise disorganizes the body of sexual difference by inducing a queasy slippage of physical limits into, against, and past one another. Dreamcrusher's self-described 'nihilist queer revolt music' aggressively sounds audience members, countering with noise (and physical confrontation) the quotidian and spectacular violence that routinely subjugates black and genderqueer bodies. Similarly, TRNSGNDR/VHS stages noise performances that insist upon inhabiting these scenes of violence without compromising reparative demands for recognition and redress, resisting both the white-washing of artistic production and the erasure of trans visibility: 'I'm just gonna do a noise project that's openly queer' (Savage Levenson 2016). Perhaps, then, if we concede Fistfuck's role in and impact on the noise scene is 'maternal', it would have to be relative to the adoptive, often aspirational relations of queer kinship and filiation that, in their enactment, give life to a divergent, underground genealogy.

Still, our purpose is not to lodge a claim to any outstanding debt, as if these current performers owe to Fistfuck their successes. Rather, what we wish to punctuate is how for these diverse musicians, noise allows the pain of traumatic history to be sounded in a queer aesthetic idiom of collective bodily pleasure. At the centre of this practice is a physical relationship wherein the body is explicitly attended to as the locus of history as it is lived in the present, in its suffering and ecstasy. These artists use noise to sound the body to arouse, provoke, and even threaten to overwhelm the sensorium of auditors as it suspends them, attentive, in the resonantly live traumatic histories of misogynistic gender subordination, white supremacy and the afterlife of slavery, cis-centric heterosexism, capitalist exploitation and reactionary xenophobic nativism.

Fistfuck's commitment to a subversive performance that fused noise and s/m, though resisting commodity fetish by staging scandalous live acts, did not mitigate, but rather accelerated, their erasure from the historical record. Yet, ironically, this is the very same practice that, we argue, promises a way of accessing the utopian intensities of the aesthetic rituals that animated Fistfuck's solicitous suspension of the otherwise unceasing propulsion of traumatic history. This is done through the potential for communal exposure to sexual and gender domination to challenge, spoil and transform – *queer* – common-sense sensibilities about the embodied historicity of power, beauty, pleasure and pain. In the interval that is this suspension we hear – *feel* – the echoes of an absent presence, and this is a corporeal, affective record of the potential for femme, queer, trans and racially minoritized subjects to, themselves, risk collaboratively sounding out the scene of the museum, stage, studio and beyond with a reparative critique that nevertheless still insists upon what will always be dissonant – *noise* – in even the best of efforts to sound-out both ordinary and spectacular trauma. What we are left with is a practice of care, a technique of communally attending to the body that does not erase what is painful for the sake of what can be collectively enjoyed, and which sustains precarious attachments to the potential for future repair by sounding the body of historical trauma.

Notes

1. All unattributed quotations are drawn from interviews J. Sannicandro conducted with Rogerson and Westwood by email between 2016 and 2018.
2. Fistfuck was also featured on the *Propagandum* (1984) cassette compilation under the name Alsatan Dogs, a joint release by Staaltape (Netherlands) and Club Moral (Belgium).
3. The Sheffield College of Art would later become the Psalter Lane campus of Sheffield City Polytechnic, now part of Sheffield Hallam University.
4. Coil were obviously queer, as the group was centred around the personal and creative partnership between John Balance and Peter 'Sleazy' Christopherson.

References

Assmann, A. (2011), *Cultural Memory and Western Civilisation: Functions, Media, Archives*, Cambridge: Cambridge University Press.
Bayton, M. (1998), *Frock Rock*, Oxford: Oxford University Press.
Berlant, L. and L. Edelman (2013), *Sex, or the Unbearable*, Durham: Duke University Press.
Berlant, L. and M. Warner (1998), 'Sex in Public', *Critical Inquiry*, 24 (2) (Winter): 547–566.

Bersani, L. (2009), *Is the Rectum a Grave? And Other Essays*, Chicago: University of Chicago Press.
Butler, J. (2002), *Antigone's Claim: Kinship between Life and Death*, New York: Columbia University Press.
Dean, T. (2000), *Beyond Sexuality*, Chicago: University of Chicago Press.
Deleuze, G. (1986), *Cinema 1: The Movement Image*, trans. Hugh Tomlinson and Barbara Habberjam, Minneapolis: University of Minnesota Press.
Deleuze, G. (1991), *Masochism*, trans. Jean McNeil and Aude Willm, New York: Zone Books.
Deleuze, G. (2000), *Foucault*, trans. Seán Hand, Minneapolis: University of Minnesota Press.
Derrida, J. (1985), *The Ear of the Other*, trans. Avital Ronell, New York: Schocken Books.
Doyle, J. (2006), 'Queer Wallpaper', in D. Preziosi (ed.), *The Art of Art History: A Critical Anthology*, 391–401, Oxford: Oxford University Press.
Edmund, M. (2016), 'Deracination, Disembowelling and Scorched Earth Aesthetics: Feminist Cinemas, No Wave and the Punk Avant Garde', *Senses of Cinema*, September. Available online: http://sensesofcinema.com/2016/american-extreme/ (accessed 24 March 2018).
Freeman, E. (2010), *Time Binds: Queer Temporalities, Queer Histories*, Durham, NC: Duke University Press.
Frith, S. and H. Horne (1987), *Art into Pop*, London: Methuen.
Halberstam, J. (1998), *Female Masculinity*, Durham, NC: Duke University Press.
Halberstam, J. (2011), *The Queer Art of Failure*, Durham, NC: Duke University Press.
Halperin, D. (1995), *Saint Foucault: Towards a Gay Hagiography*, New York, Oxford University Press.
Hegarty, P. (2007), *Noise/Music: A History*, New York: Continuum.
Johnson-Grau, B. (2002), 'Sweet Nothings: Presentation of Women Musicians in Pop Journalism', in S. Jones (ed.), *Pop Music and the Press*, 202–218, Philadelphia: Temple University Press.
Jones, A. (1998), *Body Art/Performing the Subject*, Minneapolis: University of Minnesota Press.
Keenan, D. (2003), *England's Hidden Reverse: A Secret History of the Esoteric Underground*, London: SAF Publishing.
Lieb, K. (2013), *Gender, Branding and the Modern Music Industry*, New York: Routledge.
Love, H. (2007), *Feeling Backward*. Cambridge: Harvard University Press.
Muñoz, J.E. (2009), *Cruising Utopia: The Then and There of Queer Futurity*, New York: NYU Press.
Novak, D. (2015), 'Noise', in D. Novak and M. Sakakeen (eds.), *Keywords in Sound*, 125–138, Durham, NC: Duke University Press.
Reed, A.S. (2013), *Assimilate: A Critical History of Industrial Music*, New York: Oxford University Press.
Ricco, J.P. (2002), *The Logic of the Lure*, Chicago: University of Chicago Press.
Rodgers, T. (2010), *Pinks Noises*, Durham, NC: Duke University Press.
Rubin, G. (1975), 'The Traffic in Women: Notes on the "Political Economy" of Sex', in R.R. Reiter (ed.), *Toward an Anthropology of Women*, 59–72, New York: Monthly Review Press.

Savage Levenson, M. (2016), 'TRNSGNDR/VHS and the Art of Confrontation', *Bandcamp Daily*, 15 August. Available online: https://daily.bandcamp.com/2016/08/15/trnsgndr-vhs-interview/ (accessed 12 December 2018).

Simpson, D. (2015), 'Interview: Swans' Michael Gira: "Audiences Would Flee … We Took to Locking the Doors"', *The Guardian*, 6 May.

Sharpe, C. (2010), *Making Monstrous Intimacies: Making Post-Slavery Subjects*, Durham, NC: Duke University Press.

Strong, C. (2015), 'Shaping the Past of Popular Music: Memory, Forgetting and Documenting', in A. Bennett and S. Waksman (eds.), *The Sage Handbook of Popular Music*, 418–433, London: Sage.

Thompson, M. (2012), 'Music for Cyborgs: The Affect and Ethic of Noise Music', in M. Goddard, B. Halligan and P. Hegarty (eds.), *Reverberations*, 207–218, New York: Continuum.

Wilson, S. (2015), *Art Labor, Sex Politics: Feminist Effects in 1970s British Art and Performance*, Minneapolis: University of Minnesota Press.

12

'There's No Money in Record Deals and I'm Not Looking to Be Taken Advantage Of': Princess Nokia and Urban Feminism in a New Era of Hip-Hop

Hodan Omar Elmi

Introduction

Artist Princess Nokia's LP *1992 Deluxe* redefined feminism for me, filling the silences between the personal and the political. Hearing the lyric 'Who that is ho? That girl is a tomboy' and 'My little titties and my phat belly' from the track *Tomboy* drove me to revisit and reassess my own inconsistencies with gender normativity; poor diaspora femme, second-hand mismatched clothes, loud and no fucks – exploring the love of myself in multiplicity. It is the rawness of *1992 Deluxe* that arguably brought the pedagogy of the oppressed people back to hip-hop culture. Princess Nokia's idiosyncratic engagement with her creativity and social positioning in the music industry as an Afro-Nuyorican woman with Tiano roots demonstrates the relationship between marginalization, creativity and integration into commercial music production. Princess Nokia's success is important because of her integrity and commitment to staying true to the process of cultivating a music style that is representative of herself and the values she represents. Working in the context of a weaker music industry after the advent of digitized music streaming, Princess Nokia's commercial success, in conjunction with the success of her contemporaries, is a testament to the liberatory work conducted by marginalized artists and thinkers operating in this field. This includes women and gender non-binary rappers, hip-hop feminists and young women of colour creating a global community of support for each other and their respective artistic contributions.

'Urban feminism' was coined by Princess Nokia's organization Smart Girl Club, a women's collective in New York and a radio show. Smart Girl Club's aim is to create a consciousness-raising space for women of colour that puts their needs first, whether this is in relation to spirituality, well-being, safety or economic independence. Smart

Girl primarily targets womxn who have had experiences with systemic poverty and institutional racism in New York. Urban feminism as articulated by Princess Nokia is:

> a tangible form of feminism that is accessible [to those] who do not have access to the institutionalised forms of feminism that are largely represented in higher education, the women's liberation movement and women's' studies. It does not require a class, degree or the reiteration of author or a textbook, but is happily accepted and studied. It is feminism for the oppressed ghetto woman of the inner city who knows not the word, but knows she deserves to be free of all patriarchal limitations. (Frasqueri 2017b: 29 min 47-30 min 12)

Urban feminism is what feminism should have been all along; a space in which all women were able to name patriarchy and critically assess it in their respective circumstances.

In this paper, I will unpack the epistemology of hip-hop and its integration into commercial music and cultural industries. I will dissect the racialized origins of the perceived gender problem in hip-hop, and feminist agency in the building of praxis in hip-hop culture. This includes hip-hop feminism and intragroup urban black diasporic politics as forms of intersectional resistance to white hegemony. In the latter part of the chapter, I will be assessing the commercial success of Princess Nokia's music and message, and how this was achieved outside of the larger structures of a masculine, capitalist driven music industry. Moreover, I shall be exploring how her commercial success was strengthened by her principles as a feminist, activist and positionality as a poor Latinx womxn. Her work is part of the ongoing legacy of the cultural improvisation of the oppressed – in essence how hip-hop started in defiance of the odds.

Gender trouble and the rise of hip-hop

Hip-hop is remarkable because of how it creates a relationship between black cultural aesthetics and the political through the emergence of lived theory by the means of dialogical discursive practices; using African American urban vernacular via rap, visual art (graffiti, film, fashion and dance) and music production to articulate socio-political and economic issues facing (initially) the post-industrial east coast (Rose 1994; Alridge and Stewart 2005). With its beginnings in the Bronx, hip-hop incorporates many aspects of history, including civil rights, black power and the migration of (post) colonial Caribbean people.

Rap music, in the early years of hip-hop, often created narratives about social conditions such as poverty, institutional racism and the enclosed social world of the black and Latino people residing in the ghetto. Hip-hop is advertently political because of how the lyricism, the music videos (often set in abandoned car parks, playgrounds or subway) and graffiti and its representation of an array of community members and the 'posse', reproduces the narratives, images and soundscapes of the marginalized. It is in the meanings created through the imagery of deindustrialization and racialized bodies left behind that we see the interplay between 'pleasure and power' and how this can be used as a site of transformation (Rose 1994: 22). Hip-hop's interaction with history is what George Lipsitz refers to as a 'dialogical' criticism, by which it articulates ideas concerning the social world that are overlooked. More specifically, with the case of musical production, hip-hop reflects those considered to be of 'low-culture' and allows us to decipher the tensions between marginalized people, power, expression, self-definition and institutions (Rose 1994: 148). As a cultural product, hip-hop helped consolidate an aesthetic landscape that represented the lives of young people between 1980 and 1997 (Rose 1994; Alridge and Stewart 2005).

Hip-hop's integration into mainstream popular culture was slow; rap artists experienced more censorship compared with their white contemporaries. *Yo! MTV raps* from 1988, and high profile magazines such as *The Source* and *Vibe*, proved to be successful with young people of all demographics, even in white suburbia. Rap was sold as not just a music genre that reflected the black experience but as a 'life-style' having an enormous impact on luxury brands and apparel (Chang 2005). This embrace of black culture from margin to centre is fairly novel given America's relationship with it and the people it belonged to. The following poses a few questions on the potential of hip-hop to act as a cultural resource for black and brown people to enjoy amongst each other, for them to build bridges with the rest of the world or to be used as a praxis of resistance.

As hip-hop found its way to the centre of mainstream culture, this visibility led to a cultural blacklash from White America, which incorporated a gendered element. Tricia Rose notes that 'media attention on rap music has been [focused on] extremist tendencies within rap, rather than the day to day cultural forces that enter hip-hop's vast dialogue' (Rose 1994: xiii). Hip-hop's integration into the market had many implications for the content of pop music; record companies often expressed more interest in producing audio-visual content that centred hegemonic ideations concerning the gendering of black/Latino urban cultures. The resulting representation of rap music with illicit sexual content for a wider audience must be explored as a fetish, with black sexuality represented as deviant. Hip-hop sales soared with the advent of Gangsta rap (a subgenre of hip-hop that discussed overt sexism towards women and the realities of criminal activity, even perhaps glamourizing these) and attracted a demographic – white men – previously outside of hip-hop's main audience. The 'booty' in hip-hop culture became a symbol of pathological sexuality that would entertain the mainstream white gaze. Moreover, the explicit gendering of the black body through the symbolism of the booty in fact re-centred a historic relationship to racialized difference via the sexuality (Collins 2004).

Black feminist theorist Patricia Hill Collins (2004) refers to white fixation on black sexual politics as a production of 'new racisms', which in the age of globalization and mass media utilize epistemic violence and hegemonic gendering of black women and men in racist, fixed categories, including mammy, gangsta and welfare queen. The ongoing discourses positioning hip-hop as 'misogynistic' or capitalistic are contentious ones considering the array of internal tensions and external institutional forces that work to reproduce existing trajectories relating to race, gender and the colonial. Similarly, in the video series *Cultural Criticism and Transformation*, bell hooks argues that the media's fascination with 'women' is used to colonize hip-hop culture in ways that mean 'white consumers can extract whatever they want'. However, the emergence of Gangsta Rap raised interesting questions about what made hip-hop, hip-hop. The gender problem in hip-hop was always centred on the way the question or problem was even structured to begin with, and as such the following discussions on hip-hop serve as a microcosm of similar issues of power across society (Rose in Lipsitz 2013). Hip-hop is an assemblage of the extremities of the hopes and failures of people; the contradictions and the aspirations. It is somewhere between those spheres that art, improvisation and the dialogic coalesce to give us an intersectional perspective on black and Latino urban life.

Joan Morgan's (1999) seminal book *When Chickenheads Come Home to Roost* described what we have come to understand as hip-hop feminism. This is a third-wave feminism that speaks to gender dynamics in the context of greater violence existing in the urban metropolis. Moreover, hip-hop feminism primarily speaks to young black women who feel a discomfort applying black feminist analysis to gender in hip-hop, but also the women that have not been able to articulate feminism as it would immediately be received as anti-men. It is also speaking to the wider world, and is building on a variety of feminist trajectories. As a third wave, self-reflexive, feminist praxis to be articulated outside of the binaristic moral perimeters of the second-wave, the most significant contribution of hip-hop feminism is to 'fuck with the greys' (Morgan 1999). This involves letting go of a strict moral conception of what liberation looks like and how one participates in it.

Morgan highlights that gender tensions between black men and women do not exist in isolation. For instance, many women who associate with rappers willingly utilize their sexuality for financial gain. To remove a woman's agency is to invalidate women as active participants in illicit sexual economies that promote a hypersexualized image of black women for financial gain in a capitalist system; using tools readily available in a difficult economic environment. Hip-hop feminism uses feminist consciousness-raising in conjunction with critical theory that challenges mainstream discourses that exclusively position women as passive recipients of culture and patriarchy, as opposed to becoming the agents of change within their communities. Hip-hop feminism is what Morgan refers to as an articulation against feminist 'complacency' in black, urban communities among the hip-hop generation (Morgan 1999: 23). The attack against hip-hop misogyny has racialized the phenomenon as opposed to understanding the nuances of intersectional violence against women living in this context.

Having difficult conversations concerning hip-hop and women community, building is made possible by looking 'inward' as opposed to simply denouncing men as a 'problem' (Morgan 1999). Morgan re-centres hip-hop as praxis, as a system of knowledge and dialogical interaction that is open to tension and contradiction. This is absolutely crucial because it looks to hip-hop culture to create the solutions to the problems of socially-specific gender tensions experienced by a generation of young black people. Morgan seeks to create an active dialogue between men and women of the hip-hop generation through feminist principles that liberate men from the limitations and harms (such as substance abuse and violence) of black masculinity in urban specific contexts (Morgan 1999: 61). Aisha Durham and Brittney Cooper, two hip-hop feminists, have renewed Morgan's concept of hip-hop feminism in the Crunk Feminist Collective (CFC). Today's hip-hop feminists, such as the CFC, have embraced the contradictions of desire and empowerment 'because failure to do so relegates feminism to an academic project that is not politically sustainable beyond the ivory tower' (Durham, Cooper and Morris 2013: 723). By using creativity to bring together the difference and contradiction through a 'percussive' methodology, CFC explores two different sites of inquiry that are mutually beneficial to each other.

Hip-hop feminism is 'percussive' in that it is a departure from a specific, if latent, form of normativity that permeates black social life: respectability politics. Respectability refers to a mode of behaviour that is associated with propriety, appropriateness and respect (ibid: 725). Hip-hop feminism in the digital age, on the other hand, re-imagines what we deem as representable for us by reclaiming ratchet as a cultural resource that can combat the normativity of racialized bodies. In a 2016 lecture for the RVCC Women's Center, Cooper defines 'ratchetness' as 'a range of African American practices and working class practices that exceed the bounds of respectability and propriety and they find their articulation in excess in being extra and doing the most' (Cooper 2016). The intentionality or excess is performative and is defined in opposition to respectability. It is a direct challenge and process in which working class African Americans break down respectable norms through this cultural performance of 'excess'. This includes challenging the hierarchy of knowledge within hip-hop and academia over what is considered respectable or critical enough to be deemed 'feminist'.

Hip-hop feminists have used platforms such as SoundCloud, Myspace and YouTube as a means of disseminating their music (see Durham, Cooper and Morris 2013). The internet allows access to a wider range of audiences and has showcased the talents of artists that have previously not received mainstream recognition and support by record labels based on 'sales'. The more egalitarian nature of independent platforming has, to some extent, provided internet consumers (who are largely free to listen to any given artist at a whim) with more access to hip-hop artists of all genders. The digitalization of the music industry potentially played a role in bringing unknown artists to the forefront. This doesn't necessarily mean that all new music is necessarily socially conscious, but it has opened the gate for hip-hop artists that experiment with different sounds and rap styles influenced by beat poetry, punk, queer ball culture, Bounce, Crunk and Techno–House to exist. Queer hip-hop in the United States is making commercial waves. Mykki Blanco, BBY Mufa, Princess Nokia, Dai Burger, Jungle Pussy, Cakes Da Killa, Leikeli47, Le1f, Quay Dash and THEESatisfaction (to name a few) provide social commentary about their specific socially located human experiences as black, queer women and men. Hip-hop culture's vitality and socially conscious sound has been pushed towards the centre because of the efforts of women's artistic contributions in challenging masculine hegemonic representations in commercial record industries and mainstream media – women in hip-hop have proven to be the vanguard of hip-hop by putting themselves forward to tell the stories of their communities.

Princess Nokia and *1992 Deluxe*

> Being a goddess is a tool of assistance and confidence in your life. It's a reminder to ourselves that we are something enigmatic, elusive, controlling, we're coquette, we are sweet. The goddess is comfortable with herself because she is comfortable with nature, and the woman is nature, we are nature. She knows herself, and the connection that she has to the outer earth. Are you a daughter of the earth? Well, nature better serve your secondary identity boo. Because she attunes her mind and her body and her spirit with nature, in the exchange for the powerful charge of natural light energy and magic. That's the goddess. (Frasqueri 2017a: 43 min 44–44 min 25)

Urban feminism, as defined by Frasqueri earlier in this piece, seeks to redefine women's liberation beyond the parameters of the limited scope of a privileged feminist theory that has access to institutional language and support to sustain its goals. This valid critique is the building blocks of an existing pedagogy of the oppressed that has been explored in black feminist theory and hip-hop feminist studies. What makes urban feminism unique is that it urges women to find answers within, to build critique of their gendered-racialized existence without the need for hierarchical authorship, in togetherness with other women. This also offers the possibility of developing a relationship with music that moves beyond the one typically offered in the commercialized music industries.

Princess Nokia's feminism is not merely ideational and symbolic; it directly translates to her physical artistic presence on the stage. Her performance style is a combination of all her varying feminist influences: riot grrrl, queer, cyber-punk, tomboy, femme, Tiano-Yourban goddess realness. At her concerts and performances at musical festivals, she summons all women to the front as a direct challenge to how men occupy public space at music venues. All of this contributes to a feminist live-music experience. This practice is interesting because Princess Nokia does not display any attempt to be universally palatable – in interviews she does not refer to her music or ontology as 'political' – but she uses her power as an individual and as an artist to create social impact. Her embodiment of her principles through her social location as a brown, working-class Latina woman is inherently liberating, but steering away from politics interestingly has philosophical implications for how we view empowerment outside of theoretical-institutional forms. Empowerment in this example simply locates 'power' where one finds it, it is not fought for, petitioned for but is accessible to anyone who heeds and takes power over one's self, mind and spirit.

1992 Deluxe, an LP released by Princess Nokia in 2017, and the other community building activities she has engaged in, exemplifies many of these principles. *1992 Deluxe* successfully wove together all these socially located feminisms. It was an underground hip-hop LP that took the mainstream by storm. Like her previous album projects *Honeysuckle* (2015) and *Metallic Butterfly* (2014), *1992 Deluxe* dipped into sounds ranging from techno and disco. It was released without the assistance of a record label (since then she has signed with Rough Trade Records for distribution).

However, the circumstances of the release of *1992 Deluxe* were strongly influenced by Nokia's previous experiences in music making. Prior to adopting the name and persona of Princess Nokia, Destiny released 'Bitch I'm Posh' (2012) and 'Versace Hottie' (2013) under the alias Wavy Spice. Produced in her bedroom and originally released via SoundCloud, the explosive internet popularity of the tracks came as a surprise to Destiny and allowed a visibility that secured subsequent record deal offers. When Destiny was performing under Wavy Spice, she was collaborating with her ex-boyfriend's crew, who she claims simply did not understand why she didn't want a record deal nor her desire to turn her music into a spiritual pursuit. After leaving this relationship, Destiny claims that her ex-partner accredited all her success to himself. Since then she has encouraged young women to pursue their art independently (Brown 2017). As such, Princess Nokia emerged out of a need to create without the patriarchal influences of the music industry, and the male-dominated crews that gave women access to industry (as seen with high profile female rappers in the 1990s–2000s) but would tamper with the authenticity of their work. In a 2016 interview with *Snobette* – 'Princess Nokia: "There's No Money in Record Deals & I'm Not Looking to Be Taken Advantage of"'– Nokia admits that the aesthetic behind Wavy Spice was strong but she did not have the skills to create music for monetary gain, especially under time-constraints. Lacking the mature talent she needed to really progress in her field, Destiny declined several record deal offers, subsequently going on a hiatus before beginning the aforementioned projects under the moniker Princess Nokia. The name was coined as a homage to the continuity of the analogue, using a DIY approach to creative projects as an independent musician with a Nokia phone (*Snobette* 2016).

The tenets of urban feminism can be seen throughout *1992 Deluxe* and are clearly communicated through the accompanying music videos for this album. The filmography associated with this album pays homage to hip-hop visual culture through the showcasing of New York City through the eyes of Princess Nokia, including corridors, basketball court and bridges in a quintessential continuity of hip-hop music videography. Each track carefully tells the story of Destiny's life through self-empowerment and sisterhood. The visual art of *1992 Deluxe* music videos feature her mostly brown and black friends hanging out in the streets of New York – skating, laughing and wearing baggy clothes as seen in 'Tomboy' – incurring the disappointment of her grandmother. Similarly, in the music video for 'Kitana', a posse of fresh-faced girls (friends and fellow members of Smart Girl Club) and Princess Nokia are shown all dressed in a masculine tomboy aesthetic while boxing in a local basketball court. The (re)presentation of Latinx masculine femininities is a transgressive celebration of how women collectively subvert gender expectations.

In 'Brujas' the videography centres traditional femininity of the Tiano women, Nokia reimagines black femininity in the spiritual practice of witchcraft through readapting the nineties cult classic film *The Craft* (1996), about a group of young teenage outcasts who practice witchcraft. A group of black and brown women are gathered by the water and cast spells in the forest (a representation of the earth element). The figure of the Goddess or all-positive power is represented by the femininity presented by the women, water and earth; this is a direct parallel or an integration of knowledge concerning the world and power through equilibrium. The track is a sharp contrast to feminist discourses in the west, through the deconstruction of the relationship between women and nature, from the onset ontology of feminism that Princess Nokia presents is rooted in Tiano epistemologies concerning gender, nature, culture and power. Nokia invokes Yourban goddess: 'Orisha, my alter, Got coins on the counter'. The image building in 'Brujas' presents an honest, bitter-sweet, yet celebratory representation of urban femininity. Nokia uses the theme of spirituality to explain the social realities of black and brown women in urban contexts: 'talk shit, we can cast spells, long weaves, long nails, cornrows, pigtails, baby fathers still in jail'. This representation of Orisha in 'Brujas' shifts social commentary and activism from European rationalist depictions of power. The re-centering of feminine energy has great potential for the politics of empowerment in a system of heterosexist, racist, capitalist and sexist patriarchy.

Princess Nokia's lyricism and flow are coherently inconsistent through the conscious and calculated usage of different variations of vocal register. In 'Saggy Denim' we hear a deeper tone of Princess Nokia's voice, reminiscent of Tupac. In 'Tomboy' and 'Kitana' she screams girlishly, the influence of riot grrrl culture ever present, the lines between rap music and singing blurred in this track as she marries hip-hop, trap styles of rap and Punk music. In 'Receipts' her vocal pitch drops to the lowest, as she parodies machismo hip-hop culture whilst continuing the thread of gender fluidity: 'Laughing at the rappers who got ego in they pocket, Always talking money but they never ever got it.'

Princess Nokia's multitude of gender expressions can be analysed using queer thinker Jin Haritaworn's (2008) concept of 'shifting positionalities,' in which diasporic femininity is formed mockingly, as with the case of British-Sri Lankan rapper, M.I.A. This diasporic queer femininity manifests in 'Tomboy', with Princess Nokia dressed in baggy home clothes, smoking weed in the hallways, invoking the anger of her grandmother for not performing Latinx femininity. The subversive nature of her embodiment of the experience resonated with myself and many other fans who are third-wave diasporic women experiencing patriarchal social control within our own socially disadvantaged families, and from institutions and society. The urban feminist and the diasporic subject represent the process of gendering concerning the racialization of women of colour in the United States, and Europe.

The identity that emerges across *1992 Deluxe* defies easy categorization. For example, the representations of gender in 'Tomboy' and 'Kitana' could be seen as contradictory to those in 'Brujas', but collectively they present a balance of feminine and masculine energies. The figure of the Tomboy and the Brujas speak to what Haritaworn refers to as 'aggressive heterosexual agency' (2008). This balance of gender representation is something Nokia harmonizes through Tiano spiritual teachings – the notion that there exists within us feminine energy and masculine energy (Haritaworn 2008; Medrano-Marra 2009). Similarly, Nokia embraces the multiplicity of her ethnic make-up as a mixed raced Nuyorican woman, with Arawak and West African ancestry which she alludes to on the track 'Brujas', in which she raps: 'I'm that Black a-Rican Brujas straight out from the Yoruba, and my people come from Africa diaspora Cuba, And you mix that Arawak, the original people'. She uses this project to highlight the physical space of New York, but also traces the ancestral non-physical space as a spiritual methodology to harmonize all parts of her identity as Destiny/Princess Nokia. Princess Nokia decolonizes African spirituality by referring to the motifs of magic in positive respects, via the use of urban vernacular, for example pairing 'witchcraft' and 'bitchcraft'. Through this process she creates a feminist dialogic via the interaction with the metaphysical, and the physical-social world in urban settings. This journey to inner peace, through 'magic', is a practice for the diasporic Puerto Rican/black woman that can be applied to urban, diasporic contexts in North America and the global African diaspora.

In addition to her accolades as a recording artist, Princess Nokia and her contemporaries founded urban feminist organization called the Smart Girl Club for women of colour in New York; promoting the safety, healing via magic, self-care and artistic endeavours of young women of colour in the New York area. Smart Girl Club importantly is an accessible space that allows people to grow by nurturing their creativity through sisterhood. In music and the arts women have generally been perceived as performers as opposed to creators – Smart girl Club was largely about reclaiming the creativity of women of colour in these urban spaces. Smart Girl Club embodied a safe space in which mostly young women (of colour) would build principles based on urban feminism by reflecting on the teachings of witchcraft women connect to the spirit and revision their spiritual power as women in conjunction with nature and magic. Collective togetherness exhibited by the Smart Girl Club is certainly inspired by the third wave feminist intervention of the riot grrrl movement to shake the cultural world of the male dominant punk scene in Olympia, Washington. The riot grrrl movement stemmed from a feminist response to build a culture that spoke to young women in the punk scene and universities as a voice that would platform issues affecting young women pertaining to body image, sexual abuse, self-harm, empowerment, intersectionality and creativity (citation). The principles of DIY was a crucial component to the riot grrrl scene, ranging from self-made zines, face to face meetings and radio and television programs as an alternative to patriarchal mainstream media. Smart Girl Club has promoted similar praxis relating to contemporary issues for poor women of colour in New York. By using urban vernacular and spiritual teachings that are found in West African and Tiano teachings, Princess Nokia has given fellow women the ability to seek empowerment by rediscovering heritage and the important principles followed by ancestors that can be a source of inspiration for a feminist, anti-racist space.

Conclusion

The commercial success of *1992 Deluxe* by an underground Princess Nokia redefined the notion of what accolades in music look like in hip-hop. The bridge between DIY underground artists to what she describes in an interview as an 'overnight' success is unconventional given the specific pathway she embarked on that was not connected to the industry at all. In an interview with Eddie Fu for *Genius* in 2018, Princess Nokia describes the slow process of curating *1992 Deluxe*. She recounts that she recorded the EP in her friend's house, directing the music video and finally uploading it to SoundCloud, YouTube and eventually sharing it on Instagram (Fu 2018). By enjoying the process and re-entering the joy of one's vocation, Princess Nokia was able to embody herself, and curate profound reflections about life through the meditative act of simply taking time to create music.

In conjunction to her feminist ideals and spiritual principles, Princess Nokia did not set out become a star but to create what she describes as 'nuance' in the world of hip-hop that embodied her identity without any compromise. Moreover, in doing so she gives others by example the capacity to take up that space as an individual. The authenticity demonstrated by Princess Nokia illustrates the strength and perseverance to see through what she seems as a historical moment in hip-hop till now:

> "Whether it's the music, the workshops, or the radio show," she says, "I want everyone to feel that it's fucking cool – it's the coolest thing in New York – but it isn't exclusive. (Princess Nokia 2016, *V Magazine*)

Radical self-acceptance and self-love has enabled Princess Nokia to communicate to others what is takes to survive the music industry as a woman. This is placed in stark opposition to her prior experiences with the possibility of working with labels prematurely. The notion of self-care in feminism for poor women of colour is one of the ways in which we use our own individual social consciousness and action to assist those around us. The former is important because women are socialized to attend to their needs last, and instead expected to centre themselves for the advancement of their community, as demonstrated in Princess Nokia's music and spiritual urban-feminist teachings with Smart Girl Club. The preservation of spiritual teachings placed in indigenous and African cultures, as told by Princess Nokia in an urban context, shifts the way we understand pain beyond its abject location by locating power in place of it. This understanding of Goddess power – in movement, in light through many physical spaces and social spaces – has the capacity to help us rethink power and reconsider how we can interact with power in our everyday instances and relationships with others. It is through ritual and the space of self-preservation and creativity that we have the capacity to come together and to not fall victim to activist 'burnout'. Princess Nokia shows us that through sisterhood and a principle of 'love', we are able to break down barriers between us all.

References

Alridge, D.P. and J.B. Stewart (2005), 'Introduction: Hip Hop in History: Past, Present, and Future', *The Journal of African American History*, 90 (3): 190–195.

Brown, N. (2017), 'Good Goddess: In Conversation with Princess Nokia', The Creator Class. Available online: www.thecreatorclass.com/good-goddess-princess-nokia/ (accessed 23 August 2019).

Chang, J. (2005), *Can't Stop Won't Stop: A History of the Hip-Hop Generation*, London: Picador.

Collins, P.H. (2004), *Black Sexual Politics: African Americans, Gender and the New Racism*, New York: Routledge.
Cooper, R. (2016) [lecture], 'Rethinking Intersectionality: A Conversation about Gender, Race, and Popular Culture', RVCC Women's Center. Available online: www.youtube.com/watch?v=zyCiq4hDsM8&t=1357s (accessed 23 August 2019).
Durham, A., Cooper, B. and S. Morris (2013), 'The Stage Hip-Hop Feminism Built: A New Directions Essay', *Signs: Journal of Women in Culture and Society*, 38 (3): 721–737.
Frasqueri, D. (2017a) [Radio], 'Smart Girl Radio Episode 1', *Smart Girl Club Radio*. Available online: www.soundcloud.com/princessnokia92/smart-girl-club-episode-1-jan-5th-2017-1517-1154-am (accessed 23 August 2019).
Frasqueri, D. (2017b) [Radio], 'Learning & Unlearning Part 1', *Smart Girl Club Radio*. Available online: www.soundcloud.com/princessnokia92/learning-unlearning-part-1-smart-girl-club-radio-may-1st-2017 (accessed 23 August 2019).
Fu, E. (2018), 'Princess Nokia Discusses the Success of *1992 Deluxe* a Year Later on "For the Record"', *Genius*. Available online: www.genius.com/a/princess-nokia-discusses-the-success-of-1992-deluxe-a-year-later-on-for-the-record (accessed 23 August 2019).
Haritaworn, J. (2008), 'Shifting Positionalities: Empirical Reflections on a Queer/Trans of Colour Methodology', *Sociological Research Online*, 13 (1): 13.
Lipsitz, G. (2013), 'Tricia Rose Interviewed by George Lipsitz', *Critical Studies in Improvisation*, 10 (1). Available online: www.criticalimprov.com/index.php/csieci/issue/view/193 (accessed 23 August 2019).
Medrano-Marra, M. (2009), 'Writing Our Way to Taínospirituality: Finding a Sense of Self', *Journal of Poetry Therapy*, 22 (1): 21–39.
Morgan, J. (1999), *When Chickenheads Come Home to Roost*, New York: Touchstone.
Rose, T. (1994), *Black Noise*, Middletown, CT: Wesleyan University Press.
Snobette (2016), 'No One Ever Asks Male Rappers, "What Do You Think of Female Hip-Hop?", 5 July 2016. Available online: www.snobette.com/2016/07/princess-nokia-interview-part-1/ (accessed 23 August 2019).
V Magazine (2016), 'Princess Nokia, an Artist Making a Career All Her Own'. Available online: www.vmagazine.com/article/princess-nokia/ (accessed 23 August 2019).

Discography

Destiny (2015) *Honeysuckle*. Vice Records.
Princess Nokia (2013) 'Versace Hottie'. Self-released.
Princess Nokia (2014) *Metallic Butterfly*. Vice Records.
Princess Nokia (2017) *1992 Deluxe*. Rough Trade Records.
Wavy Spice (2012) 'Bitch I'm Posh'. Self-released.

Filmography

The Craft (1996), [Film] Dir. Andrew Fleming, USA: Columbia Pictures.
Bell Hooks: Cultural Criticism and Transformation (1997), [Film] Dir. Sut Jhally. USA: Sut Jhally.

13

'Kill It in a Man's World': Gender at the Intersection of the British Asian and Bollywood Music Industries

Julia Szivak

Oh, the Asians? They hated me in the beginning, but now, that I'm successful, they claim that I'm a Punjabi too ... This is how it works, first they dismiss you 'cuz they don't get you. 'Why are you doing black people's music? You a ho? Nobody will marry you.' [...]They want me to act like a girl but when they need me, they want me not to act like a girl and to be 'hard core.' And what does that even mean to act like a girl?![1]
(Hard Kaur, personal interview, 2019)

No matter how successful she has become in India, her initial struggle in the UK still evokes vivid memories in Hard Kaur. When we met in an upscale North Mumbai bar, India's first female rapper had just returned to India from Birmingham, her childhood hometown. As she was recounting her experiences of being a female performing artist in the British Asian and Bollywood music industries, I understood that her experiences are typical of the gender and sexual politics of these respective scenes. However, her career also provides an interesting contrast to traditional career trajectories in these industries – primarily on account of its transnational nature. As an artist of the diaspora who became popular in the homeland, her transnational career was partly a product of her personal biography. It has also been influenced by the storied dynamics of cultural relations between the UK and India, as well as Punjab and the rest of India, in which British Punjabi artists such as Hard Kaur have played an important role.

Hard Kaur was born in 1979 as Taran Kaur Dhillon in Kanpur, India, but relocated to Birmingham with her family in her early childhood. She grew up in the racially and culturally diverse environment of Handsworth, Birmingham, and as a result of the exposure to hip-hop music there Hard Kaur decided to pursue a career in rapping. After a prolonged period of struggle on the British Asian music scene and in the mainstream hip-hop world, the turning point in her career was her collaboration *Ek glassy* with the British Asian hip-hop group the Sona Family in 2005, where she rapped in Hindi. Despite its place of production, the song became a hit in India, and in 2007 music directors Shankar-Ehsaan-Loy invited her to produce a hip-hop track for the Bollywood film, *Johnny Gaddar* (Khan 2010).

From this point the number of her performances and work assignments in India increased and she moved to Mumbai, the entertainment capital of India. Along with her work in Bollywood, she performed all over the country, participated in reality shows, acted in films and became a nationwide celebrity. She is now credited with not only being the first female Indian rapper, but also the artist who established hip-hop as part and parcel of Bollywood film soundtracks (Ghosh 2019). As a result of her popularity in India, her appearances on the British Asian music scene have increased, and she now regularly performs at British Asian festivals and weddings. She has been dividing her time between the UK and India, performing and recording music, as well as developing artists in both places.

Hard Kaur's artistic journey seems even more special because achieving lasting success on the male-dominated British Asian scene has been close to impossible for women, while female artists who did not fit a very specific set of aesthetic and behavioural expectations were sidelined in the Bollywood music industry. In spite of the challenges, she has been present on both the British Asian and the Bollywood music scenes for more than twenty years. Throughout the course of this chapter, I argue that this is a result of a variety of interrelated factors that are connected to gender politics of both scenes and the transnational aspect of her career. Despite Kaur's non-conventional decision to pursue hip-hop, it is somewhat ironic that it was her refusal to fit in to established genres and related modes of femininity which led to her subsequent breakthrough. As a female, British Asian rapper, she could not quite fit in the bhangra-dominated British Asian musical landscape or the mainstream hip-hop scene. It was, however, the same factors that in India made her a unique phenomenon in the eyes of the Bollywood music industry that was eager to incorporate new sounds and performers. I argue that the key factor in the success of this transition was her transnational, diasporic position. Building on the traditionally vibrant cultural exchange between the British Asian diaspora and the audiences of the homeland of India, she could capitalize on greater mobility and technological developments of the twenty-first century and achieve a status of transnational stardom.

Her career exhibits the characteristics of other transnational musicians, who 'are able to exploit the possibility offered up by the contraction of time and space to lead a near simultaneous existence across multiple spaces, across different localities and nations', where the key feature of these experiences is that they are 'constitutive rather than exceptional' (Meinhof 2017: 463). In fact, her success in India impacted on her standing on the British Asian music scene, where, previously shunned, she is now considered as a Punjabi performing artist. I argue throughout this chapter that this is the result of her transcultural capital (Meinhof 2017: 468), a mixture of cultural and social capital that derives from her position of being at home in both the diaspora and homeland. This contributes to her ability to translate her successful transnational career into economic capital. In support of this argument, the chapter traces Hard Kaur's artistic journey from Britain to Bollywood through ethnographic material and an analysis of news media coverage, and thereby looks at the challenges of female participation on both scenes and the possibilities that the intersection of the two offers.

Gender on the British Asian music scene

> Look at us now, it feels so good. At that time all the girls my age were, 'Well, we are getting married next year but ain't nobody will marry you.' And I was like, 'Who the fuck wants to get married anyway? I've got a fucking tune coming out next week! That's way more important.' And they were like, 'Whatever, that's not how life works.' And look at us now. I don't get this mentality, it's like a fucking Ekta Kapoor serial.[2] (Hard Kaur, personal interview, 2019)

British Asian music – produced, performed and consumed by members of the British South Asian community – is not an easy territory for women. Most successful performers, producers and music industry professionals are male, and the lack of women on the scene is mirrored in the lack of academic attention to this phenomenon. The public and academic discourse around British Asian music has largely been celebratory in nature (clearly demonstrated in the UK documentary *Pump up the Bhangra* 2018) and the gender politics of the scene has not been explored thoroughly. The most extensive monograph on gender and British Asian music, *Bhangra and Asian Underground: South Asian Music and the Politics of Belonging in Britain* by Bakrania (2013) did not discuss female performing artists, stating that this was because there are only a 'few and relatively unknown women artists in the bhangra and A[sian] U[ndergound] scenes' (Bakrania 2013: 21), while adding that it is more productive to look at women as consumers of this type of music. The current chapter therefore aims to bridge this gap in academic literature and, in addition to tracing Hard Kaur's career across the music industries of the diaspora and the homeland, to chart some of the structural problems that women in the British Asian music industry face.

The British Asian music scene is not alone in displaying a gender bias, as it has been argued that it is harder for women to be successful performers on other music scenes as well (see, for example, Bayton 2006, Katz 2006, O'Shea 2008 and the other chapters in this volume). There are, however, three main factors that hinder the progress of females in British Asian music specifically: the origins of British Asian music in traditionally male-dominated musical genres; the conservative attitudes in the community where girls were traditionally not encouraged to pursue careers in performing arts (Housee and Dhar 1996: 87); and girls not having equal access to spaces of music performance and consumption (Bakrania 2013).

British Asian music has drawn much of its inspiration from bhangra, deriving from a traditional Punjabi folk music and dance genre which used to be performed by all-male bands and dancers celebrating the harvest and the Punjabi new year. Traditional bhangra performances were displays of force, virility and masculinity (Roy 2011: 95) and as British Asian bhangra bands sought to evoke certain nostalgic associations, most British Asian bhangra bands comprised male members only. This led to a gender imbalance in access to training and technology, as it was usually young males who were mentored by established artists and producers. This often happened through family networks as well. Scheffler (2012: 347) has pointed out that a major difference between the trajectories of the Punjabi folk music scene in India and in the UK diaspora was that diaspora musicians did not belong to hereditary musical lineages or castes like they did in India. Despite this, British Asian musical families – like the Bhamrahs, where the father Kulwant was the lead singer of the band, Apna Sangeet, and the son, Dipps is a presenter and DJ on BBC Asian Network, or the exceptional case of Parv Kaur, the first female *dholi* in Britain, daughter of Balbir Singh, *dhol* player of the band Bhujangy – still came into being.

However, the women members of these families, and South Asian girls in the diaspora in general, were discouraged from pursuing performing arts as women were traditionally considered to be the bearers of tradition and cultural authenticity (Bakrania 2013: 6). On account of its historical trajectory that blurred the boundaries between performing and prostitution in India (Vanita 2018), the involvement of women in performing arts continued to be considered immoral in the diaspora, especially as it involved leaving the private sphere, which was the traditional purview of femininity (Bakrania 2013: 18). As a result, music – especially popular music – was not considered an appropriate career choice for a girl from a respectable family. The fact that performances sometimes happened late at night, which potentially involved the consumption of alcohol and possible free mingling of men and women, often increased the suspicion of the community about the dubious nature of performing arts.

In addition to historical prejudices, some of these fears and restrictions were grounded in the gendered nature of the spaces of British Asian music production and consumption. Bhangra nights have been identified by researchers such as Bakrania (2013) and Dhar and Housee (1996) as hypermasculine and violent spaces, where female performers or club-goers frequently still find themselves in a difficult position. In addition to safety, another main concern about the involvement of women in music-making and performing was the perception that girls who make music would be less desirable on the marriage market in their refusal to conform to traditional gender expectations (Dhar and Housee 1996: 85).

According to industry experts and scene participants, this perception has changed with time and it is now more acceptable for British Asian girls to try their hand at making music. However, they still have a shorter period than men to prove their merit and they are expected to revert to assuming traditional gender roles if their artist careers do not work out as imagined ('The Future of British Asian Music' 2017). Achieving quick success on the scene is hampered by audience demands, who fear that women are not capable of performing music with the same energy and virility as males (Dudrah 2007: 54, 58). As Kiranee Dhanoa (a British Asian female performing artist who now works in India as an Artist and Repertoire specialist for a major label) noted in an email interview with me in 2019, male artists are still booked more often and paid more for live events.

Interestingly enough, this does not hinder female performers from Punjab to the same extent – either in India or in the British Asian diaspora. Recordings of Surinder Kaur (1929–2006), a singer who had been instrumental in giving birth to modern era of Punjabi folk singing (Schreffler 2012: 343), have always been extremely popular in the diaspora. Similarly, contemporary female singers – such as Miss Pooja, Jenny Johal and Nimrat Khaira from Punjab or Jasmine Sandlas from the US Punjabi diaspora – are frequently booked for live performances in melas and weddings, the traditional spaces of live music consumption in the British Asian context.

Hard Kaur's career, too, bears testimony to the presence of the hurdles described above. She however pushed back against the community's moral judgement, breaking with the prevalent gender expectations by choosing a career in the performing arts. An alternative avenue for women in other traditionally male-dominated scenes was to achieve a status where they are perceived as 'one of the boys' on account of their musical proficiency that transcend boundaries of gender (O'Shea 2008: 58). In addition to striving for equality in terms of skills, Hard Kaur also adopted a tough, masculine image. This includes her stage name, which while referencing her ethnic origins, as Kaur is the surname traditionally given to Sikh women, is also homonymous with the quality and approach of being 'hard core', which is traditionally associated with masculinity. She has cultivated a low-key physical appearance that purposefully pre-empties the claims that she wants to go forward in life through her beauty (Deepak 2016), thus subverting the traditional associations of female beauty and talent going hand in hand (Dunbar 2011: 174). Moreover, she has been showcasing other traits that are usually associated with male participants of the British Asian scene, such as being loud and outspoken, and consuming alcohol openly. She reflects on the prevalent expectations and her subsequent decisions in the following way:

> If you're a rapper, you're a prostitute, if you're a mehndi artist, you're a prostitute[3] [in the eyes of the community] […] So from day one, I decided to fuck up my own reputation. I didn't want to be all clean, all perfect … I'll go to a function with no makeup, I'll be drunk if I want to be. If I'm a hoe already then might as well ….
> (Hard Kaur, personal communication, 2019)

Her confrontational attitude posed a number of obstacles as the British Asian music scene had traditionally been quite small, and the production and distribution of music occurred through personalized networks (Banerjee 1988: 212). This often resulted in cancellation of shows and collaborations. Another issue that led to her marginalization was her unusual choice of genre. Whereas during the 1990s Asian households usually listened to Punjabi or Bollywood music, she became interested in rap, which was considered alien (black people's music), masculine (even Asian boys were not doing it) and subversive. Even though African American and African-Caribbean musical influences had been present in the work of male British Asian artists and producers – case in point are Apache Indian's Patois-language songs or Bally Sagoo's RnB-infused remixes – British Asians' appetite for hip-hop produced within the community was quite small. As a result, there was no other Asian performing artist, and certainly no female artist who was successful pursuing the genre within the community. In addition, as Hard Kaur noted during our conversations, within the mainstream hip-hop world, Asian artists were marginalized as their ethnic origins were not considered authentic enough.

Nevertheless, Hard Kaur stuck to the genre as it was intricately intertwined with her own marginal position in the Asian community. Being a 'freshie', a first-generation immigrant with weak English language skills, she was not accepted into the fold of British Asian communities in school and was more closely associated with Black British and Caribbean school groups, who were heavily invested in hip-hop culture. She learned English through hip-hop lyrics and subsequently decided to become a rapper. In spite of her firm decision, she spent years honing her skills to the point where she felt that she would not be judged on account of her gender and her skills would vouch for themselves. A similar coping mechanism has been recorded elsewhere, whereby women confine their endeavours to their private sphere until their skills render their gender irrelevant (Wolfe 2012). Her skills, however, did not bring Hard Kaur the success she had hoped for. After a period of struggle in the British Asian music scene and the mainstream hip-hop world, she transitioned to the Bollywood music scene. She was quick to take the opportunity that offered to turn her disadvantages into advantages. Her position as an Indian-origin female performing artist, who grew up in the West among a variety of non-Asian musical influences, enabled her to circumvent the gender-specific expectations that female Indian performing artists had had to conform to in the Bollywood music industry.

Bollywood music and gender

> In England they hate each other and don't care, they have the chip on the shoulder attitude. In India, we work together because there is a scene, even though we kinda' hate each other. And anyhow, in England how far a brown girl can go? I got tired of not gettin' the respect there and puttin' up with all that shit. I get that respect here, it's cool. (Hard Kaur, personal communication, 2019)

In contrast to the almost exclusively male domain of British Asian music, the Bollywood music industry has always been in need of female singers. The reason lies in the intricate intersection of Hindi cinema and film music. Hindi films feature multiple song sequences that are sung by playback singers and picturized on the characters of the film. Actors and actresses lip synch and perform dance choreographies to these songs, which usually forward the narrative in a variety of ways (Dudrah 2006). As songs are performed by male and female characters alike, this demand provides a constant source of employment for female playback singers too. However, there are deep, structural imbalances in the Bollywood music industry that result from its close association with the film industry. The Bollywood film industry is male-dominated, and it prefers the foregrounding of men both in its production and narratives. This is visible throughout the production process, where it is the male 'hero' of the film who gets signed first because the enormous amount of star power male Bollywood actors possess will impact on the popularity of the film. To this end, films tend to focus their narratives around the male characters whereas females have traditionally played a supporting role (Ganti 2016: 264). The female singer's repertoire is limited by the less extensive and less diverse roles that women play in Hindi cinema (Thomas 2017). Female roles traditionally were categorized as the eroticized, Westernized vamp or the chaste Indian heroine (Gehlawat 2015: 6). These modes of portrayal impacted upon the music industry as well, where voices of female singers were similarly typecast and only those singers whose voices conformed to these stereotypes could stay in the industry (Srivastava 2004: 2022).

Moreover, access to the Bollywood music industry has been extremely difficult for aspiring singers as they would typically have needed family connections or powerful mentors to enter the industry (Booth 2019: 259). However, as has been recorded on other music scenes, if there are not many established female scene participants who could provide mentoring, young women might feel uncomfortable as a result of the patronizing attitudes of the male mentors or of the close proximity in which they have to work with them (Katz 2006: 585). The association of young women with senior, powerful male mentors can be especially problematic in the eyes of Indian society that valorizes chastity and the segregation of genders outside of familial relations. In addition to the perceptions of society come the very real problems resulting from power imbalances between a male mentor and a female mentee that have recently been exposed by the #MeToo movement in India. According to the testimonies of female singers, leading music directors and established singers have abused their position of power and influence and taken advantage of the aspirations of young singers in a variety of ways that led to considerable mental and emotional distress (*Indian Express* 11 October 2018).

In addition to these issues, the music recording process has also changed and it is even more challenging now for upcoming talent to break the industry. The currently popular multi-composer and multi-singer soundtracks only allow singers to sing so-called scratches, or small portions of a song instead of full songs on the albums, leading to less exposure and hindering singers on their way to an established position. Moreover, the laxity of copyright laws and lack of royalty payments make it hard for performers to earn a stable income from playback singing only. Performing artists then must go on live tours and perform at weddings in search of income instead. In addition to leading to lifestyles which are incompatible with traditional expectations of settling down and having a family, performing at such gigs might be physically dangerous as well, as alcohol consumption, which is rampant at such live music venues, often leads to the audience throwing bottles and other objects on the stage (Shetty 2017b).

In spite of all these challenges, the Bollywood music industry is still very lucrative for young singers and it has recently become more penetrable. As the construction of femininity shifted in Bollywood cinema towards a less polemic and more accommodating approach with regards to female sexuality, the moralizing associations of 'good' and 'bad' women have also loosened. This resulted in the Bollywood music industry opening up for a wider variety of female voices in the early 2000s (Gehlawat 2015: 53). In addition to the more nuanced approaches to the portrayal and perception of femininity, economic considerations also played a significant role in the inclusion of new voices. During the late 1990s, a number of non-film albums, commonly labelled as belonging to the Indipop genre, achieved considerable success on the Indian music market. The Indipop artists such as Alisha Chinai, Shaan and Daler Mehndi were not the invisible, low-profile singing voices of famous actresses and actors any more but had their own star persona and were celebrities in their own right. The Bollywood music industry was eager to incorporate these new sounds and new performers who rose to fame in an unprecedented way (Beaster-Jones 2015: 146, 154). It is plausible that the fact that Hard Kaur also became famous in her own right through *Ek glassy* and not via the traditional Bollywood route also impacted on the way she was incorporated into Bollywood music and represented in film soundtracks.

Hard Kaur was radically different, and represented another approach to femininity, to the previous playback singers who could be categorized as voices of 'good' or 'bad' women. Even though her brazen attitude and suggestive lyrics did conform to the traditional audio-visual registers of the vamp, her approach marked a departure. While the vamp had always sought to seduce the male hero, Kaur most often presented a casual, almost deliberate indifference to engaging in such an exercise. In her Bollywood music videos, she goes clubbing, consumes substances, dances and raps in order to enjoy life on her own terms. She does not live to entertain men. In fact, her behaviour undermines traditional gender expectations and behaviour. Whereas drinking alcohol is traditionally understood to be the privilege of men, in Bollywood music videos usually represent the consumption of alcohol by women as a way to lose their self-control and to be more easily approachable for men. In her music videos, Hard Kaur, on the other hand is shown drinking and partying, but not in order to lose her moral inhibitions. She is shown drinking because she likes to have a good time and does not believe that women should adhere to different codes of conduct than men.

This break with expectations of behaviour might stem from her own personal history but its acceptance in the music industry could be explained by her position as a woman coming from the diaspora. Her choice of musical genre, her sartorial choices and her behaviour all identified her as an emancipated, modern and highly Westernized woman. However, her physical appearance, the way she referenced Punjabi culture and spoke the vernaculars of the country established her as Punjabi and Indian. Her position as a member of the diaspora served to not only bridge certain cultural contradictions between the UK and India, but to also to carve a niche out for herself in the Bollywood music industry as a result of her transnational position and transcultural capital. While she was familiar with the musical styles of England and could bring a new, Western style into Bollywood music, she was also acquainted with the Indian cultural context and audience expectations. This fit in well with what music directors and film producers were looking for in relation to film soundtracks in the early 2000s.

After India's economic liberalization in the 1990s, the Bollywood music industry has been increasingly eager to incorporate new, international sounds into its repertoire, while ensuring that audiences should be able relate to these innovations. Indian audiences demand that Bollywood films and music have a certain 'Indian touch' to them (Rao 2010: 1), which can stem from familiar musical instruments, rhythms, language, lyrics, cultural codes or cultural references in terms of music. The Indian diaspora, and especially the UK Punjabi diaspora, has always played an important role as a transnational influence, when it came to musical innovations that still had this certain 'Indian touch' to them. It has been argued that the British bhangra revolution had a profound effect on the development of the Punjabi music scene in India (Schreffler 2012: 352), as well as the UK- and US-origin South Asian remix culture having a deep effect on the nascent Indian club scene and on the Bollywood music scene. Following the example of Bally Sagoo, Apache Indian, Jazzy B, Rishi Rich, Jay Sean and other male British Asian performing artists who became popular in India as well, Hard Kaur was also in the position of bridging diaspora and homeland by bringing together Western musical genres with Punjabi cultural references. This catered to the growing appetite for dance music among Indian audiences in the wake of music television and club culture (Beaster-Jones 2015: 154).

While bringing the fresh sounds of hip-hop music, Hard Kaur's Hindi and Punjabi language skills established a connection with Indian audiences and placed her within the broader tradition of performance culture, therefore music directors were eager to incorporate her tracks (Sen 2018). As she was radically different from previous female singers both in terms of musical genre and star persona, her film songs also did not conform to earlier categories of female songs: she did not perform the songs associated with the chaste heroine, nor the vamp but was mostly performing the novel category of the party hip-hop songs. Unlike traditional songs that were picturized on actors and did not show any of the performing artists, her songs featured her as the artist and were featured during end credits (*Move Your Body* [Johnny Gaddar, dir. Sriram Raghavan, 2007], *Laung da Lashkara* [Patiala House, dir. Nikhil Advani, 2011]), used as background score (*Kaara Fankaara* [OK Jaanu, dir. Shaad Ali, 2017]) or as semi-diegetic music, where the actors are seen lip synching the songs, but it is clear that the music is coming from the PA system of the party venue (*Char baj gaye hain* [F.A.L.T.U., dir. Remo D'Souza, 2011]).

Her voice also set her apart from previous singers, as her deep, throaty timbre, easily mistaken for a man's voice, is diametrically opposed to the mellifluous, classically trained voices that were audible before. This way, her voice, that was quite unique in itself, eluded connections to any of the typical female characters of the narrative. Coupled with her song lyrics, which were written in a mixture of Hindi, English and Punjabi, Kaur was able to create a unique position for herself with her unique career trajectory serving as a backdrop to the evocation in the audience of something which defied easy categorization but was self-created and defined. Subsequently, a number of female performers from various South Asian diasporas, such as Jasmin Sandlas from the United States, Shirley Setia from New Zealand and Jonita Gandhi from Canada have also been incorporated into the Bollywood music industry on account of their transcultural capital. They could draw on similar experiences as children of first-generation Indian immigrants, who grew up listening to Hindi and Punjabi music, speaking heritage languages but also picking up Western musical education (Shetty

2017a, 2018) that provided them with additional value for the Bollywood industry that valorizes fresh sounds and tries to incorporate new, cosmopolitan influences but necessitates the presence of the 'Indian touch'.

Conclusion

> Kill it in a man's world ... better than the rest.
> Determined in my mind so I know what my future is.
> ('Kattey', Hard Kaur 2011)

Having traced Hard Kaur's artistic journey through two very different, although similarly male-dominated, music scenes, it can be argued that she managed to create a musical and artistic space for herself in the Bollywood music industry on account of her own personal biography and transcultural capital. Growing up in Britain, she became familiar with the genre of hip-hop, which was not yet popular in the Asian community in England nor in India. As a result of this, she was conceived as not authentic enough by a British Asian music industry that has traditionally been male dominated, as the result of the prevalent genres and production structures. However, the exceptional circumstances of the Bollywood music industry being hungry for new sounds with the 'Indian touch' and the privileged place of the UK Punjabi diaspora in Indian popular culture enabled her to build a transnational career.

Nevertheless, the gender politics of the two scenes remain crucial to the current discussion. In addition to charting the gender politics of two interconnected musical scenes, it is important to locate Hard Kaur an as exceptional figure on both scenes, not only in terms of music or image but also in terms of professional aspirations. In spite of her successful Bollywood trajectory, she remained a relative outsider to the film music industry in the sense that she has been maintaining her presence on the independent music scene as well. Her success in India impacted on her standing in the UK as well, where now she is an established member of the British Asian music scene, but still the only well-known female artist on the scene. Interestingly, even though on multiple occasions she spoke about the difficulties of being a female performing artist in the British Asian music industry, she is not looking to mentor females specifically, as to her 'talent has no gender as ain't nobody better than me, no man or woman.'

The chapter also sought to demonstrate how transnational capital can subvert established structures and open up new opportunities, while making a case for looking at personal histories within larger, industry-wide discussions. Hard Kaur's artistic journey, which is also a product of her personal biography, should be read within the context of the process of the diaspora and homeland coming into closer cultural contact than ever before, transforming and moulding the perceptions and aspirations of both. The tensions of modernity, authenticity and belonging in the context of gender which are played out in Hard Kaur's career are indicative of larger processes within the relationship between diasporic and homeland artists that can contribute to discussions about identities negotiated through musical idioms.

Notes

The current chapter is based on findings of my ongoing PhD research at the School of Media, Birmingham City University. I would like to express my gratitude to my supervisors, Professor Rajinder Dudrah and Dr Annette Naudin for their assistance with the preparation of this manuscript.

1 The interview with Taran Kaur Dhillon AKA Hard Kaur took place on 9 January 2019, in Mumbai and I would hereby like to thank Hard Kaur for her time and contribution to the research. All unattributed quotes in this piece are from this interview.
2 Ekta Kapoor has created a number of successful Indian television shows, that usually revolve around themes of marriage and domestic life, which are discussed in a highly dramatic manner, hence the sarcastic reference.
3 Reference to her mother who supported the family by running her own mehndi-business that was quite unusual at the time, when being a housewife was a norm and being an independent, self-supporting woman was frowned upon.

References

'#MeToo: Here Is the List of All Men from the Film Industry Who Have Been Accused of Harassment' (2018), *Indian Express*, 11 October. Available online: https://indianexpress.com/article/entertainment/bollywood/me-too-accused-men-list-harassment-5396034/ (accessed 12 March 2019).

Bakrania, F. (2013), *Bhangra and Asian Underground. South Asian Music and the Politics of Belonging in Britain*, London and Durham: Duke University Press.

Bayton, M. (2006), 'Women Making Music. Some Material Constraints', in A. Bennet (ed.), *The Popular Music Studies Reader*, 347–354, New York and London: Routledge.

Beaster-Jones, J. (2015), *Bollywood Sounds. The Cosmopolitan Mediations of Hindi Film Song*, Oxford: Oxford University Press.

Booth, G. (2019), 'Bollywood and the Life of Music in Twenty-First-Century Mumbai', in B. Leshua (ed.), *Sounds and the City. Popular Music, Place and Globalization. Vol. 2*, 253–275, Houndmills: Palgrave and Macmillan.

Deepak, S. (2016), 'Top Young Musicians from the Region Talk about What Drives Them', *India Today*. 2 September. Available online: https://www.indiatoday.in/magazine/supplement/story/20160912-hard-kaur-badshah-sufi-music-punjab-music-industry-top-young-musicians-829523-2016-09-02 (accessed 11 February 2019).

Dhar, M. and S. Housee (1996), 'Re-Mixing Identities: "Off" the Turntable. Mukhtar Dhar and Shirin Housee Talk to Bally Sagoo and Radical Sista', in J. Hutnyk et al. (eds.), *Dis-Orienting Rhythms: The Politics of the New Asian Dance Music*, 81–104, London and New Jersey: Zed Books.

Dudrah, R. (2006), *Bollywood: Sociology Goes to the Movies*, Delhi and London: Sage.

Dudrah, R. (2007), *Bhangra. Birmingham and Beyond*, Birmingham: Birmingham City Council Library & Archive Service.

Dunbar, J.C. (2011), *Women, Music, Culture. An Introduction*, Routledge: New York and London.

'The Future of British Asian Music' [Radio programme] (2017), BBC Asian Network, 5 October.

Ganti, T. (2016), 'Fair and Lovely. Class, Gender and Colorism in Bollywood Song Sequences', in K.L. Hole, D. Jelaca, E.A. Kaplan and P. Petro (eds.), *The Routledge Companion to Cinema and Gender*, 256–265, Abingdon and New York: Routledge.

Gehlawat, A. (2015), *Twenty-First Century Bollywood*, Abingdon and New York: Routledge.

Ghosh, D. (2019), 'Before "Gully Boy": Rap's Journey in Hindi Films', *Scroll.in*, 9 February. Available online: https://scroll.in/reel/910396/before-gully-boy-raps-journey-in-hindi-films-1968-continuing (accessed 6 April 2019).

Katz, M. (2006), 'Men, Women and Turntables: Gender and the DJ Battle', *The Musical Quarterly*, 89 (4): 580–599.

Khan, N. (2010), 'Hard Kaur', *Desi Blitz*. Available online: https://www.desiblitz.com/content/hard-kaur (accessed 11 February 2019).

Meinhof, U. (2017), 'Globalised Culture Flows, Transnational Fields and Transcultural Capital', in A. Triandafyllidou (ed.), *Handbook of Migration and Globalisation*, 458–472, Cheltenham: Edward Elgar Publishing.

O'Shea, H. (2008), '"Good Man, Mary!" Women Musicians and the Fraternity of Irish Traditional Music', *Journal of Gender Studies*, 17 (1): 55–70.

Pump Up the Bhangra! (2018) [documentary] BBC4, 26 August.

Rao, S. (2010), '"I Need an Indian Touch": Glocalization and Bollywood Films', *Journal of International and Intercultural Communication*, 30 (1): 1–19.

Roy, A.G. (2011), 'Meanings of Bhangra and Bollywood Dancing in India and the Diaspora', *Topia*, 26 (Fall): 85–104.

Schreffler, G. (2012), 'Migration Shaping Media: Punjabi Popular Music in a Global Historical Perspective', *Popular Music and Society*, 35 (3): 333–358.

Sen, D.S. (2018), 'Bollywood Gets Hooked onto Rapping', *Times of India*, July 21 2018. Available online: https://timesofindia.indiatimes.com/entertainment/hindi/music/news/bollywood-gets-hooked-onto-rapping/articleshow/65067136.cms (accessed 6 April 2019).

Shetty, K. (2017a), 'Talking Music with Shirley Setia' [Radio interview], *JioSaavn*, 18 October.

Shetty, K. (2017b), 'Talking Music with Aditi Singh Sharma' [Radio interview], *JioSaavn*, 13 December.

Shetty, K. (2018), 'Talking Music with Jonita Gandhi' [Radio interview], *JioSaavn*, 2 May.

Srivastava, S. (2004), 'Voice, Gender and Space in Time of Five-Year Plans: The Idea of Lata Mangeshkar', *Economic and Political Weekly*, 39 (20): 2019–2028.

Thomas, S.M. (2017), 'Bollywood's Female Playback Singers Explain Why Arijit Singh Is on Every Damn Song', *BuzzFeed*, 14 June. Available online: https://www.buzzfeed.com/soniathomas/bollywoods-female-playback-singers-explain-why-arijit-singh?bffbindia&utm_term=.gsw3jyjPKr#.xuGQvKvy5E (accessed 6 April 2019).

Vanita, R. (2018), *Dancing with the Nation: Courtesans in Bombay Cinema*, New Delhi: Speaking Tiger.

Wolfe, P. (2012), 'A Studio of One's Own: Music Production, Technology and Gender', *Journal on the Art of Record Production* (7). Available online: https://www.arpjournal.com/asarpwp/a-studio-of-ones-own-music-production-technology-and-gender/ (accessed 29 November 2017).

14

Keychanges at Cheltenham Jazz Festival: Issues of Gender in the UK Jazz Scene

Sarah Raine

This chapter explores issues of gender in the UK jazz scene as narrated through the (anonymized) experiences of four female musicians. Emerging out of a partnership research project, these issues then set the scene for a critical reflection on the first stage of Cheltenham Jazz Festival's engagement with the Keychange initiative. This study clearly recounts the ways in which music festivals are engaging with an international initiative aimed to address the notable (and global) gender imbalance within the music industries. It also represents a comparatively rare study of women's everyday experiences of negotiating music-making within the jazz scene. Engaging with issues of gender representation within the UK jazz scene forces us to consider jazz practice beyond the male voices that dominate jazz histories and scholarship, and beyond the extraordinary context of the jazz festival stage. As an ongoing dialogue between scene, research and industry, this study demonstrates the isolation and subsequent knowledge gaps that have become the key barriers for women in jazz and highlights positive strategies for supporting women jazz musicians, in both industry and scholarship contexts.

Keychange and Cheltenham Jazz Festival: A brief framing

This chapter represents the initial findings of a UK Arts and Humanities Research Council (AHRC) funded collaborative research project, undertaken in 2019 and in partnership with Cheltenham Jazz Festival (CJF). This project aims to articulate the complex barriers that lie in the paths of women jazz musicians active in the UK. Such insights will form the basis of a public report for CJF and a series of recommendations for festival programming and message, outreach and education. Beyond the festival's Keychange strategy, this project will provide the first detailed academic study of this gender imbalance at UK jazz festivals. The four interviews here are a representative sample of the wider research in relation to career stages and instrumental or vocal specialism. The emerging themes detailed here were reflected in my other conversations with musicians scheduled to play at the festival in May 2019. This chapter is also informed by my own experience attending and organizing jazz performances (as a music fan and a research network coordinator, respectively), my conversations with the programming and marketing team at CJF, my experience with the Royal Birmingham Conservatoire as a member of staff at Birmingham City University, and a roundtable event organized at the beginning of this project which involved music academics, educators, promoters, musicians and festival organizers from a range of genres, including jazz.

The Keychange initiative was developed by PRS Foundation (PRSF) and launched at the EU Parliament in 2017. As the philanthropic arm of PRS for Music (Publishing Rights Society) in the UK, PRSF engages in outreach, education and talent development. It exists within a member-led, industry-focused organization which is also a member of UK Music, a key organization in representing industry interests and concerns at a national and international industry and government policy level. Keychange is an international campaign which both invests PRSF funding in emerging female talent (supporting sixty emerging artists and innovators through a series of collaborations, showcases and creative labs) and encourages music festivals and conferences to pledge a 50:50 gender balance in their programming by 2022. As an initiative launched by an industry membership body, Keychange is currently a recommended policy for the music industries, but the *Keychange Manifesto* (2017) explicitly makes demands of the EU Parliament in relation to gender equality in pay, support and representation at senior levels of management. It remains to be seen how this initiative will influence legislation or policy at local and national levels.

The target element of Keychange is primarily aimed at music festivals and conferences across the world as a concerted attempt to inspire change within a male-dominated industry. At the time of writing this chapter, CJF was one of five UK jazz festivals to pledge their support for Keychange. This project will therefore inform the festival's gender-focused scheduling agenda and marketing, educational and outreach activities going forward. Cheltenham (established in 1996) is the second largest jazz festival in the UK, with over sixty-five main venue events and a lively Fringe offering. The annual Cheltenham-based festivals (of Jazz, Literature Music and Science) attracted over 215,000 attendees in 2018 and engage with 25,000 people through a year-round education and outreach program. CJF is also presented in association with BBC Radio 2 and is broadcast on Radio 2, 6 Music and Radio 3, with a potential reach of over 25 million listeners. The festival therefore represents a significant platform for jazz musicians, with festival programming teams acting as critical gatekeepers – alongside agents, promoters and the specialist media – to progression within the UK jazz industries. The program manager for CJF, Emily Jones, acted as the industry partner lead for this project.

As a registered charity and a business that is part-funded by sponsors and which employs a substantial festival team, the programming and development aims of the festival are also subject to both financial and community-focused responsibilities. The annual program of the jazz festival must therefore be both financially successful and in line with their altruistic (and public) mission statement. It is within this context that the CJF team must negotiate their Keychange pledge and, in stark terms, ensure that the flow of talent continues to feed future Cheltenham festivals. Alongside these restraints of music festival programming, Jones also negotiates the suggestions and aims of Festival Curators – UK radio producer and DJ Gilles Peterson, UK musician Jamie Cullum and US musician Gregory Porter – and long-standing Programme Advisor Tony Dudley-Evans, in addition to overseeing the work of two freelance programmers for the family and fringe events. It is also worth noting that CJF programs an 'accessible' line-up from across the wide church that is jazz music, from free jazz to jazz-inspired chart-toppers. Furthermore, it is within the particular gender politics of the jazz industries that CJF must work to support women musicians, a complex situation to which we first turn.

Being a woman in the UK jazz scene

Academic studies have highlighted issues with retention of female students in formal jazz education environments (McKeage 2004), lower levels of female student confidence in their performances (Wehr 2016), reduced engagement level in classes and a decreased likelihood of solos during school jazz festivals (Steinberg 2001). Contributors to this book (see Chapters 2–4) have similarly highlighted the detrimental impact of male-dominated educational settings. While data on the gender balance of students in formal jazz courses can be purchased from the Higher Education Statistics Agency, this – alongside staff demographics – has not yet been the focus of a dedicated study. Beyond formal educational settings, data on music professionals more generally in the UK are primarily reliant upon industry organizations and bodies (such as Access Creative College, PRS for Music and the Music Managers Forum) surveying their members. Respondents to such surveys are therefore unrepresentative of the community as a whole – they are aware of such bodies, they have money for membership and they have time and a desire to fill in a survey. More significantly for our understanding of the demographic breakdown within jazz, the data gathered by these surveys is rarely genre-specific. And as we will see, one of the biggest issues for the women that I spoke to is a lack of access to and knowledge of such organizations and other industry gatekeepers.

In establishing some understanding of the jazz landscape which women musicians emerge into and move through, it is useful to consider the central industry gatekeepers of festivals, specialist media and promoters in relation to gender. The power of all three in the successful development of a jazz career was commented upon during the four interviews that inform this chapter. As demonstrated by the figures provided here for CJF and other emerging studies on the gender balance of jazz festivals (see Björck and Bergman 2018), the gender ratio of jazz festival stages is far from balanced. This imbalance at music festivals more generally has acted as the catalyst for the Keychange initiative and the focus for a range of current academic studies (e.g. the current Humanities in the European Research Area (HERA) funded project, *European Music Festivals, Public Spaces and Cultural Diversity*).[1] The gender ratio of jazz promoters is similarly unequal, with men making up 63 per cent of the members of the national Jazz Promotion Network (JPN 2019), despite recent attempts by industry body Help Musicians UK to encourage a new generation of promoters aware of diversity and gender balance issues through their Jazz Promoters Fellowship. This continued dominance of men within the roles of jazz gatekeepers is further reflected in the all-male editorial team of the most prominent, and indeed progressive, specialist magazine. *Jazzwise*, as 'the UK's biggest selling jazz monthly and the leading English language jazz magazine in Europe' (www.jazzwisemagazine.com), is central to the public understanding of jazz and the image of the jazz musician. Looking at the front covers of the magazine over a five-year period (Jan 2014 – Dec 2018) it is clear that this publication constructs a noticeably masculine 'articulation of gender' (Tucker 2002: 397) in relation to jazz, with eight of a total fifty-five issues (15 per cent total) featuring women (issues 233, 231, 228, 223, 213, 202, 194 and 190).

In terms of scholarly and specialist narrating of jazz genre and scene, Willis notes that, 'rather like the Bermuda Triangle, jazz is a mysterious, curious area of complicated intersections where women frequently disappear' (2008: 293). Speaking as an English Literature scholar, Willis explores this disappearance by considering the barriers of the jazz language – as a 'masculine space' – which permeates the ways in which jazz is spoken about and, importantly, defined. This gendered language of jazz not only positions women and their contributions as 'not jazz', but confers upon male musicians and male (song/music) writers the accreditation of 'jazz'. And, as Willis notes, this masculine space becomes the language through which jazz is written about by others, from Colbert's (1975) *Who Wrote That Song?* to Gioia's *The History of Jazz* (1997). In such publications, the experience of women is relegated to the footnotes of jazz, a peppering of one-off examples and the wives of male musicians. In a scholarly translation of this jazz language, jazz academia has become the music and lives of particular Great Men (Tucker 2002). It has become particular musical practices such as improvisation and jamming, or certain time periods of jazz music-making. It is a celebration of genius and the extraordinary events of jazz history.

In her 2002 article and later in a co-edited book (2008), Tucker (and her co-editor Rustin) calls for academics to 'listen for gender'. Building on the growing body of research that identified the masculine space of the jazz scene and scholarship, *Big Ears: Listening for gender in jazz studies* considered gender analysis as a tool for exploring how the jazz music has been 'shaped, directed and recorded by fans, critics, historians and musicians' and examined the 'conditions of possibility' for jazz artists (2008: 2). The subsequent research that has 'listened for gender' has done so by asking different questions, consulting different types of sources or archives, considering different roles in jazz (see Attrep 2018) and questioning dominant narratives. For my own research, I explore the experiences of women in jazz by focusing on music-making practices of the everyday.

Gebhardt, in his consideration of the everyday aesthetics of Ornette Coleman's loft apartment in early 1970s SoHo, asks us to attend to music through the in between times; the 'uneventful or ordinary period of time' (2019: 387) that happens on either side of the brief and temporary extraordinary moments of performances or social gatherings.

Ornette Coleman's album *Friends and Neighbors* (1970) that emerged out of a time of music-making in his SoHo loft has since become extraordinary, but by considering this period within the everyday of this domestic, social and creative space, Gebhardt places the production and message of this music back into the everyday. In relation to this project, asking women about their everyday experiences as jazz musicians meant that we were able to discuss the pathways into and through jazz, their engagements with 'gatekeepers', their strategies for filling a venue, for recording an album and for 'getting through the hard times'. Similarly, by moving beyond a sole focus on the spectacle of the jazz festival and the separate performances of these individual musicians, it is possible to identify the gender politics of the UK jazz industry culture and the potential barriers that exist within this context for women musicians.

Four women have contributed their experiences to this chapter, yet the key themes explored here are echoed throughout the wider research project. Rather than adding more layers or details to 'Great Man narratives', the accounts of musicians engaging with the jazz of their everyday moves dramatically away from the common tropes of jazz genius and the extraordinary moments, focusing instead on the ordinary times and trials of being a woman in the UK jazz industries. Such an understanding of the everyday is central to identifying and addressing issues with gender imbalances within the scene, and for Cheltenham, at UK jazz festivals. Natalie (a vocalist crossing over from a more popular genre), Marnie (a composer and instrumentalist), Sara (a self-taught improviser) and Valerie (an experienced instrumentalist and composer) discussed their everyday music-making and how this related to their gender (all pseudonyms). Three interconnected main themes emerged and have been subsequently related to the current gender imbalance at UK jazz festivals.

Music education: Male dominance, support networks and the formalizing of jazz

All of the four women identified as self-taught in terms of their jazz repertoire, having studied theoretical (rather than practice-focused) programs of formal study beyond school or specialized in other areas of music practice. Sara had undertaken a postgraduate qualification at a conservatoire but found it to be a male-dominated environment. Two – Sara and Valerie – had since become involved in casual teaching at conservatoires but both highlighted the gender imbalance evident within their classes. Equally, they both suggested that this lack of female students is due to the frequency of all-male interview panels for initial student selection (which are not blind auditions), the shortage of female role models on the staff and the scene, and the institutional formalizing of jazz from an improvised and experimental music form to the competent replication of standards for public performances and assessment.

For Sara, this very particular understanding of jazz music led to a loss of confidence and a belief that she (and her music) did not 'belong' or 'fit' and was not of value within the formal conservatoire setting. This feeling drove Sara to leave the jazz scene for several years and, upon her return to public performance, contributed to her reluctance to engage with the scene and to identify herself as a 'jazz musician' more generally. This formalization of jazz and a valuing of certain types of playing, performance and skills has, for Sara, meant that the performance of self and identity through music, and a discovery of this during formal education, has been overtaken by the shaping of a certain type of 'valued' musician through the processes of Higher Education. Despite a worry that she would not 'fit' within the setting and the all-male nature of the cohort, Sara more recently accepted an invitation to teach at a London-based conservatoire, which was a very positive experience. However, this temporary position was further limited by the loss of the member of School staff who had invited Sara to teach. Sara noted in her interview that due to her feelings of being out of place within such formal educational settings, she is not comfortable initiating contacts and future opportunities to teach. With the loss of this particular gatekeeper with whom Sara was familiar, her inroad into teaching was disrupted and another potential woman role model prevented from redressing the balance.

For those that did not attend a UK conservatoire, their inability to access the support and networking system offered to the students and alumni of those institutions also placed them at a disadvantage. All four women relied upon DIY methods of musical development, scene mentoring and trial and error in order to perform and record their music. Even the informal settings of jamming were considered to be a 'boys' club'. The comparative lack of scene support networks, the reliance on DIY methods, and the dominance of homo-social musical environments are all directly linked to the rate of career development and the visibility of women musicians. As I note in relation to CJF's initial Keychange programming strategy, this issue of visibility is key to the underrepresentation of mid-career women jazz musicians at UK jazz festivals and the scene more widely.

'I get off the phone and I am so upset': The emotional labor of 'Doing-it-Yourself'

Sara, Valerie and Marnie did the vast majority of every day work relating to their career. This included writing and distributing press releases, approaching promoters and festival programmers, promoting their latest release, booking (and indeed paying for) venues and recording time, and finding collaborators. As Natalie – who was supported by an agent in her more profitable parallel popular music role – notes, this is not uncommon for the jazz industries which are generally less lucrative and more unstable than classical or musical theatre. However, faced with tokenistic or misogynistic 'gatekeepers' and a reduced support system, each woman that I spoke to reflected upon the emotional and physical strain of doing everything, especially when releasing a new album or making the most out of an award. Not only did these women have to maintain several support roles beyond that of the musician, but they had to develop these skills through a trial-and-error approach and to rely upon their family (rather than jazz scene) support network when the emotional toll became too much.

Beyond dealing with agents who had 'a female pianist on [their] books already', being ignored by sound technicians, frequently finding themselves without a women's dressing room, and side-stepping sexual advances from event organizers, each woman had to manage their own profile within the industry carefully. Social media played a crucial, if double-edged, role in this, but managing the specialist media takes a more sustained approach. All of the women interviewed had read reviews of their performances that began with a critique of their outfit – from criticisms of too revealing dresses to suggestions that trouser suits are indicative of homosexuality – and had therefore become highly conscious of their choices whilst on stage. Natalie also spoke of her desire to be 'taken seriously' as she crossed-over into the jazz scene, choosing a trouser suit. Marnie detailed her strong identity, built upon the confidence of an established career and the increasing support of the London jazz community, but noted that there was conflict between her and editorial teams to maintain control of this. Valerie's comment that she was an object first and a musician second permeated these attempts to manage a music career. The success of each woman in managing the everyday emotional labour of being a woman in jazz was dependent upon their access to skill development, industry-based support systems, knowledge transfer, tenacity, and the support of gatekeepers. Any programming strategy at CJF must be therefore coupled with supporting musician skill and knowledge development, the critical negotiation of misogynistic processes within the industry and reaching out to those musicians who are particularly isolated from the wider scene.

The role of festivals

Each woman impressed upon me the importance of the UK jazz festivals in their career development, with a slot at Cheltenham viewed as a recognition of their place within the jazz industries. Yet each woman also discussed their engagement with jazz festivals in relation to either gendered barriers to access or a set (and equally gendered) definition of jazz. Marnie had cultivated a good working relationship with CJF and had been approached for her 2019 slot. However, her view of other UK-based jazz festivals had been affected by experiences of fellow female musicians who had reported a tokenistic approach to programming women jazz musicians. Natalie had negotiated her acceptance into the festival over a period of time, proving 'her chops' not through a significant fan following, but rather her well-publicized collaboration with well-known, male jazz musicians which she saw as instrumental in Cheltenham accepting her 2019 pitch. Sara and Valerie, both as experienced instrumentalists, expressed the most frustration at the lack of access to and communication with the festival. Furthermore, Sara was unsure of her (and her music's) fit within the program, and had therefore planned composed pieces – with 'a beginning, a middle and an end' – rather than her usual improvisation style.

As an emerging vocalist, Natalie was programmed in one of the smaller venues, and as an established and well-known instrumentalist, Marnie was invited to perform one of her compositions in the second largest venues. Both were aware and supportive of CJF's long-term plans to nurture women jazz musicians through the tiers of the festival. Sara and Valerie, on the other hand, were mid-career instrumentalists and viewed CJF as 'inaccessible' without the support of an agent or a 'way in'. They also voiced a level of caution in relation to Cheltenham's long-term plans, and noted that '[i]f Cheltenham and jazz festivals want 50/50, they have to actively go and find it. It's not going to come to them because we don't know how to go to them' (Valerie). For those women jazz musicians who find themselves outside influential, male-dominated support networks, who fight for respectful and music-focused press coverage, and who manage each element of their career, it was clear that Cheltenham must actively seek out and communicate directly with them. Furthermore, within a scene that is both dominated by male gatekeepers and heavily associated with male musicians, particular instruments, and homo-social practices and spaces, the challenges that face CJF are significant and complex.

These interviews and the themes that emerged were gathered in the run up to the 2019 festival. The section that follows explores the first stage of Cheltenham's Keychange strategy for a gender balanced program, as yet uninformed by this research project and the experiences of the women programmed to perform at the festival. This initial approach works within the current structure and ethos of the festival.

Scheduling a 'gender-balanced' festival program

The Keychange campaign has widely been interpreted within the media as a push for a gender balance of individual musicians on festival stages. However, the interpretation of '50/50 gender balance' is down to the pledging institution. This makes comparative data collection, reporting and measuring the success of this campaign difficult, and has the potential to perpetuate rather than address pervasive gender issues within the music industries. However, as CJF head of programming Emily Jones noted, this interpretative nature of the pledge goes some way in making a scary target more palatable for institutions and offers them a level of control, even if she and many others are aware of the limitations of their institution's interpretation. For CJF, an act is counted as 'female' for the purposes of measuring gender balance if there is at least one female performer on stage. This raises the possibility that while the festival may be technically meeting its 50/50 target, the performers may still be overwhelmingly male if many acts are ensembles dominated by men. For the programming data that follows, the CJF interpretation of 'gender balance' will be used, but the limitations of this will be examined in relation to the wider gender politics of the UK jazz scene, the experiences of the women interviewed and the long-term plans of CJF.

From the seventy-two scheduled ticketed gigs in the 2019 CJF program, forty-two involved sessions with at least one woman on stage, representing 58 per cent of the program. This is a 17 per cent increase on the 2013 schedule (at 41 per cent) and, to provide a longer-term contrast, a 43 per cent increase from the very first CJF program in 1996 (at 15 per cent). This initial decrease in the gender gap for the festival program primarily represents the concerted efforts of Jones in her role as head of programming (since November 2013). In terms of their definition of 50/50, CJF have already met their target. The Keychange pledge supports the work that Jones had already established through her role at Cheltenham and as the Chair of the Jazz

Promoters Network (JPN). As a drummer, DJ and an active participant in the jazz scene, Jones is keenly aware of the 'leaky pipeline' of women, with female participation in jazz visibly decreasing as they progress through formal education and finally make it to the festival stage (see also McKeage 2004; Wehr-Flowers 2006; and Teichman 2018, amongst others). With the support of her management and the work of the wider festival team, Jones has placed gender at the heart of her programming since beginning the role. CJF's strategy for their first year of Keychange relates to programming and talent development support, and attempts to balance between immediate impact and sustainable investment. However, as the four narratives included within this chapter show, CJF and other UK jazz festivals face a range of pervasive and entangled barriers that continue to work against the success of women musicians.

Supporting women musicians through festival programming

The CJF 2019 program features over seventy pay-in performances over six days, across a range of venues. Faced with what she saw as comparatively lower numbers of established women jazz musicians in the UK and the economic restrictions of running an international music festival, Jones focused on targeted programming of emerging women musicians in the smaller venues and booking mixed gender bands. As we shall see, both strategies represent an initial and problematic step in the first year of CJF's pledge. However, it is key to note that these limitations reflect wider issues with the ways jazz is defined and valued within the scene which will hopefully be addressed as part of CJF's longer-term strategy.

Firstly, the current Keychange strategy aims to develop more women musicians through a progressive talent development pathway. This includes earmarking slots in the smaller venues at the festival and offering targeted opportunities for women. For the 2019 program, this strategy was most visible through a larger number of emerging women musicians in the smaller venues at the festival and through the 'Showcase' project which, according to the 2019 brochure, 'opens the doors for two emerging artists' who have previously been involved in the festival Fringe. Whilst seemingly benefitting only emerging artists, Jones noted that this was part of a longer-term attempt to address the current gender inequality evident in the UK jazz industries more generally. These program strategies are also supplemented by year-round talent development activities, such as one-to-one advice sessions with key industry figures. In giving emerging women musicians a major performance opportunity, CJF would be creating the next generation of mid-career women musicians able to command significant audiences, and eventually developing headliners for the future. Based upon her own experience as a musician – and in attempting to address their underrepresentation within the current UK jazz industries – Jones was particularly keen to program female instrumentalists.

Reflecting upon the previous programs, Jones had also focused on booking mixed-gender bands and supporting large, gender balanced ensembles playing music composed by women. However once again, the majority of these mixed bands were emerging rather than established groups. Trawling through the band websites to gather data for this project suggests that such gender roles persist, the common image of the 'mixed' band being a row of male musicians and a woman vocalist or one-off instrumentalist staring back from band photos. However, in relation to the CJF interpretation of 50/50, Jones was aware of the tokenistic approach of 'one woman on stage' and the potential for this to feed current gendered roles within the scene – the female vocalist of an all-male band (see Willis 2008, amongst others). Jones noted that addressing the gender imbalance within 'mixed bands' and the persistence of gendered roles within jazz musicianship would take longer than the remaining four years of Keychange. Alongside a gender-focused program, she aimed to use this first year to set in motion a series of future projects and funding applications that focused on professional development and career support for women musicians.

This initial strategy both supports an emerging generation of women musicians (particularly instrumentalists) and naturalizes a mixed-gender stage. However, this support of female instrumentalists needs to be carefully considered if it is to cascade into the industry more widely. As Willis (2008) has noted, women instrumentalists have long been written out of the jazz language of the specialist and national media as they break with the expected image of the male jazz musician and the pantheon of greats they follow. Similarly, a tokenistic approach of gatekeepers within the current industries was noted by the women that I spoke to, with agents stating that they 'already had a female pianist' on their books. Jones herself also noted the comparative power of these agents, with up to 50 per cent of the program negotiated through agent offerings. Within such a context, CJF – and the other UK jazz festivals that have signed up to Keychange – could play an extremely significant role in providing a platform for women instrumentalists. In order to initiate significant change, they must be both aware of and actively challenge the current hegemonic jazz discourse.

Reflecting on my interviews, it is also clear that the perceived lack of mid-career women jazz musicians by gatekeepers such as CJF is indicative of a more pervasive issue within the jazz industries. Like rock (Cohen 1997; Leonard 2007; Reddington 2012), male musicians have been placed at the centre of the ways in which jazz music is defined, from the influential musicians remembered for their contributions to the various epochs of jazz to associations between improvisation and masculinity (see Tucker 2002 and Hollerbach 2004). Jazz has become viewed by jazz critics and audiences alike as a male genre. Women musicians (particularly instrumentalists) are a novelty rather than a normality on the festival stage, conservatoire courses and magazine covers. As peripheral players, their career is not consistently followed by jazz media and they are not placed as successors (or innovators) in the timeline of 'jazz greats'. For mid-career musicians – those who had been on the scene for over a decade and had previously commanded audiences necessary for mid-sized venues (1,000 capacity) – this is most keenly felt. Sara and Valerie were both mid-career musicians, yet did not feel that their value as established jazz musicians had been acknowledged by CJF or gatekeepers of the jazz scene more widely. They linked their lack of value within the industries, comparative 'invisibility', and limited progression to being a woman in a music scene that values male instrumentalists and that is controlled by men in positions of power and access.

It is not that the UK jazz scene is lacking in experienced women instrumentalists, it is that they do not fit with gendered definitions of jazz music and musician. To compound matters, the achievements of women instrumentalists are less visible in media and they are not always part of the male-dominated circles of musicians that have come to epitomize the scene and offer work opportunities. This comparative invisibility is also in part due to the DIY strategies employed in an attempt to deal with a male-dominated and at times misogynistic music scene. For Cheltenham, the Keychange pledge represents a call to action, at point from which to engage in a more concerted way with issues of access, development and success for women in the UK jazz scene. A more difficult task for the festival is to work beyond the normal channels of jazz media and agents to identify musicians, to communicate their less visible long-term aims to women musicians and to gain their trust that such strategies are indeed rooted in making a difference.

Conclusions and ways forward

This collaborative project articulates the complex barriers that lie in the paths of women musicians who are part of the UK jazz industries. Ultimately, their peripheral place on UK jazz festival stages is due to their comparative 'invisibility' and reduced access to skill development support, networks and performance opportunities required for their professional development. This reduced access and visibility, in turn, is due to the continued gendered nature of the jazz industries and formal education. As Valerie noted in her interview, jazz continues to be a 'boys' club', from the conservatoire interview panel to the jam-session. Not only do women feel uncomfortable within spaces dominated by men, but the formalization of jazz – musically in relation to formal jazz education and through the male-dominated front covers and lead editorial of the specialist media – has further positioned women on the edges of jazz scene and, at times, music.

In addressing the visible gender imbalance on the festival stage, even following their Keychange target 'success', CJF will have to engage with these gender politics of the UK jazz scene and, importantly, act as a role model for the other central gatekeepers. Supporting emerging women jazz artists through the career stages of the festival and pushing for 'mixed gender' bands are elements of this. These issues of visibility and the traditional gendering of jazz roles are more entangled and complex, yet must be considered by Cheltenham if they wish to implement enduring strategies and to establish themselves as a role model in a wider engagement with the gender politics of jazz. Becoming a champion for jazz musicians irrespective of gender will mean an investment in and support of women jazz musicians from emerging to established. It will require an understanding that access varies dependent upon the individual, a push for both the naturalization of gender balanced bands *and* a questioning of gendered roles in jazz, public statements of support for Keychange and other initiatives, and the clear communication of long-term strategies for supporting change with the women it aims to encourage. In acting as an industry role model, CJF will also have to establish and uphold particular expectations of promoters, agents, educational institutions and policy makers on their subsequent roles that feed into the annual festival program. For jazz festivals engaging with Keychange more generally, some shared understanding of what is meant by '50/50' is essential for both accurate data sharing and for addressing key issues of gender within the jazz industries. This is further necessitated by the Keychange request of gender data from all the pledged festivals. An institution-driven interpretation may make this initiative more palatable, but will, without careful consideration, replicate pervasive inequalities.

As one of the largest jazz festivals in the UK, Cheltenham holds a very influential role in terms of assigning value and influencing the ways in which UK jazz is defined. In agreeing to work in partnership with myself and my institution, the festival has demonstrated a desire to understand the complex issues that have led to the underrepresentation of women active in the UK jazz industries. Individuals such as Emily Jones (who personally spoke in support of this partnership) and, by extension, the festival as an organization, recognize the value of both academic research and an ongoing dialogue with women musicians. What, then, can jazz festivals and musicians expect from their relationships with academics such as myself?

As a researcher interested in the ways in which women engage with music scenes, I often consider the role of the scholar and, by extension, the duty of the university or funding body. Reflecting upon my conversations with these women musicians, it is clear that the first contribution I can make is to write about their experiences. As Valerie noted in our conversation, being written about means that other women can read your stories and will know that they are not alone, that other women *have* been there before and that it can be done. Although academics are increasingly 'listening for gender', if we are to understand the UK jazz industries as they stand and the inequality that is laid bare on the jazz festival stage, we must also attest to the jazz of the everyday, the in-between and the ordinary. Jazz and its gender politics are not just the product of a pantheon of musicians, music, places and times, but also the realities of being a musician in contemporary jazz, and as such both need to be taken seriously by academics and festivals alike.

As my own project develops, it is also clear that my time, contacts and my access to city-centre venues and funding could provide the essential ingredients for crucial knowledge and skill development. Universities are perfectly positioned to provide (ideally free) inclusive and accessible events during which information is shared, knowledge exchanged and skills developed. It is encouraging to see initiatives such as Keychange emerging from the industries as individuals and industry bodies recognize the severity of this lack of diversity, gender and otherwise, however much more can be done by academics to address the same issues. In the current landscape of the UK university system, engagement with community issues and demonstrable indicators of impact in the 'real world' encourage us to think carefully how we plan our research projects, how we spend our allocated funding and how we can use the resources available to us to produce within a short space of time impactful change that, most importantly, can exist without the researcher and beyond the life of the research project. Furthermore, in light of jazz scholarship as it stands, it is through a return to the everyday production and consumption of jazz music that the detail of such issues becomes clear. Coupled with a concerted focus on contributing to access as well as knowledge, it is possible for music scholars, too, to make a difference.

Note

1 The data for the gender imbalance at music festivals in the UK has been so far developed by media outlets and industry bodies. For example, the BBC published a report on the gender gap in music festival line-ups in 2018. From nine of the largest music festivals, 77 per cent of acts advertised were male – https://www.bbc.co.uk/news/entertainment-arts-44655719.

References

Attrep, K. (2018), 'From Juke Joints to Jazz Jams: The Political Economy of Female Club Owners', *IASPM@Journal*, 8 (1): 9–23.

Björck, C. and Å. Bergman (2018), 'Making Women in Jazz Visible: Negotiating Discourses of Unity and Diversity in Sweden and the US', *IASPM@Journal*, 8 (1): 42–58.

Cohen, S. (1997), 'Men Making a Scene: Rock Music and the Production of Gender', in S. Whiteley (ed.), *Sexing the Groove: Popular Music and Gender*, 17–36, London: Routledge.

Gebhardt, N. (2019), 'Friends and Neighbours: Jazz and Everyday Aesthetics', in N. Gebhardt, N. Rustin-Paschal and T. Whyton (eds.), *The Routledge Companion to Jazz Studies*, 389–398, New York: Routledge.

Hollerbach, P. (2004), '(Re)voicing Tradition: Improvising Aesthetics and Identity on Local Jazz Scenes', *Popular Music*, 23 (2): 155–171.

Leonard, M. (2007), *Gender in the Music Industry: Rock Discourse and Girl Power*, Aldershot: Ashgate.

McKeage, K.M. (2004), 'Gender and Participation in High School and College Instrumental Jazz Ensembles', *JRME*, 52 (4): 343–356.

PRS Foundation (2017), *Keychange Manifesto*. Available online: https://keychange.eu/wp-content/uploads/2018/11/1052-keychange-A5-v15-web.pdf (accessed 11 March 2019).

Reddington, H. (2012), *The Lost Women of Rock Music: Female Musicians of the Punk Era*, Sheffield: Equinox Publishing.

Steinberg, E.N. (2001), '"Take a Solo": An Analysis of Gender Participation and Interaction at School Jazz Festivals' (Doctoral dissertation). Retrieved from ProQuest Dissertations and Theses database (UMI No. 3029732).

Teichman, E. (2018), 'Something's Missing from My Jazz Band's Bulletin Board: An Autoethnographic Reflection on Making Space for Girls and Women in Jazz Education', *Canadian Music Educator*, 59 (4): 8–12.

Tucker, S. (2002), 'Big Ears: Listening for Gender in Jazz Studies', *Current Musicology*, 71–73 (Spring 2001–Spring 2002): 376–408.

Tucker, S. and N. Rustin (2008), *Big Ears: Listening for Gender in Jazz Studies*, Durham, NC: Duke University Press.

Wehr, E. (2016), 'Understanding the Experiences of Women in Jazz: A Suggested Model', *International Journal of Music Education*, 34 (4): 472–487.

Wehr-Flowers, E. (2006), 'Differences between Male and Female Students' Confidence, Anxiety and Attitude toward Learning Jazz Improvisation', *JRME*, 54 (4): 337–349.

Willis, V. (2008), 'The Location of Women and Subversion in Jazz', *The Journal of American Culture*, 31 (3): 293–301.

15

Queer(ing) Music Production: Queer Women's Experiences of Australian Punk Scenes

Megan Sharp

Introduction

I distinctly remember the first time I saw a woman working behind the scenes at a gig. She was fierce and formidable, commanding and all business. I was a 22-year-old cis-woman who had been involved in a regional punk scene for over five years already, and I was struck by her. How could I have not considered what women do to this sound, to the space I was standing in? Why had I never thought about where they were if they were not in the audience or on the stage? This chapter explores the experiences of queer women who labour in punk music scenes as sound engineers, stage technicians and venue managers. In recording these narratives, the entanglements of pleasure and labour are made known through examinations of gender, queerness, technology and resistance.

Unsurprisingly, informant narratives suggest that doing queer womanhood in punk spaces is complicated by social expectations of femininity and heterosexuality. This is not a new finding: authors before me have documented widely the nexus of power and resistance that queer women are bound by when navigating punk participation (see Ciminelli and Knox 2005; Halberstam 2005; Shoemaker 2010; Wiedlack 2011; Taylor 2013). Further to this, women experience sexualization (see Gavanas and Öström 2016), dismissal (see Abtan 2016) and hostility (see Wajcman 1991) regardless of sexuality, music genre or trans-local punk settings (Marcus 2010). I do not intend here to assert that what heterosexual and queer women do to resist male-domination in punk is markedly different. Instead, I attend to queerness as a particular framework for resistance, one which envelopes sexuality, politics, affect and experience. The following analysis expands upon themes of marginalization to consider the nuance of *how* queer women seek pleasure in resistance in an Australian punk scene.

Drawing broadly on gender and sexuality as signifiers of credentials and authenticity, informants discuss their extracurricular labour as situational to both job security and futurity, as well as community building. The women interviewed suggest that it is through their queerness that they create scope for a continuum of labour, that queerness itself acts as a framework for establishing themselves as removed from the archetype of punk producer and creator which in turn makes their contribution to sound desirable. They explain how they leverage assumptions of gender and sexuality in male-dominated spaces through a kind of socio-spatial preconfiguration; creating strategies of resistance within the margins of dominant punk narratives to attract parts of the community which seek the same.

In curating a queer sound, and a network of queer sound producers, informants are cataloguing new punk archives from which opportunities for work, pleasure and collaboration emerge in a process of stickiness. Ahmed (2004) suggests that stickiness is an ether of queer affect, where sonics and bodies can become tethered. The use of the term sticky in this way communicates an affective transference of emotions through individual and collective *doing*. De Nora (2000: 68) explains this doing of emotion in relation to music as 'musical materials provide[ing] terms and templates for elaborating self-identity – for identity's identification' (De Nora 2000: 68). Adding a queer(ed) perspective to De Nora's claim, this chapter attends to queerness' ability to permeate atmospheres of sound and embodiment which affords both space for new music archives, and the fracturing of historically heterosexual and masculine archives – for example records and books – where gendered power dynamics are a tangible product of place and sound (Halberstam 2005: 326).

Considering affect as stickiness, and in collaboration with Tia De Nora's (2000) theoretical framework of music as a partly written narrative, this chapter contributes to a small and relatively niche body of work concerning queer women as producers and curators of sound and space beyond their audience or performer status. Concentrating data to the Melbourne punk scene, and incorporating an 'insighter' (Hodkinson 2005) ethnography – a methodology which engages reflexively with the researchers' own biographical entanglements of place – this chapter provides a snapshot of lived experience and captures the nuance of queer music production in a local Metropolitan music scene.

Insighter methods

Using qualitative, ethnographic and insighter methods, the stories of fifteen self-identified queer women collected between 2014 and 2017 are reflected in the analysis throughout. I use the term insighter purposefully as I am a part of the punk scene in Melbourne, am both queer and cisfemale, and have close relationships with many informants of this study. However, I am not a sound engineer, stage technician or venue manager and so I cannot assume a wholly insider research status nor do I write from an auto-ethnographic perspective. Such considerations are implicitly epistemological in that my approach to the construction of knowledge is one of lived experience; a nexus of my own knowledge and my informants' knowledges (Taylor 2011). Using the subcultural work of Bennett (2002) and Hodkinson (2005), I theorize insightership malleable practice, warranting attention to the limitations that inhere in both insider and outsider positions. For example, how nuance (re)constructs and distorts knowledge (Sullivan 2003), and how boundary work can challenge knowledge distortion. In addition, the intricacies of self-making and performativity (Butler 1990) form the basis for understanding how technologies of collective embodiments mobilize to step away from domination.

An insighter position affords much potential to expand on the nuances of conversations and interactions, apply historical knowledge to temporal or fleeting circumstances, and utilize the possibilities of a dynamic research population. However, these affordances and possibilities are not without limitations (Jones 2010: 122), even compromises. I have pre-existing relationships with queers in punk, some of which have been intimate, and at times, uneasy. I am at once an insider and an outsider in my research; sometimes I can feel the nuance of a participant experience which informs the depth of our engagement, other times I have little context for their narratives. In that way, I am caught between worlds of knowing which requires considerations of researcher relationality and mobility, ever-shifting across place, space and time.

In addition to the detailed stories of queer women presented below, all of whom identify as cisfemale, my engagement with those who identify as gender diverse, transfeminine, transmasculine and genderqueer, as performers and audience members also informs my wider research. Within this chapter, only the narratives of those who described their experiences as sound engineers, venue managers and stage technicians have been used in order to capture a snapshot of lived experience within specific parameters of labour and technology (see Sharp and Nilan 2015, 2017; Sharp and Shannon, forthcoming).

The theory of DIY and DIT

White, heterosexual cis-men dominate at most punk gigs, on stage, in technical support, in front-of-house and in the audience. This is nothing new in punk, (see for example Halberstam 2005; Sharp and Nilan 2015, 2017; Avery-Natale 2016) or in broader music scenes such as electronic dance music (Abtan 2016), rock (Smith 2009) and hip-hop (Sharpley-Whiting 2007). Yet some queers make a living in the punk scene, sometimes for many years (Taylor 2013) and maintain a queer politic to do so. For example, in specifically queer music scenes, 'both queercore and dyke-core set out to create a queer countercultural sphere constituted via networks of bands, performers, fans, activists, film-makers, zine-makers, writers and clubs that drew on punk's do-it-yourself ethos' (Taylor 2013: 200). In this chapter, I examine the doing of queer resistance, of claim and counter-claim in punk scenes, to foreground punk as a site of contestation and affective production of sound.

The narratives that have been openly shared with me, as a researcher and a queer cis-woman, give weight not only to the struggles of marginalized people to be considered legitimate in punk scenes, but provide insight into how legitimacy is being re-visited in collective terms. Building on the original embedded resistance to commodified culture found in Do It Yourself (DIY) culture (Threadgold 2017) while also critiquing it, a Do It Together (DIT) approach forefronts a practical way that space and sound can become queer(ed). An analysis of DIT as an embedded on-the-job skill set provides some explanation of how queer women are able to work within the margins of – and renegotiate – dominant tropes. In doing so, DIT presents an eminently collective method of claiming space and time in tangible ways, for example, the use of safe(r) spaces policies at gigs. In this way, I theorize the epistemological meanings of DIT with a specific focus on the queer *doing of togetherness*; relationship maintenance, visibility work, (re)claiming credibility and dismantling gendered boundaries located in punk scenes. It is argued that this is a 'sticky' process in Ahmed's (2004) terms.

Using Ahmed's theory of affect as a stickiness; collective affects that become 'sticky' (Ahmed 2004), the potential for space to be considered queered is evident. The use of the term sticky in this way communicates an affective transference of emotions through doing. Ahmed (2004: 91) describes the stickiness of emotions and the expectations of them as, 'what objects do to other objects … a relation of doing in which there is not a distinction between passive or active'. Rather, a 'sticky' attachment evolves in the doing. The intangible becomes 'sticky' in that 'emotions are not only about movement, they are also about attachments or about what connects us to this or that' (ibid: 11). Using this concept means that queer(ed) space can be mapped by materializing abstract terms such as embodiment, space and even, queer. And even more so, these sticky experiences can be mapped as a collective intensity which mobilizes emotions. The movement of affective transference in queer punk spaces and times illustrates how affective atmospheres (Anderson 2009; Ash 2015) come *into* doing.

Considering that sound engineers, stage technicians and venue managers also at times, form part of the audience, I acknowledge their interchangeable roles in the embedded power dynamics of the wider social space that frames audience and performer sites. In doing so, I take the notion of affective atmospheres to describe the ways that embodied senses of self and their prescribed performativity rub together in social spaces (see Massumi 2002; Anderson 2009; Pile 2010; Ash 2015) or become 'sticky' (Ahmed 2004). Punk + queer achieves a hybrid metaphorical space that transcends the physical space of the venue through extensions of *affect* that are collaboratively accomplished. The kinds of social and cultural capital brought to this space by embodied queer women and gender diverse people are combined in the collective practice of DIT to achieve unexpected new distinctions of bodily habitus and cultural taste in the field of punk, which has always been a fertile site for political contestation in any case.

Notably, like those who have written about queer time and space in subcultural scenes before me, I do not assume that all queer people live radically different lifestyle to their straight counterparts. As Halberstam points out, 'queer subcultures produce alternative temporalities by allowing their participants to believe that their futures can be imagined according to logics that lie outside of those paradigmatic markers of life experience – namely, birth, marriage, reproduction, and death' (2005: 2). Similarly, this research is being conducted at the intersection of labour, class and gender norms.

Pleasure and labour

For informants, earning an income in the punk music scene establishes a complicated relationship between pleasure and labour. There are the obvious gender imbalances and performative roles implicit in a heteronormative, masculinized workplace, however these women describe a nexus of joy in their work, beyond simply their 'passion' for music, sound production and event organizing. Informants suggested to me – perhaps fearing that their skills would be erased in my interpretation of their stories – that while they did have a passion for their work, this should not be taken as the sole rationale for their continued participation in difficult subcultural terrains. Instead, they urged me to look beyond passion and to address their expertise as knowledge producers, particularly their commitment to effective communication and skills in critical community building. As a result, this chapter section interrogates firstly an example of hegemonic gender relations in punk spaces to contextualize a gig space and subsequently, an analysis of what queer women do to find pleasure in their labour set apart from their passion for music and sound.

Speaking to gendered codes and as a sentiment echoed by all fifteen informants of this research, D reflects on the differences between interactions of male and female sound engineers, and the labour that is invested in fracturing these tropes of behaviour. Speaking from the perspective of an off-the-clock sound engineer who is participating as an audience member D notes:

> There is a big difference between the kind of tone and language that men use to address men, and how they address women. There is nothing odd about seeing a man publicly dismiss a woman in a way he would never do to another man. (D, Sound Engineer)

In D's example, one of many provided to me by informants on this topic, if the audience can see a female or gender diverse band member asking a male sound engineer to adjust the volume or effects, they can then observe the sound engineer's overt or covert dismissal of her request. Audience members of different genders and from different experiential backgrounds may react to this kind of interaction in varying ways; anger, agreement, distaste, humour, apathy and so on. The bodies at a gig that experience an event, such as that which D described, rub together in active praxis (Massey 1999) and in doing so, create an affective atmosphere (Anderson 2009). The experience of the band members, the audience and the sound engineer intermingle to form an intense atmosphere of collective, bodily engagement or disengagement. This atmosphere becomes highly affective in varied responses to gendered stereotypes. Some of those present may feel anger at a man dismissing a woman, whereas others may think he is 'just doing his job'. Some may fail to notice. As an instance of non-interlocking contestation, she emphasizes the affect and effect of telegraphing a gendered insult: 'he would never do that to another man'.

In this way, discourses of gender difference become produced and reproduced at the intersection of power and knowledge (Foucault 1998). Unless there is a disruption, embedded power structures are (re)produced using these codes, and authority and privilege are withheld because female/queer/gender non-conforming participation is routinely undermined. D goes on to suggest that at times like these, she must make a choice to go beyond her technological expertise and dip into her 'queer lived experience' to do the work of destabilizing paternalistic reinforcement. In terms of labour, this decision-making process invokes the body's memory and,

> extends the body's role beyond that of a vessel that treads the past/present line, instead transforming it into a tool, which physically produces queer futures from the debris of queerness' history, the still-warm corpse of the immediate past, and the ever-shifting moment in which the body operates. (Rosenberg and Sharp 2018: 165)

D is clear that in these moments of decision making, it is not her passion that decides her willingness to disrupt gendered codes. Rather it is her own biography that determines her capacity; whether she has been in this situation before and what she knows about calling out language from her experiences with both queer and punk cultures. It is from her biography that D develops skills which she then applies in these potentially hostile places of participation. For D, there is pleasure in this process. She notes,

> at least I can think about how to manage calling someone out in a gig space, because my friends and I talk about doing this stuff all the time. I learn about my work from my social circles as much as I make friends through work. (D, Sound Engineer)

Here, D draws on knowledge building as a reflexive entanglement between work and embodiment. Through the process of knowing, D feels confident to do labour beyond her role in a way that leverages her lived experiences while still doing her job – something that is required to maintain employment security and futurity. This conceptual queer past-present-future triad can be seen to produce a type of queer affective atmosphere (Anderson 2009), where the feelings of fear and unsafety meet their positive counterparts, through the agentic role that queer bodies have in the construction of desirable futures. So, while informants noted that they were consistently *making an investment* (D, Sound Engineer) in punk, they are also investing in their future and the futures of a community of non-cismale experts. In making spaces more accessible to non-dominant identities, queer women provide themselves and others with space to work within the margins. In this way, queer women concentrate on labouring subversively in order to maintain community and build networks.

Strategies of resistance

Following on from pleasure and labour, queer women fracture, understand and reconfigure masculinist repertoires of behaviour through, what Halberstam (2005) asserts as 'strategies of resistance'. Informants explain how they negotiate socio-spatial preconfiguration; taking up strategies of resistance within the margins of dominant punk narratives as opposed to simply being relegated there by the majority. In this way, informants see themselves as actively seeking out a space in the periphery of punk as a supposition of labour, rather than attempting to infiltrate the centre.

In studying DJ culture, similar patterns of establishing a career as a woman were noted. Gavanas and Reitsamer (2016: 5) document female DJs in Berlin, London, Vienna and Stockholm using 'a typical method to compensate for her exclusion from male-dominated scene networks: she organised her own regular club nights, to which she invited other DJs and where she herself performs, and she set up her own networks.' Smith (2009: 150), in their work on female sound engineers in rock scenes in New Zealand notes that historically, women 'tended to enter the field of sound engineering through academic training and hands-on experience at women's music festivals. These routes into sound engineering are forms of resistance to women's exclusion from mainstream avenues into sound'. Drawing on this literature, the below cases of informants L and C extend discourse to include a queer(ed) strategy of resistance, one that is specific to a punk and queer setting. L and C's stories are representative of a broad theme of strategies echoed by informants.

L is a queer, cisfemale sound engineer who lives in Melbourne after moving from a small town in New South Wales in the early 2000s. L regularly attends gigs as an audience member, but is also a member of several bands. She has been working as a sound engineer for the last five years. She mixes bands several nights a week,

> I get the sweetest feedback from bands really regularly, and I have a constant stream of work coming in because people have either heard a good mix at a show or heard of me from someone else. But those nice things are often offset by bands and performers who have never met me and I can see the shock on their faces when they realise a woman is mixing [for] them. Shock and then concern. (L, Sound Engineer)

Reputation plays a significant part in L's career opportunities. Her credentials have paved the way for her to continue working in the job that she loves. L acknowledges her capabilities by saying that 'people have heard a good mix'. Overwhelmingly this statement reflects that her nexus of social capital is the most powerful tool she has to obtain employment. By stating that newcomer acts express shock when she appears as their sound engineer, L highlights an understanding of ongoing gender stereotypes within the punk community, even in Melbourne where many informants have relocated in order to escape small town career and music barriers. The fact that newcomers are 'surprised' to see her as the sound engineer of a show indicates the underrepresentation of women working in this scene.

And yet there is a complication for L in her role as a sound engineer, one that Smith (2009: 269) found in their research of New Zealand female sound engineers, where 'a number of women respondents related incidents of male audience members and sound engineer colleagues attempting to elbow their way behind the mixing desk'. L suggested to be that there are times 'where you are so angry that someone is undermining you, you tell them to fuck off and worry about professionalism later'. While Smith's respondents – who were primarily involved in rock and hard rock scenes and whose sexualities were reported as mostly heterosexual – reported 'it was fairly typical for such behaviour to be downplayed, considered a triviality' (2009: 269) by female sound engineers, informants in this research were more likely to assert their boundaries, rather than consider whether they would be hired back at the venue again.

There are a multitude of potential reasons for queer women's likelihood of taking space invasion seriously, however I would suggest that the two most obvious are the radical community building strategies queers employ, and the flipped social script of heteronormative femininity. Gavanas and Reitsamer (2016: 11) find similar alliance building strategies and expenditure of emotional labour in DJ work, 'where "queer" is understood as a strategic term for alliance-building with cultural producers who identify themselves as transgender or refuse membership or approval seeking according to the criteria and gatekeepers in the heteronormative and male-dominated scenes'. Queerness therefore becomes communication, where the discursive production of difference is challenged by queer boundaries. In the same vein as above, C, a sound engineer and stage technician told me about her experience of learning sound production in a tertiary setting as well as the use of online sound engineers groups for non-cismale contractors.

> There were very few women in my cohort at TAFE, and it got less and less as time went on. They had to separate us into a group just for women so that we had a chance to speak and work things out. So I guess that flows into a work space where, to feel like you can ask a question without this assumption that your gender is hindering your knowledge, you have to create a place to ask. (C, Sound Engineer/ Stage Technician)

C describes that with these tactics, those who are marginalized actively refute the engagement of cis-men in certain networks. This non-interlocking strategy lends itself less to queerness specifically, and more to gender inequality which represents a disruption to cismales being privileged in the scene on the basis of their gender. C pointed out that she needed to do additional labour to feel confident in asking questions about her profession, and that this can impact the end-goal of her learning and her work. Interestingly, C notes that generally she has good experiences with cismale sound engineers in punk settings and that the labour she does is in anticipation of being dismissed, rather than being sure of dismissal. Therefore, these preconfigurations present extra labour that potentially cismale engineers and technicians do not engage with. Extending from the concept of emotional labour, queer – and arguably heterosexual – women who continue to be active members of punk scenes imply that they do not simply participate, rather they make an investment in changing the dynamic of the male homosocial punk landscape.

C sees the strategy of women as technical assistants and engineers bonding together as 'nipping it in the bud' (negative female gender stereotyping), by excluding cis-men from their dialogue around obtaining work or playing a show. It seems that a sense of community is being built within both the virtual and physical communities, and that 'the grrrl gang' of female sound engineers (as well as trans and non-binary people) flourishes. Some of those strategies include forming groups on social media sites, such as Facebook, exclusively for queers, women and gender diverse people. These sites afford private spaces where, for example, employment can be offered and shared amongst those who may be overlooked in other situations. This practice demonstrates resistance to the male-gendered nepotism that commonly exists within the scene. These groups are not only practical resources, but also sites of intimacy where women and other marginalized groups can feel safety in sharing or acquiring knowledge.

Another example of this kind of community based networking is present in the LISTEN project which has a female and gender non-conforming audio and sound engineer database called Listen Lists. The global, online database aims to 'subvert the 'go to' culture that continues to allow men to dominate key areas of the music industry' (www.listenlistenlisten.org), and engineers can self-subscribe in order to publish their contact details. The practice of creating private or exclusive forums in order to share opportunities reveals the need for women to act in a way that remains covert, or at the very least within the margins of the broader music scene.

Queer(ing) sonics and archives

Lastly, I analyse the impact of a queer identity on a historically heterosexual and masculine music space where gendered power dynamics are a tangible product of place and sound. These sonic affects and gendered codes go beyond a gig space and into a virtual realm as S explains below. S explores this affective space of *doing more,* as D recounted above, in detailing how she obtains knowledge about her profession. In attempting to gain more technical experience, S must navigate a masculinized online archive of knowledge regarding sound production. S's articulation of the masculinist landscape of technological proficiency was a commonality among informants, who noted that there are multiple entry points into a discussion about gender and sexuality inequality in music scenes, some of which are more obvious than others.

> It's not just the show space or even the working part of being a sound engineer. Like, having to learn about things, look them up online, you're just bombarded with men attributing knowledge to masculinity. Like, online tutorials are all addressing men, assuming that men are the only ones watching. (S, Sound Engineer/Stage Technician)

Here I posit that there is a broader structural force at play, one that ascribes technical proficiency to cis-men, while assuming a technical ineptness for women. S's statement reflects a body of work which has accounted for this. Smith (2009) in drawing on Wajcman's Technofeminism thesis notes, even in writing about the technologies of sound from a sociological standpoint, we often (re) produce gendered coding.

Wajcman (1991: 23-24) asks us to consider technology, and the way it is studied, with greater attention to the interplay between gender and skill.

> This blindness to gender issues is … indicative of a general problem with the methodology adopted by the new sociology of technology. Using a conventional notion of technology, these writers study the social groups which actively seek to influence the form and direction of technological design. What they overlook is the fact that the absence of influence from certain groups may also be significant. For them, women's absence of influence from observable conflict does not indicate that gender interests are being mobilised. For a social theory of gender, however, the almost complete exclusion of women from the technological community points to the need to take account of the underlying structure of gender relations. (Wajcman 1991: 23-24)

I contend, as Wajcman (1991) and Smith (2009) do, that the production of sound and sonic knowledge and even more broadly, inanimate technology, re-establishes a kind of technological determinism where technology is assumed to be gender neutral, and thereby also assumes 'that where gender is concerned, technology is democratic' (Smith 2009: 160). However, I go further with this line of critique to say that technology, and the distribution of its knowledge, are implicitly heteronormative.

> You are never going to get the same mix twice, that's just the way that sound works. But I think it's important to recognise gender and sexuality in a mix, not that it's the be all and end all, but that the way queers hear and learn about music impacts the way they approach music. (S, Sound Engineer)

S contributed greatly to this theme of queer(ing) sound by interrogating linkages between lived experience and technology. She highlighted throughout her time with me that in her role as a sound engineer, she utilizes a DIY/DIT approach to her work while also drawing on her biographical assemblies of knowledge. In this way, the sounds that she curates are amplifications of belonging, resistance and community which she telegraphs to the inclusion of some (queers and other non-dominant groups) and the exclusion of others (cis-men).

There are obvious ways she can do this, for example, being selective with the bands, performers and genres she chooses to work with. However, there are also nuanced elements of choice embedded in the work that she produces. A practical application of this is S's own growing up queer narrative, where the music of her past informs the sound that she amplified, the influences that she draws on, and the curation of the recording and engineering process. For example, finding queercore as a young person influenced S's interpretation of sound, what it meant to find it, what the audience looked like, felt like, acted like, what they enjoyed and connected to. These knowledges inform S's production approach, where certain sonic manipulations are suggested to artists in the form of references to the sound of other artists. As Sylvia Massey, a US-based sound engineer who has built a career from her craft states,

> I am a designer of experience, a documentarian who captures fleeting moments of audio that I transform into an enduring legacy. I write from the perspective of an operator who is creating an audio postcard to the future. It was a shared experience when it was recorded, and you get a sense of those special moments every time it is played back. (Massey 2016: 2)

From such a perspective, and in S's case, we must then consider De Nora's claim of music being a partly written narrative. In this sense, music is *doing*; an active ingredient in the reflexive construction of space-making. The influence of music transcends performance within a set space, punctuating the composition of bodies and passages of time. Music is then a soundtrack to embodied social action (De Nora 2000: 17), even while music itself acts as an affective fabric that embeds itself in broader cultural artefacts. Style, aesthetic and culture mobilize around music, as do constitutions of self and other, highlighting the transformative characteristics of the make-up, take up and archival of music (De Nora 2000).

Kumbier (2014) explores the multitude of alternative mediums queer people utilize as archives of queer history, such as oral accounts of now-destroyed artefacts and collaborative archival curation. Through archiving, we become 'archival/archiving subjects', both narrators and actors in a set of stories which would otherwise never be recorded. One approach to these actions is 'archiving from the ground up' (2014: 124); within this praxis, the people within the group determine the choice of materials, language and narratives archived. As S describes above, mixes are recorded and stored, shared and heard, left unplayed and used in the future. In this way, S creates an archive, but also becomes archive; looking back on sound to judge its future qualities. Ultimately, what I suggest here is that the production of music can be considered beyond the technical, and into a frame of archival which implicitly stores identities and has the potential to queer the broader cultural landscape of punk.

Conclusion

There is so much more to be said of women who are mobilizing their gender and queerness in labour, particularly punk scenes; durability, resilience and desire for inclusive spaces are especially important to wider contexts of gender, feminism, music and sexualities. Importantly, it is the dismissal and relegation faced which leads to rich and reflexive practices of resistance, thus creating a collective resource which challenges the ongoing heteronormativity of the punk scene. The fifteen informants who were venue staff, sound engineers or organizers of events described examples of redistributing labour and safety to other non-cismale groups. Naming these as strategies of resistance (Halberstam 2005) provides a lens with which to view seemingly disjointed tactics as a single holistic function – equity praxis. Importantly, *working within the margins* is described by informants as a key resistance to dominant tropes of behaviour. Rather than attempting to infiltrate the centre, queer women remain outliers in order to maintain community and build networks. In doing so, this research positions queer(ing) sound and space as subversively disruptive to the encoded normativity of the Melbourne punk music scene.

Describing how bodies – queer and otherwise – fill (or do not fill) these sonic places where transformative moments happen offers a rich and deepened analysis that goes beyond the usual account of queer people, and women, as marginalized. Instead, they are shown to be making active and political choices concerning their participation in punk, choices which entangled with the affective transference of biographies and music. Moreover, the production of sound is considered through a queer identity where it becomes part of the history of punk and contributes in some way to how music affects those who engage with it, as well as those who do not. Queer sound engineers, stage technicians and venue managers' choices are the result of investments made in certain knowledges, collectives and performances. Informants invest labour in their scene, which acts as individual and collective doing work, helping to reconfigure spaces to be safe(r) for marginalized people. And while their marginality still matters, as we see in the examples of minority focused online groups, it acts as a site of preconfiguration to oppression, rather than simply being a product of it.

References

Abtan, F. (2016), 'Where Is She? Finding the Women in Electronic Music Culture', *Contemporary Music Review*, 35 (1): 53–60.

Ahmed, S. (2004), *The Cultural Politics of Emotion*, New York: Routledge.

Anderson, B. (2009), 'Affective Atmospheres', *Emotion, Space and Society*, 2 (2): 77–81.

Ash, J. (2015), 'Technology and Affect: Towards a theory of Inorganically Organised Objects', *Emotion, Space and Society*, 14: 84–90.

Avery-Natale, E.A. (2016), *Ethics, Politics, and Anarcho-Punk Identifications: Punk and Anarchy in Philadelphia*, Maryland: Lexington Books.

Bennett, A. (2002), 'Researching Youth Culture and Popular Music: A Methodological Critique', *The British Journal of Sociology*, 53 (3): 451–466.

Butler, J. (1990), *Gender Trouble. Feminism and the Subversion of Identity*, New York: Routledge.

Ciminelli, D. and K. Knox (2005), *Homocore: The Loud and Raucous Rise of Queer Rock*, Los Angeles: Alyson Books.

De Nora, T. (2000), *Music in Everyday Life*, Cambridge: Cambridge University Press.

Foucault, M. (1998), *The History of Sexuality: The Will to Knowledge*, London: Penguin.

Gavanas, A. and A. Öström (2016), *DJ-liv. Historien om hur diskjockeyn erövrade Stockholm* (DJ Life. The Story about How the DJ Conquered Stockholm), Stockholm: Gidlunds Förlag.

Gavanas, A. and R. Reitsamer (2016), 'Neoliberal Working Conditions, Self-Promotion and DJ Trajectories: A Gendered Minefield', *Postscriptum*. Available online: https://www2.hu-berlin.de/fpm/popscrip/themen/pst12/pst12_gavanas_reitsamer.pdf (accessed 5 December 2018).

Halberstam, J. (2005), *In a Queer Time and Place: Transgender Bodies, Subcultural Lives*, New York: New York University Press.

Hodkinson, P. (2005), 'Insider Research in the Study of Youth Cultures', *Journal of Youth Studies*, 8 (2): 131–149.
Jones Jr, R. (2010), 'Putting Privilege into Practice through Intersectional Reflexivity: Ruminations, Interventions, and Possibilities', *Reflections: Narratives of Professional Helping*, 16 (1): 1–5.
Kumbier, A. (2014), *Ephemeral Material: Queering the Archive*, United States: Litwin Books.
LISTEN, www.listenlistenlisten.org (accessed 6 September 2018).
Marcus, S. (2010), *Girls to the Front: The True Story of the Riot Grrrl Revolution*, New York: HarperCollins.
Massey, D. (1999), 'Space-Time, 'Science' and the Relationship between Physical Geography and Human Geography', *Transactions of the Institute of British Geographers*, 24 (3): 261–276.
Massey, S. (2016), *Recording Unhinged: Creative and Unconventional Music Recording Techniques*, Milwaukee: Hal Leonard Books.
Massumi, B. (2002), *Parables for the Virtual: Movement, Affect, Sensation*, Durham, NC: Duke University Press.
May T. (ed.) (2002), *Qualitative Research in Action*, London: Sage.
Pile, S. (2010), 'Emotions and Affect in Recent Human Geography', *Transactions of the Institute of British Geographers*, 35 (1): 5–20.
Rosenberg, S. and M. Sharp (2018), 'Documenting Queer (ed) Punk Histories: Instagram, Archives and Ephemerality', *Queer Studies in Media and Popular Culture*, 3 (2): 159–174.
Sharp, M. and P. Nilan (2015), 'Queer Punx: Young Women in the Newcastle Hardcore Space', *Journal of Youth Studies*, 18 (4): 451–467.
Sharp, M. and P. Nilan (2017), 'Floorgasm: Queer(s), Solidarity and Resilience in Punk', *Emotion, Space and Society*, 25: 71–78.
Sharp, M. and B. Shannon (forthcoming), 'Becoming Non-Binary: An Exploration of Gender Work in Tumblr', in N. Ferris, A. Herrera and D. Compton (eds.), *Race, Gender and Sexuality in the Digital Age*, New York: Springer.
Sharpley-Whiting, T.D. (2007), *Pimps Up, Ho's Down: Hip-Hop's Hold on Young Black Women*, New York: New York University.
Shoemaker, D. (2010), 'Queer Punk Macha Femme: Leslie Mah's Musical Performance in Tribe 8', *Cultural Studies and Critical Methodologies*, 10 (4): 295–306.
Smith, D.M. (2009), *Decibelles: Gender and Power in Sound Engineering for Popular Music in New Zealand*. PhD Thesis. Retrieved from: https://ourarchive.otago.ac.nz/bitstream/handle/10523/373/Decibelles+final.pdf?sequence=1.
Sullivan, N. (2003), *A Critical Introduction to Queer Theory*, New York: New York University Press.
Taylor, J. (2011), 'The Intimate Insider: Negotiating the Ethics of Friendship When Doing Insider Research', *Qualitative Research*, 11 (1): 3–22.
Taylor, J. (2013), 'Claiming Queer Territory in the Study of Subcultures and Popular Music', *Sociology Compass*, 7 (3): 194–207. https://doi.org/10.1111/soc4.12021
Threadgold, S. (2017), *Youth, Class and Everyday Struggles*, London: Routledge.
Wajcman, J. (1991), *Feminism Confronts Technology*, Cambridge: Polity Press.
Wiedlack, M.K. (2011), 'LOL – Lick It Out Loud: Punk Rock as a Form of Queer Activism', in B. Scherer and M. Ball (eds.), *Queering Paradigms II: Interrogating Agendas*, 209–224, Bern: Peter Lang.

Index

Abramo, J. M. 18–20, 23, 30
Agamben, Giorgio 154
Ahmed, S. 202, 204
Aldredge, M. 104
all-girl music technology 21–2, 120
Ambrose, J. 93
American Utopia (Byrne) 131, 140
anti-music approach 147
Anu, Christine 83
APRA AMCOS (The Australian Performing Rights Association and Australian Mechanical Copyright Owners' Society) 60, 76, 78
Arena, Tina 83
Armstrong, V. 20, 64–5
Art Labor, Sex Politics (Wilson) 150
art school training (Fistfuck) 149–54
Assmann, A. 150
Australian Women Screen Composers: Career Barriers and Pathways (Strong & Cannizzo, 2017) 76

Bain, Vick 40 n.4
Baker, S. 35–6, 111
Balance, John 160 n.4
Banyard, V. L. 98
Bartmann, D. 111
Baxter, Stewart 35, 40 n.4
Bayton, M. 20
BDSM (Bondage and Discipline, Domination and Submission, Sadism and Masochism) practices 8, 147, 154
Beard, M. 33
Beckett, Samuel 153
bedroom production 55
Beegle, A. 17
Bennet, S. 98
Bennett, A. 202
Bernstein, B. 18
Bersani, Leo 154

Biddle, I. 34
black and minority ethnic (BAME) women 123
Bloomaert, Jan 16
Bloustien, G. 111
Bogdanovic, D. 30, 32, 36
Bollywood 4, 9, 175–6, 180–4
Bondage and Discipline, Domination and Submission, Sadism and Masochism. See BDSM practices
Born, G. 31, 65, 109
Both Sides Now programme 35
Bourdieu, P. 18, 105–6, 109, 137
boys' club' 1, 6, 29, 31, 37, 64, 66, 69, 76, 78, 103, 131–2
British Asian music scene, gender
  Bhamrahs 178
  Bhangra and Asian Underground: South Asian Music and the Politics of Belonging in Britain 177
  coping mechanism 180
  factors 177
  fears and restrictions 178
  female performers 179
  Hard Kaur 179–80
  lack of women 177
Burnard, P. 104
Butler, Judith 105
Byrne, David 131, 137, 140

Campbell, P. S. 17
camping spaces 97
Chadwick, Helen 151
Cheltenham Jazz Festival (CJF) 9, 187–9, 197
Choueiti, M. 2
Christopherson, Peter 'Sleazy' 160 n.4
Cloonan, M. 40 n.1
cluster sampling approach 135
Cobb, G. 19
Cohen, B.M.Z. 35–6, 111

Coleman, Ornette 190–1
Colley, A. 21
Collins, Patricia Hill 165
Comber, C. 21
community performance nights 104, 106–7, 111–12, 113
composers 6, 132, 136, 149
    Australian screen composers study 59–60
    educated women 60–4
confidence 6, 21, 33, 36, 64, 76, 78–80, 83–4, 111–12, 189, 191, 193
Connell, C. 17
Connell, J. 104
Conor, B. 37, 40
Cooper, Brittney 167
Cooper, R. 91
creative industries 3–4, 9, 37, 63, 69, 77
Crenshaw, K. 123
cultural scaffolding 7, 90
    of sexual violence 91, 93–6

Dalimore, Claudia Sangiorgi 73
dance 93, 177, 180, 182–3
Darley, J. 98
Davies, Dai 40 n.4
De Nora, Tia 202, 211
Deleuze, G. 155–6
1992 Deluxe (Princess Nokia) 163
    DIY 171
    gender expressions, multitude 170
    Goddess power 172
    lyricism and flow 170
    shifting positionalities 170
    Smart Girl Club 171
    social impact 168
    SoundCloud 169
    spirituality, theme 170
    success of 171
    urban feminism 168–9
    visual art 169
Devine, K. 31, 65, 109
Dewey, John 19
Dhanoa, Kiranee 178
Dhillon, Taran Kaur. *See* Hard Kaur
Dibben, N. 30, 109
Do It Together (DIT) approach 203–4
Do-It-Yourself (DIY) 9, 147, 192–3, 197, 210
    creative projects 169
    and DIT 203–4
    principles 171
    record production 150
Dobner, Sarah-Jane 135
Doehring, Andre 138
Donze, P. L. 121
Doyle, Jennifer 153
Dudrah, Rajinder 185
Durham, Aisha 167
Dyer, R. 35

Edmund, M. 149
electronic music 1, 45–7, 49, 148
Ellis-Petersen, H. 140
Eltham, Ben 84 n.2
England's Hidden Reverse: A Secret History of the Esoteric Underground (Keenan) 151, 153
Eno, Brian 149
Equality and Diversity Charter 119
Evans, K. 93

femininity 9, 18, 34–6, 45, 48, 52, 91–2, 105, 109, 121, 169–70, 176, 178, 181–2, 201, 208
feminism 8, 163–4, 166–72, 209, 211
    liberal 125
    self-care in 172
    urban 8, 163–4, 168–9
feminist theories 105, 168
festivals 9, 73, 78–9, 82, 90, 93, 95–8, 112, 118, 122, 131, 135–42, 168, 176, 191–2, 198, 207
    Cheltenham jazz festival 187–9
    role of 193–4
    gender balance/imbalance 189, 194–7, 199 n.1
    scheduling/scheduling conflicts 79, 187–8, 194–7
Finkel, Rebecca 105
Fistfuck 147–9, 151, 153–4, 157, 159, 160 n.2
Foster, P. 137
Foucault, M. 154, 156
Fraser, N. 125
Frasqueri, Destiny 8
Freeman, Elizabeth 155

Friends and Neighbors (Coleman) 191
Frith, S. 91, 150

gatekeepers 7–9, 64, 107, 113, 131–2, 135–42, 188–94, 196–7, 208
Gavanas, A. 207–8
Gavey, Nicola 90, 98
Gebhardt, N. 190–1
gender
    inequality (*see* inequalities)
    in music higher education 30–1
    norms and stereotypes 32–7, 91–4
    and sexuality 29
gender-balanced festival program
    50/50 gender balance 194
    gender gap 194
    supporting women musicians 195–7
gender-diverse students 2
gender imbalance 48
    addressing 53–4
    music technology education 53–4
    scheduling conflicts 82
    UK jazz scene 191, 199 n.1
gender mainstreaming (GM) 117–19
    BAME women 123
    conceptualizing equality 121–3
    motivations 120–1
    practices 7, 120–3
    strategies 119
Gender Matters (2015) 74
gendering musical labour 7, 59, 83, 105, 108, 110–12, 118–19, 121–2, 125, 127, 193, 205–6, 208, 211
gendering of instruments 30–4, 36, 38–9, 45, 109–10, 118, 194–7
Gibson, C. 104
gig economy 4
Gill, R. 37, 40, 64, 78, 84 n.2
Giroux, H. 69
Green, L. 16, 30, 39, 65
Grimes 45
The Guardian 140

Haenfler, R. 92
Halberstam, J. 157, 204, 206
Halperin, David 154
Hannam, James 40 n.4

Hard Kaur 4, 9, 175, 182, 185 n.1
    artistic journey 176, 184
    bridging diaspora and homeland 183
    career 179, 184
    language skills 183
Hargreaves, D. J. 21
Haritaworn, Jin 170
Hawkins, S. 39
Hebert, D. G. 30
Hegarty, Paul 148
hegemonic masculinity 34, 49, 94, 105
Her Sound, Her Story (Hunder & Dalimore) 73–4, 83–4
heterosexuality 19, 49, 91, 170, 201–3, 208–9
hidden curriculum 6, 54–5, 59, 65–9
hip-hop 163–72, 175–6, 179–80, 183–4, 203
The History of Jazz (Gioia) 190
Hodkinson, P. 202
Hollows, J. 20
Homan, Shane 84 n.3
Honan, Nuala 132, 135
Honeysuckle (Princess Nokia) 168
Horne, H. 150
How Popular Musicians Learn (Green) 16
Hunder, Michelle Grace 73
Hunt, G. 93
Hutton, F. 93

inequalities 1, 3, 117
    addressing 55, 69
    arts and cultural industries 78
    in creative work 75
    evidence 90
    indices to measure 74
    issues of 18, 23
    in music higher education 30–1
    in music scenes 209
    of participation 76–7
    with sexual violence 91
    socio-cultural 39
    stereotyping 35
    weaker networks 39
interactions with (male) classmates
    female presence in male spaces 51–2
    male classmates, experiences with 49–50

male spaces and women's behaviour 50–1
intersectionality 3, 117, 123–4, 127, 164, 166, 171

James, M. 125
Jarman, Derek 151
Jarman-Ivens, F. 34
Jones, Amelia 154
Jones, Emily 188–9, 194–5

Kapoor, Ekta 185 n.2
Kaur, Surinder 179
Keenan, David 151–2
Kelly, L. 90
Ketiboah-Foley, Jasmine 135
Keychange 141–2
    and Cheltenham Jazz Festival 187–9
    gender balanced program 194–7
Keychange Manifesto (2017) 188
Kumbier, A. 211

Lady Gaga 29
Latane, B. 98
Leblanc, L. 92
Leonard, M. 2, 38
Leyshon, M. 106, 108
LGBTQ+ community 20, 23
Lieb, K.J. 121, 150
LineupsWithoutMales 82
Lipsitz, George 165
LISTEN 80–1
Listen Lists 209
live music scene, Australia 7, 89, 91, 94
Liverpool Institute for Performing Arts (LIPA) 31, 37–8
Lowes, Kate 35, 40 n.4

male-dominated spaces
    Bollywood film industry 180
    British Asian scene 176–7, 180
    femininity in 48
    learning environments 33
    music education 191–2
    in music technology schools 55
    in punk 201
    women's experiences 46, 92

malestream processes 50
Maloney, M. 93
Mansfield, Carrie 40 n.4
Mantie, R. 16
Marsh, C. 35–6, 38
Masculine Domination (Bourdieu) 105
masculine subjectivities 4, 64
masculinity
    culture 68–9
    de-facto 126
    and femininity 91
    improvisation and 196
    and popular music 34
    technology and 33, 45, 65
    toxic 34
Massey, Sylvia 210
Maton, K. 105
McRobbie, Angela 105
mentorship programs 68, 78
meritocracy 3, 79, 83
Metallic Butterfly (Princess Nokia) 168
Miller, D. L. 138
Minogue, Kylie 73
Monaghan, U. 109
Morgan, Joan 166
Morris, Evelyn 80
Morrison, Lindy 73–4, 83
Moschella, E. A. 98
Munoz, Jose Esteban 154
music education 2, 4, 15, 29–30, 34–7, 39–40, 45–7, 54–5, 59–63, 73–4, 78, 127, 183, 187–9, 197–8
    gendered dynamics 1, 64
    hidden curriculum 65
    inequalities 31, 69
    institutions 64–9, 117, 119
    masculine dominance 65
    popular music (*see* popular music education)
    PRSF 188
    UK jazz scene 188–9, 191–2
music industry 4, 40 n.1, 117
    Australian 73, 75–6, 82, 91, 98
    Bollywood 175–6, 180–4
    'boys club' 29, 31, 37
    digitalization 167
    gatekeeper level (*see* gatekeepers)

gender mainstreaming 118–19, 127
inequalities 40, 55, 81, 109, 117
limits 8
sexual violence 93
UK 132, 136
music socialization 45
music technology education
   classroom experiences 47–9
   data and methods 46–7
   gender imbalance, addressing 53–4
   interactions with (male) classmates (*see* interactions with (male) classmates)
   leaky pipeline analogy 45–6, 54–5, 59, 195
   predominantly male teaching staff 52
   teachers and gendered experiences 52–3

Naudin, Annette 185
networking and networks
   community based 209, 212
   exclusionary networks 66
   homosocial networks 59, 122
   industry networks 64, 69
   informal networks 64, 66, 131, 139
   and oppurtunities 37–9, 104
   support networks 191–2, 194
The Night Porter (Cavani) 147
Noise Music: A History (Hegarty) 148
noise music scene 148
   art school to fetish club 149–54
   and s/m 149
norms and stereotypes, gender 32–7, 91–4
NVivo 60

O'Brien, D. 83
O'Connor, Justin 84 n.2
open mics 7, 103
   music making and performance, gendered nature 109–10
   performances and experiences, access 105–6
   performers 103
   pubs and gender 103–5
   setting scene 106–7
   space, place and confidence 111–12

Orgad, Shani 78
O'Shea, H. 107–8

Pegley, K. 20
Penna, A. 69
Performing Rights Society (PRS), UK 7, 132–3
   average earnings 134
   Keychange 9, 122, 141–2, 188
   membership numbers by gender 134
   Women Make Music 119, 132, 141
Petterson, Blair 113
Pieper, K. 2
Pinckney, Jazlyn 135
political economy, sex 158
pop music (Australia) 74–8
popular music education
   German 15
   North American 15–24
   Scandinavian 15
popular music pedagogy (PMP) 16
   goals 21
   groupwork 18–19
   popular musics and 18
Porter, Gregory 189
postfeminist sensibility 3
Propagandum 160 n.2
PRS Foundation (PRSF) 188
pubs 104
   environment and timings 112
   masculine domination and 107–9
   women participating, lack 112
punk 4, 89, 92, 135, 147, 149–54, 158, 171. *See also* Do-It-Yourself (DIY)
   Australian 9, 90, 201–8, 211–12

QMusic 78
queer 9, 149–50, 153, 159–60, 203
   femininity/woman 170, 201–6, 208
   hip-hop 167
   and punk 149, 203–4, 206, 211–212
   sonics and archives 209–11
   sounding 148, 154–8, 202, 212
The Queer Art of Failure (Halberstam) 157

rap 9, 163–70, 175–6, 179–80
Reitsamer, R. 207–8

Richardson, Elvis 82
Riches, G. 92
Rodgers, Tara 150
Rogerson, Diana 8, 147, 149–53, 155–6, 158–9
Rubin, Gayle 158

Salo (Pasolini) 147
Save Live Australian Music (SLAM) 80
screen composition, Australia
    educated women composers 60–4
    education institutions and educators 64–8
    hidden curriculum 59
    leaky pipe phenomenon 59
    screen composers study 59–60
sexual assault 7, 78, 80–1, 89–90, 93, 95–8
sexual violence
    alcohol, drugs and 94–6
    campaigns 89–90
    cultural scaffolding 90, 94–6
    defining 90
    perpetration and normalization 98
    space, design and dynamics 96–8
Simoni, M. 21
Sisters Are Doin' It for Themselves (Morrison) 73
Skipping a Beat: Assessing the State of Gender Inequality in the Australian Music Industry (Cooper, Coles & Hanna-Osborne) 74–6, 82
Smith, D. M. 207–10
Smith, G. D. 30
Smith, S. 2
social encounter 32
social media 79–80, 82, 193, 209
social networks 5, 47, 131, 139–40, 151
sociolinguistic theory 16
songwriting 2, 62, 18, 20–1, 34, 37, 103–4, 106, 108–10
sound engineers 2, 9, 46–7, 201–12
Stapleton, Steven 151
Sutcliffe, Peter 152

Tanglewood Symposium 16
Taylor, M. 83
Taylor, S. 37, 40

Technofeminism 209
technology 20–2, 120. *See also* music technology education
technophobia 20–1
Thatcher, Margaret 149–50
Thompson, Marie 156–7
Throbbing Gristle 147, 150
Tobias, E. S. 19
    all-girl spaces 22
    hybrid approach 23
    male-dominated fields 21
    songwriting and technology course 20–1
tokenism 51
trans persons 3, 10 n.1, 23, 31, 34, 117, 124–6, 159, 203, 208
Tucker, S. 190
Turning Pointe (Westle) 74
Twisting The Black Threads of My Mental Marionettes (Rogerson) 152

UK jazz scene 9, 195–8
    being woman in 189–94
    Keychange and Cheltenham Jazz Festival 187–9
UK Music 29, 31, 40 n.2
UK Music's Music Academic Partnership 29, 40
urban feminism 8, 163–4, 168
    tenets 169

Verloo, M. 123
von Appen, Ralf 138

Wajcman, J. 209–10
Waksman, S. 109
Westwood, Jill 8, 147, 149–53, 156, 158–9
When Chickenheads Come Home to Roost (Morgan) 166
Who Wrote That Song? (Colbert) 190
Williams, Carla Marie 29
Williamson, J. 40 n.1
Willis, V. 190
Wilson, Siona 150
Wittel, A. 64
Women in Australian Film Production (Ryan, Eliot & Appleton) 74

Women in the Victorian Contemporary Music Industry (Music Victoria) 74, 76
Women in Theatre (Lally & Miller) 74
Women make Music (PRS) 119, 132, 141
women musicians 9, 79–80, 120, 195
    Cheltenham Jazz Festival 189
    DIY strategies 197
    gatekeepers 196
    generation 196
    mid-career musicians 196
    one woman on stage approach 196
    Showcase project 195
Women Working in the Australian Mass Media (Ryan, Eliot & Appleton) 74
Woodward, S. C. 30
Wyn Evans, Cerith 151–2

young musicians research project 31–2
Younker, B. A. 21

Zimmerman, John 94

www.ingramcontent.com/pod-product-compliance
Lightning Source LLC
Chambersburg PA
CBHW052038300426
44117CB00012B/1871